THE MEMOIRS OF GOD

"Remarkable for his range of interests, erudition, and mastery of detail, Mark Smith here makes available to non-specialists new thinking on two key issues in biblical interpretation: collective memory and monotheism. Smith skillfully shows how profoundly these issues affect the meaning of divinity in the Bible, the concept of history, and the formation of Israel's concept of God. On the way, the reader is constantly brought up to date on a wide variety of biblical topics. Highly recommended."

— RICHARD CLIFFORD
Weston Jesuit School of Theology

"Mark Smith's view of the evolution of monotheism in Israel is highly persuasive, and should command a consensus. In this book he enriches the discussion by explaining the process of selective memory that shaped the biblical account. An important contribution to the study of the religion of Israel."

— JOHN J. COLLINS
Yale Divinity School

"In this extremely well-written book, Mark Smith brings his groundbreaking work on the religion of ancient Israel to the general public. Going beyond his earlier work, this book also applies the revolutionary work of historians on collective memory to understanding the history and religion of ancient Israel. Readable, yet scholarly, this delightful book deserves to be read by both Christians and Jews, scholars and students, or anyone interested in understanding the Bible."

— WILLIAM M. SCHNIEDEWIND
University of California, Los Angeles

THE MEMOIRS OF GOD

*History, Memory, and the Experience
of the Divine in Ancient Israel*

MARK S. SMITH

Fortress Press
Minneapolis

THE MEMOIRS OF GOD
History, Memory, and the Experience of the Divine
in Ancient Israel

Cover art: *Tel Gezer* by Sandra Bowden. Copyright © Sandra Bowden.
Used by permission.
Cover design: Kevin Vanderleek
Type design: Allan Johnson, Phoenix Type, Inc.
Maps: Lucidity Information Design, LLC

ISBN: 0-8006-3485-3

Library of Congress Calaloging-in-Publication Data
Smith, Mark S., 1955–
    The memoirs of God : history, memory, and the experience of the
divine in ancient Israel / Mark S. Smith.
        p. cm.
    Includes bibliographical references and indexes.
    ISBN 0-8006-3485-3 (alk. paper)
    1. God—Biblical teaching. 2. Bible. O.T.—Theology.
    3. God (Judaism)—History of doctrines. I. Title.

BS1192.6.S553 2004
221.6--DC22

                                                2004018093

Manufactured in the U.S.A.
08 07 06 05 04   1 2 3 4 5 6 7 8 9 10

*In great gratitude and appreciation
to my graduate and undergraduate students
and to my departmental colleagues
at New York University,*

Daniel Fleming most of all

Contents

Acknowledgments

*. . . and all my memories are closed courtyards
at summer's high noon.*
— Yehudah Amichai, "Jerusalem Is a Cradle"

earthquake:

As I remember it, this book started in the fall of 2000, my first semester at New
York University. I was looking through a bookshop off Washington Square, and
I came across *Religion as a Chain of Memory* published by Danièle Hervieu-
Léger in 2000. I stopped; I was transfixed by what I read and I thought to myself—this is what the Bible is, a collection of Israel's memories about its past, in
T. S. Eliot's words, "mixing memory and desire." Or, in the terms used by the
tradition of the *Annales* school standing behind Hervieu-Léger's work, the
Bible is Israel's record of its collective memory. What I am presenting in this
book is a synthesis of insights and research that began with *Religion as a Chain
of Memory* and led me back to works by biblical scholars that helped me to
think about history and memory about Israel and its Deity. Many studies informed my discussion of the issues, and I happily recall my debt to the scholars
listed in the bibliography. Chief among them are Rainer Albertz, Elizabeth
Bloch-Smith, Avraham Faust, Baruch Halpern, Friedhelm Hartenstein, Ronald S.
Hendel, Baruch Levine, Bernard Levinson, Nadav Na'aman, David Schloen, Karel
van der Toorn, and Franz Wiggermann.

In many respects, this book is the result of my years of teaching at New York
University. In various graduate and undergraduate courses, I have benefited from
discussions devoted to the issues presented in this work. For this reason, I am
very grateful to my students at NYU. The first two chapters have been improved
by constructive readings of four of my departmental colleagues at New York University: Robert Chazan, Hasia Diner, David Engel, and Lawrence Schiffman. My
NYU colleague Daniel Fleming has been an inspiration to me in many ways;
not least has been his collegial attitude and aid. He read an earlier draft of this
work, and as usual, he added many good comments and criticisms to which I

viii

have tried to respond in rewriting this book. My investigations into collective memory, marked especially in chapter 4, began with my inaugural lecture as professor at New York University. I also gave a form of this talk at the national meeting of the Catholic Biblical Association of America in 2001 (subsequently published in *Catholic Biblical Quarterly* in 2002). A number of colleagues at the meeting offered helpful suggestions. In particular, I am grateful for the bibliographic aid that Gregory Sterling provided to me in the area of New Testament studies pertaining to memory. I am further indebted to the Catholic Biblical Association for its strong support over the past two decades.

Contacts with colleagues elsewhere have also contributed to this work. Chapter 3 is based on lectures given 8–12 November 2003 at the universities of Hamburg, Marburg, and Göttingen. I especially wish to thank Dr. Klaus-Peter Adam (at Marburg) as well as Professors Friedhelm Hartenstein (at Hamburg) and Hermann Spieckermann (at Göttingen) for arranging these talks. I am further indebted to Dr. Adam for arranging my visit to the University of Giessen on 12 November 2003. There, in the academic home of Hermann Gunkel, I gave a lecture on collective memory in ancient Israel, which is included here as chapter 4. The Sonderforschungsbereich Erinnerungskulturen at Giessen provided the basic funding for the entire trip, and I am grateful in particular to its director, Dr. Almuth Hammer, for her interest in my work on collective memory. As one of the largest research institutes in Germany today, the Sonderforschungsbereich Erinnerungskulturen at Giessen has assumed the massive task of studying collective memory across a score of academic disciplines, and it promises to illuminate the ways in which the academy understands itself as implicated in the transmission of our cultures' past. All four of the lectures and the ensuing discussions provided me with wonderful opportunities to air the questions and information addressed in this book. Particularly helpful, as well as delightful, were my visits with Professors Klaus Koch and Friedhelm Hartenstein in Hamburg; with Professors Hermann Spieckermann, Reinhard Kratz, and Rudolf Smend at Göttingen; with Professors Erhard Gerstenberger and Jörg Jeremias at Marburg; and with Professor Jeremias and the Sonderforschungsbereich Erinnerungskulturen at Giessen. I also enjoyed my many conversations with Dr. Adam, who served generously as my guide throughout this trip to Germany.

In the fall of 2003, I also had the opportunity to discuss a number of issues with Jan Assmann, Marc Van De Mieroop, and David Carr following a lecture delivered by Professor Assmann at Union Theological Seminary. In chapter 3 readers will recognize the vast differences between the views of Professor Assmann and myself. Despite our differences in outlook on biblical monotheism, I found our conversation enormously engaging and helpful. Karel van der Toorn and I spent hours in discussion during his visit to the United States in November of 2003. After his return to the Netherlands that fall, he read a draft of this work and offered several helpful remarks, for which I am grateful.

Finally and most of all, I offer my deepest thanks to my wife, the archaeologist Liz Bloch-Smith. We have turned time and again to the issues raised in this work, and I learn much from our discussions. In addition, she commented on chapter 1 and offered many helpful suggestions. As our children observe, our discussions are not like the conversations of their friends' parents. I save a word of thanks for our daughter, Shula (now in sixth grade), who helped me with the title of this work; after she perused a thesaurus, she suggested "memoirs."

4 July 2004
Skirball Department of Hebrew and Judaic Studies
New York University

Abbreviations

AB	Anchor Bible
ANEP	*The Ancient Near East in Pictures Relating to the Old Testament,* 2d ed. with supplement, edited by James B. Pritchard
ANET	*Ancient Near Eastern Texts Relating to the Old Testament,* 3d ed. with supplement, edited by James B. Pritchard
B.C.E.	Before the Common Era (= B.C.)
Bib	*Biblica*
BR	*Bible Review*
CAT	*The Cuneiform Alphabetic Texts from Ugarit, Ras Ibn Hani and Other Places,* edited by Manfried Dietrich, Oswald Loretz, and Joaquín Sanmartín
CBQ	*Catholic Biblical Quarterly*
CBQMS	Catholic Biblical Quarterly Monograph Series
C.E.	Common Era (= A.D.)
ConBOT	Coniectanea Biblica: Old Testament series
FAT	Forschungen zum Alten Testament
HSM	Harvard Semitic Monographs
HSS	Harvard Semitic Studies
IEJ	*Israel Exploration Journal*
JBL	*Journal of Biblical Literature*
JSOTSup	Journal for the Study of the Old Testament Supplements
MT	Masoretic text
NJPS	New Jewish Publication Society translation of the Hebrew Bible
NRSV	New Revised Standard Version of the Bible
OBO	Orbis biblicus et orientalis
OTL	Old Testament Library
Praep. ev.	Eusebius, *Praeparatio evangelica (Preparation for the Gospel)*
SBLDS	Society of Biblical Literature Dissertation Series
SBLMS	Society of Biblical Literature Monograph Series
TA	*Tel Aviv*
VTSup	Vetus Testamentum Supplement
WMANT	Wissenschaftliche Monographien zum Alten und Neuen Testament

Time Lines:
Periods, Events, and Writings

Middle Bronze Age (2000–1550 B.C.E.)

Late Bronze Age (1550–1200 B.C.E.)

1400–1200	Heyday of Ugarit, cosmopolitan city-state on the Syrian coast, produces hundreds of texts
1213–1203	Reign of Pharaoh Merneptah; the Merneptah stela (with first reference to Israel), ca. 1208
ca. 1300–1200	Earliest traditions of Israel?

Iron I Period (1200–1000 B.C.E.): Premonarchic period

ca. 1200–1000	Premonarchic tribes of Israel and Judah
ca. 1150–1000	Poem of Judges 5 and sayings in Genesis 49
	Early inscriptions (e.g., personal names on arrowheads)
ca. 1030–1010	Saul as king over "Gilead, the Ashurites, Jezreel, Ephraim, and Benjamin" (2 Samuel 2:9)

Iron II Period (1000–540 B.C.E.): Period of the monarchy and "exile"

ca. 1010–970	David as king of Judah and Israel ("United Monarchy"), treaty with Tyre, hegemony over other neighbors
ca. 970–930	Solomon as king of Judah and Israel ("United Monarchy"), treaty and trade network with Tyre, diplomatic relations with Egypt
ca. 960s	Jerusalem Temple built

ca. 930	Death of Solomon, division of the northern kingdom (Israel) and the southern kingdom (Judah)
ca. 930–913	Jeroboam I, first king of the northern kingdom (Israel)
925	Pharaoh Shishak invades Judah
ca. 900s–800s (?)	The Gezer Calendar inscription
	Early royal psalms (for example, Psalm 18 = 2 Samuel 22)
	The "J" "source" (?), composed in the southern kingdom
882–871	Omri, king of Israel, establishes new northern capital to Samaria, pays tribute to Assyria
873–852	Ahab, king of north, coalition with Tyre via marriage to Jezebel
853	Battle of Qarqar: western coalition, including Ahab, holds off Assyrian encroachment to the west (the Levant)
mid-800s	The prophet Elijah in the northern kingdom in reign of Ahab
ca. 800s	The "E" "source" (?), composed in the northern kingdom
842–814	Jehu overthrows Omride dynasty and rules as king of north
mid/late-800s	The prophet Elisha (disciple of Elijah) in the north
early 700s	Kuntillet Ajrud inscriptions (in the Sinai)
786–746	Reign of Jeroboam II; last flowering of Israel before Assyrian conquest of the west (the Levant)
770s	Samaria Ostraca inscriptions (years 9, 10, 15, and 17 of Jeroboam II)
ca. 750s	Prophecy of Amos during reign of Jeroboam II in Israel
745–727	Tiglath-pileser III, king of Assyria, conquers the west (the Levant)
ca. late 740– early 730s	Prophecy of Hosea in Israel; core of Deuteronomy written (?)
ca. 734–732	Isaiah delivers oracles of consolation to King Ahaz, including "Immanuel oracles" of Isaiah 7 and 9, to support the king during the war waged against Judah by Israel and Syria (Syro-Ephraimite War)
732	Assyria comes to the aid of the Judeans, resulting in the fall of Israel to the Assyrians
732–722	Hoshea, last king of Israel and vassal of Assyria

722	Assyrian conquest of the north, twenty-seven thousand taken as captives, northern refugees flee to Judah, Israel incorporated into the Assyrian Empire as provincial territory
ca. 727/715	Beginning of the reign of Hezekiah as king of Judah
late 700s	Khirbet el-Qom burial inscription (in Judah)
ca. 705–701	Hezekiah prepares for Assyrian invasion of Judah by fortifying the walls of Jerusalem and extending its waterworks
	The Siloam tunnel inscription reflecting this work
701	Assyrians under Sennacherib invade, lay siege to Jerusalem, take over two hundred thousand Judeans to Assyria, with Judah remaining as vassal to Assyria
	Isaiah's prophecy to Hezekiah during Sennacherib's invasion, as reported in Isaiah 36–39 = 2 Kings 18–19
	First edition of the Deuteronomistic History (Joshua–2 Kings) produced during Hezekiah's reign inspired by "victory" over Assyrians
	Proverbs transmitted by "men of Hezekiah" (Proverbs 25:1)
ca. 698/687	End of Hezekiah's reign in Judah
689/687–642	Manasseh as king of Judah, vassal to Assyria
640–609	Josiah as king of Judah
late 620s	Assyrian withdrawal from the west; Judah as small regional power
ca. late 620s–610s	Revision of Deuteronomistic History in time of Josiah
	So-called discovery of the Torah (some form of Deuteronomy) in Jerusalem Temple reported in 2 Kings 22; so-called reforms of Josiah (2 Kings 23)
ca. 610–586	Prophecy of Jeremiah in Jerusalem
late 610s	Collapse of Assyrian Empire, rise of Babylonian Empire
604–562	Nebuchadnezzar II of Babylon
597	Conquest of Jerusalem by the Babylonians under Nebuchadnezzar II, about 3,000 Judeans taken to Babylonia (reported as 10,000 or 8,000 by 2 Kings 24:14-16, about 3,000 according to Jeremiah 52:28)
593–563	The priest Ezekiel's career as prophet in Babylonia

587–586	Further conquest of Jerusalem by the Babylonians
	About eight hundred Judeans taken to Babylonia (Jeremiah 52:29)
	Destruction of Jerusalem and Temple (2 Kings 25)
582	About seven hundred Judeans taken to Babylonia (Jeremiah 52:30)
586–538	Captivity of Judean elite in Babylonia
582	Babylonian incursion into Judah, with further captivity of about 750 Judeans (Jeremiah 52:30)
ca. late 580s	Book of Lamentations and Psalm 74 composed in Jerusalem
	Psalm 137 composed in Babylonia
	Amos 9:11-15 and Isaiah 11:1-9 added (?)
ca. 561	King Jehoiachin released from prison in Babylon (2 Kings 25:27-30)
559	Cyrus comes to the throne of Persia
ca. 550s	Exilic supplements to the Deuteronomistic History (including 2 Kings 24–25; see especially 2 Kings 25:27-30)
556–539	Nabonidus, last king of Babylon

Persian Period (540–333 B.C.E.): Yehud as Persian province

539	Conquest of Babylonia by Cyrus the Persian
538	Edict of Cyrus granting permission for captive peoples to return to their homelands
	Isaiah 40–55, composed in Babylonia, celebrating prospect of return to Judah; Psalm 126, anticipating return
	First group of Judeans return to the province of Yehud (Judah) under the leadership of Sheshbazzar, first governor (Ezra 5:14)
530–522	Cambyses succeeds Cyrus
525	Persian capture of Egypt
522	Revolt within Persian Empire following death of Cambyses
	Darius assumes office as Persian king, consolidates power through 521
522–486	Darius I as king of Persia

ca. 520–515   Rebuilding of Jerusalem Temple led by Zerubbabel, second governor of Yehud, and the priest Jeshua, religious leader of Yehud, and inspired by the prophecy of Haggai and Zechariah 1–6 (520–518)

late 500s–(?)   Priestly arrangement of the Torah (Pentateuch)

Postexilic expansions to the Deuteronomistic History (e.g., 1 Kings 8)

New preface added to Deuteronomy (Deuteronomy 1:1—4:43)

Isaiah 56–66

The book of Job in its present form (?)

Late 500s–   Documents of Judeans written from Elephantine (in southern early 300s   Egypt)

ca. late 440s   Nehemiah as Persian governor of Yehud, leads rebuilding of Jerusalem's walls

ca. 440–416   Murashu documents (from Nippur in Mesopotamia)

ca. 419   "Passover letter" from Elephantine

ca. 409   Elephantine letter about rebuilding Elephantine temple

mid-400s (or   Mission of Ezra to Jerusalem; religious reforms said to be early 300s)   undertaken

400s   Song of Songs

Qohelet (also known as Ecclesiastes)

300s (before 333)   1 and 2 Chronicles

Court tales of Daniel 2–6

The book of Esther

The Levitical compilation of the book of Psalms (?)

Hellenistic Period (333–165 B.C.E.): Judea as contested territory

333   Alexander the Great conquers Egypt and the Levant

ca. 330   Conflicts in the priestly ranks in Jerusalem lead to Samaritan Jewish priestly establishment, which continues relations with Jerusalem priesthood

323   Death of Alexander, his vast empire split among his generals, who establish four dynasties, including Egypt (Ptolemies) and Syria (Seleucids)

ca. 312–200	Judea under control of Egyptian Ptolemies, growing Jewish community in Alexandria (Egypt)
late 300s–200s	Zechariah 9–14
early 200s	Shift of control of Judea to Syrian Seleucids
mid-200s	Earliest Dead Sea Scrolls (?), beginning of Septuagint translation of the Bible into Greek in Alexandria
ca. 180	Ben Sira (also known as Sirach or Ecclesiasticus) written
175–164	Antiochus IV Epiphanes (Seleucid)
171	Murder of the priest Onias III
167–164	Judean revolt against Seleucids and their Jewish priestly and upper-class allies led by the Maccabees (1 Maccabees 1–4, composed ca. 100)
late 167	Seleucid dedication of the Jerusalem Temple to Zeus
ca. 167	Apocalyptic visions of Daniel 7–12 against Seleucids
late 164	Death of Antiochus IV Epiphanes
200s–100s	Torah, Historical Books, Prophets, and Psalms recognized as authoritative Scriptures, with many biblical works circulating in multiple forms

Maccabean Monarchy (165 B.C.E.–63 C.E.): Judea independent

164	Maccabean victory over the Seleucid armies
	Restoration of the Jerusalem Temple (1 Maccabees 4–6)
	Seleucid offer of truce and amnesty rejected by Maccabees and their forces (2 Maccabees 11)
164–160	Judas Maccabeus rules Judea
ca. 160	Restoration of the Jerusalem Temple celebrated in 1 Maccabees
160–142	Jonathan (brother of Judas) rules Judea, battles Nabateans, fortifies Jerusalem
ca. 154	The Jewish priest Onias IV builds a temple in Leontopolis in Egypt, sign of division in priestly ranks
ca. 150	Further split in priestly ranks, signaled by the establishment of Dead Sea Scrolls community/movement
ca. 150–(?)	Early phase of the Dead Sea Scrolls community/movement

142–135	Simon rules Judea, gains recognition of Judean independence by Seleucids, later defends against Seleucid incursions
135–104	John Hyrcanus rules Judea
104–76	Alexander Janneus expands boundaries of Judean state

Roman Period (63 B.C.E.–70 C.E.): Judea as Roman territory

63 B.C.E.	Roman general Pompey establishes Roman control over Judea
37–4 B.C.E.	Herod ("the Great") rules Judea under Roman patronage, rebuilds the Jerusalem Temple, builds Caesarea, Masada, and Herodium
4 B.C.E.–6 C.E.	Herod Archelaus rules Judea, Samaria, and Idumea as ethnarch under the Romans
4 B.C.E.–39 C.E.	Herod Antipas rules Galilee and Perea as tetrarch under the Romans
ca. 4 B.C.E.– 30 C.E.	Jesus
26–36 C.E.	Pontius Pilate, Roman governor of Judea
ca. 50–100	New Testament books written
66–73	Jewish revolt against Rome
68	End of the Dead Sea Scroll community
70	Romans recapture Jerusalem and destroy Jerusalem Temple
ca. early 90s	Josephus's *Antiquities*
200–300s	Jewish and Christian canons of the Hebrew Bible defined
ca. 210	Mishnah redacted
ca. 390	Jerusalem Talmud completed
ca. 500	Babylonian Talmud completed

Ancient Near East

Israel & Judah

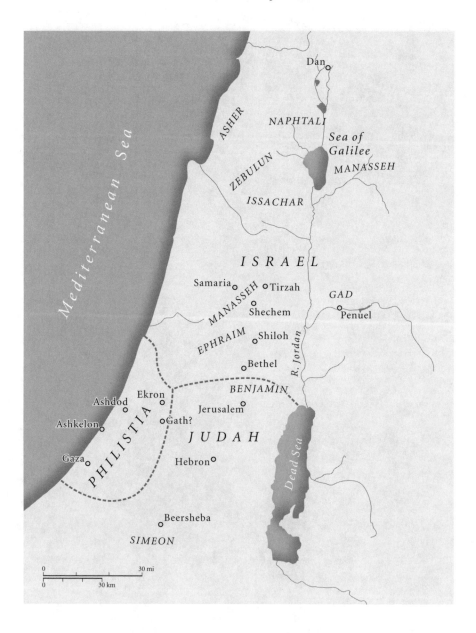

Mediterranean Sea

ASHER

NAPHTALI

Dan

Sea of Galilee

ZEBULUN

MANASSEH

ISSACHAR

ISRAEL

Samaria   MANASSEH   Tirzah

GAD

Shechem   Penuel

EPHRAIM   Shiloh

R. Jordan

Bethel

BENJAMIN

Ashdod   Ekron

Ashkelon   Gath?   Jerusalem

PHILISTIA   JUDAH

Gaza   Hebron

Dead Sea

Beersheba

SIMEON

0   30 mi
0   30 km

Introduction

If I forget you, O Jerusalem . . .
   —Psalm 137 (and Yehudah Amichai)

For quite some time, perhaps about two decades, a new discussion about the history of Israel and the understanding of God in the Bible has been going on in scholarly circles. Despite the great significance of this discussion, a limited amount of it has made its way to the general public. On one side, the discussion has involved efforts at understanding the historical context of the Bible and how the Bible represents Israel's past. On another side of the discussion, the representation of the monotheistic God of the Bible has been reevaluated and probed with fresh perspectives and insights.

These matters about Israel and God are intertwined within the Bible, and although these could be separated out as two sets of issues, it seems to me that a discussion of the two together would be mutually illuminating. Unlike my earlier books on these intertwined subjects, I offer this work for an audience that goes beyond my circle of fellow Bible scholars and graduate students. Toward this end I have made an effort to write this work in a more accessible style, with little technical jargon and no footnotes. I do mention the names of various scholars over the course of the chapters, and the works of these scholars can be identified by consulting the bibliography at the end of this book. Also, for the sake of simplicity, I have omitted diacritical marks for the representation of Hebrew words. I also decided to include a basic time line, for periods, events, and biblical writings. I hope that this will make it easier to keep straight the basic time frame for the different events mentioned in this book.

Before explaining the plan of this book, I would like to mention an important matter of terminology. When scholars write about the Jewish Bible or the Christian Old Testament, they use many words that refer to phenomena that in fact did not exist at the time when the books of the Bible were written—for example, the word "Bible" itself! This word denotes a single work, a closed canon containing revealed writings. In fact, there was no closed canon until long after the books of the Hebrew Bible were written. Thus, in one sense I should not use the word "Bible." This is the best-known term, however, for what this book is discussing, and so I continue to use it. The same problem applies to the word "book," as when I speak of a "biblical book." In the period represented by the writings that later became known as the Bible, there were no books, since a book constitutes a single bound volume. Instead, one of the main technologies for writing sacred texts in ancient Israel was the scroll, as in the Dead Sea Scrolls. Thus, perhaps I should also abandon the expression "biblical book," since it contains not one, but two anachronisms! I could use the word "Scriptures" instead, and I sometimes do use this word. Still, the words "Bible" and "book" are conventional, and hence I employ them in the chapters that follow.

The same problem extends to many other words found in this book. "Monotheism" and "polytheism" are words that basically postdate biblical works. Currently, it is hotly debated whether these terms should be used at all. However, these are the terms that people today in Western countries use for the notion of worshiping and believing in either one deity (monotheism) or multiple deities (polytheism). So these remain helpful terms at least for entering into this area of religion. While few ancients would probably have understood the question "Are you a monotheist or a polytheist?" they would have understood what it means to offer worship to and believe in more than one deity, since these sorts of terms are found in ancient religious literature. So, to enter into this entire discussion, I use these terms while also recognizing their inadequacies. Many other terms that we regularly employ denote things that did not really exist at the time of the Hebrew Bible. "Religion," which implies a discrete group of phenomena separate from other spheres of human life, is another anachronism. The list could go and on. So, with an awareness that all these terms have their limitations, we can enter into this investigation of Israel's representation of its past and the changing perceptions of its divinity.

I devote the first two chapters to the representation of Israel's past in the Bible. In chapter 1 I survey the Hebrew Bible's presentation of Israel's history, which for the purposes of this discussion begins at just before 1200 B.C.E., the time of the first reference to Israel outside the Bible and roughly speaking the period of the earliest compositions in the Bible. The discussion ends generally with the Persian period (ca. 540–333 B.C.E.). At various points in this book, I mention some of the Bible's later works, such as Daniel, but the Persian period marks the end of biblical narratives about Israel's past, which are the central concern of this book. In order to highlight certain features of the Bible, I have taken the further liberty of occasionally mentioning the Dead Sea Scrolls, which date roughly from about 250 B.C.E. (though perhaps later) to 68 C.E. These later texts often illustrate the longevity of many of the ideas from earlier periods. Thus they often help to show some important developments.

As we will see in chapter 1, the narratives of the past in the Bible, especially Genesis through 2 Kings, show an interesting mixture of historical information and cultural memories. Within Genesis–2 Kings, the mixture also involves the medium: many sections seem to reflect scribal, written production while other biblical texts seem to show an oral background frozen in writing at some secondary point. In addition to these books, other biblical works not usually included in a treatment of history also offer portraits of Israel's past (such as Ruth, Song of Songs, and Ecclesiastes, also called Qohelet). These contain indicators of Israel's ideas about its past, just as Genesis–2 Kings do. The larger point in this discussion involves seeing the Bible's presentation of history not only as the record of Israel's past or as literary representations of this past, but also as a response to the past, or a series of responses to it.

In chapter 2 I follow up this approach to Israel's past by focusing on the many challenges to Israel's existence. Here various historical narratives and other biblical works can be viewed in the context of crises facing Israel. Biblical history, then, does not simply record crises; it is also Israel's responses to them, and these responses in turn shaped Israel's perception and representations of its past in the Bible. One of the most basic representations was the shifting definition of who or what an Israelite was. While the Bible seems to answer this question clearly as the twelve tribes, the label "Israel" is applied to different groups and tribes in different ways in different times. Some attention to this shift not only shows deeper political and social dynamics at work; it also indicates how various representations of Israelite identity during its history were shaped by a number of challenges to that identity. The representation of Israel's past in the Bible shows the imprints of its response to ongoing challenges to its existence; Israel's understanding of the past changed in light of its circumstances. These two initial chapters also provide a backdrop to the rest of the study, since the way Israel faced different crises and remembered its past profoundly shaped biblical monotheism and the memory of God in the Bible, the topics of chapters 3 and 4.

In chapter 3 I look at biblical monotheism and how it fits into Israel's larger religious history. Monotheism, the belief in a single deity, has long been considered a hallmark of biblical religion. This is quite correct. All too often, however, monotheism is presumed by readers of the Bible to constitute part of the revelation at Mount Sinai that took place in the Late Bronze Age (as presented in the books of Exodus and Leviticus), prior to the entry into the land (as recounted in the book of Joshua). This reading of the biblical representation of monotheism, especially in the book of Exodus, is not quite correct, as Exodus assumes or admits to the existence of other gods; it does not deny their existence, unlike later clear expressions of monotheism in the Bible. The monotheistic assumption brought to the reading of Exodus also obscures the fact of Israel's primordial polytheism, especially as it is attested in the earliest recollections of highland Israel during the premonarchic period. Its multiplicity of gods and goddesses was not simply a departure from norms known earlier from Sinai (as suggested, for example, by the present form of the book of Judges).

Indeed, the standard of monotheism was not fully articulated in Israel until the period of the monarchy, beginning probably in the eighth or seventh century, and at that point it was projected onto Israel's memory of the revelation at Mount Sinai. In order to understand Israel's monotheism, largely a religious perspective that developed initially during the seventh and sixth centuries, it is important for modern students of the Bible to take Israel's polytheism seriously, because the biblical writers themselves took seriously the power of Israel's other gods, not only the gods of the other nations that it later criticized. To appreciate Israel's polytheism, then, helps us to understand the depth of the response represented by biblical monotheism.

Chapter 3 is based largely on my book *The Origins of Biblical Monotheism*, but here I approach the issues in a significantly different manner. I examine the four levels of the pantheon from the pre-Israelite texts of ancient Ugarit, through the polytheism of early Israel, and down to the competing polytheistic and monotheistic pantheons of late-monarchic and exilic Israel. With this approach, I chart the shifts in the configurations of divinity in ancient Israel, from roughly the premonarchic period through the sixth century. Each period shows changing configurations in the understanding of divinity (represented in chapter 3 by four levels or tiers of divinity); biblical monotheism can be seen as a new configuration of divinity. To be sure, each period also shows some shifts in the configuration of Israel (discussed in chapters 1 and 2) as well as shifts in the range of persons, social groups, and social segments voicing different religious viewpoints, whether they were monolatry (worship of only a single deity), various forms of polytheism, or different visions of monotheism.

In general, this diachronic, historical approach to biblical monotheism stands in opposition to the views of the Egyptologist Jan Assmann, views that have received a tremendous amount of attention in recent years, especially thanks to his book *Moses the Egyptian*. Professor Assmann brings innovative perspectives to bear on the question of biblical monotheism, and his insights have made a major impact on the study of ancient religion in both Egypt and the rest of the ancient Near East. For example, his discussion of the "translatability" of deities across ancient cultures has proven to be both historically correct and heuristically helpful for understanding biblical monotheism (Assmann 1997, 3, 28, 44–54). I have incorporated this perspective into my discussion in chapter 3. In chapter 4 I take up many of the questions about cultural memory that Assmann has addressed in his work (although I am more directly influenced by the French *Annales* school on this issue). At the same time, it will be clear to readers in chapter 3 that my views differ vastly from those of Professor Assmann. He views biblical monotheism as revolutionary, while I bring forward evidence for biblical monotheism as both revolutionary and evolutionary. Assmann does not situate biblical monotheism within its historical and cultural context in Israel, while the material evidence shows how such contextualization is fundamental for understanding monotheism in Israel. This contextualization of the actual evidence allows us to see the lines of continuity and change that issue in monotheism as it was remembered in the Bible.

To follow up the discussion in chapter 3, in chapter 4 I introduce the social phenomenon of collective memory into the discussion of the Bible's representation of divinity. The academic study of collective memory offers important intellectual help for understanding the biblical representations of Israel's past, which includes its past recollections of its God. In this chapter I examine the double role that collective memory plays in the formation of Israelite monotheism. Collective memory first helped to shape biblical monotheism, and then it influenced Israel's understanding of its own polytheistic past. Collective memory—or the lack of it (in other words, collective amnesia)—helped Israel to forget about its own polytheistic past, and in turn it served to induce a collective amnesia about the other gods, namely, that many of these had been Israel's in the first place.

One weakness in my presentation of the issues in chapters 3 and 4 is my tendency to present the history of divinity in an overly linear and schematic fashion. I am aware of this shortcoming. Competing ideas about the configuration of the pantheon were operative at any given time, both prior to and during ancient Israel. Nonetheless, the approach taken in this short study may serve to clarify the situation as it was unfolding in ancient Israel. I do not think that, for the purposes of this discussion, adding more layers of hypotheses and data would advance the basic ideas that much farther. Further layers would also reduce the accessibility to the fundamental points of the presentation.

Because these historical issues are ultimately of importance for understanding the God of the Bible, I offer some thoughts in a brief postscript following chapter 4. The issues raised there are ultimately religious and theological in character, as they impinge on the contemporary search for God. Readers will see in this section that I step away from my basic task of examination of the primary evidence and reflect on some of the implications that the analysis in this book holds for religion, theology, and history. As is so often the case for those interested in such questions (whether religious or not), the Bible remains an indispensable beginning point, the "Genesis."

In a book of this sort, a writer might have devoted one chapter to each period of Israel's culture. Instead, I begin each of the four chapters with early Israel and trace its development in a different way. In chapter 1 I trace the Bible's representation of Israel's past. In chapter 2 I examine the history of challenges to Israel, how Israel addressed those crises, and how Israel's writings as represented by what are now biblical books not only contain Israel's recording of its difficulties but also constitute its response to these crises. With monotheism already noted in chapter 2 as a major dimension of Israel's response to the crises of the seventh and sixth centuries, in chapter 3 I back up to the beginning of Israel's religious history and trace its understanding of divinity, from the antecedent polytheism of the region (now best attested in the Ugaritic texts), through Israel's early polytheism down to Israel's monotheistic expressions best seen in the seventh and sixth centuries. In chapter 4 I offer one final sweep of Israelite culture, this time by examining some of the ways in which this culture remembered its religious past and especially how the later monotheism of the seventh and sixth centuries altered Israel's recollection of its earlier understanding of divinity.

As a result of this approach, I begin this book with what is most familiar about the Bible and its representation of Israel and God through time, and move to the less familiar terrain of the cultural mechanisms that led to the biblical representations of the past. What seems at the beginning to look like history ends up looking like a mixture of historical facts with cultural echoes and memories from different periods. The Bible's ultimate purpose was not primarily to record a dispassionate or a single version of the past. Instead, the ongoing dialogue in ancient Israel over the different versions of the past involved impassioned efforts designed to enable Israel to face the crises it experienced over time and to reach to the future with hope, accompanied by the God(s) whom it had recalled from its earliest remembered past.

The powerful human and divine narratives of the past, as Israel remembered it, made a massive impact on Israelite efforts to cope with crises and to find meaning in its existence as well as comfort in the knowledge of its covenant with God. Over the course of time, these stories of Israel and its Deity became enshrined as authoritative religious writings and eventually books of the canonical Bible. These became recognized as God's revelation about Israel's past, and as a result they were transformed, in a sense, into the memoirs of God.

The Biblical Backdrop to the Story of Israel

The LORD caused festival and
sabbath to be forgotten in Zion
—Lamentations 2:6

Introduction: The Bible and the Task of History

Until relatively recently, a typical description of Israel's history would essentially follow the outline of the Bible, supplemented by archaeological information and texts outside the Bible. With the Genesis stories of creation and flood providing both backdrop and rationale (Genesis 1–11), "biblical history" begins with the divine choice of Abraham and his descendants marked by an eternal covenant (Genesis 12–36). The Israelites, Abraham's line named after his grandson Jacob-Israel, travel to Egypt to escape famine (Genesis 37–50), only to be enslaved later by the Egyptians (Exodus 1–2). Moses emerges to lead the Israelites out of Egypt with divine aid (Exodus 3–15). After traveling to Mount Sinai, the people receive the covenant from God through Moses (Exodus 16–Numbers 10), who then leads them toward the land promised to their ancestors (Numbers 10–36; the narrative of Exodus through Numbers is retold and telescoped in Deuteronomy). The conquest and settlement of the land (Joshua) is followed by temptations to idolatry, as practiced by Israel's neighbors, which issues in divine punishments in the form of foreign oppression (Judges). This difficulty sets in motion the rise of the glorious monarchy of David and Solomon crowned by the building of the Jerusalem Temple (1–2 Samuel and 1 Kings 1–11). After the death of Solomon, the monarchy fissures into two kingdoms, with the north falling to Mesopotamian conquerors first and the south following suit about 150 years later (1 Kings 12–2 Kings 25). This second disaster is marked by the fall of Jerusalem, the destruction of the Temple, and the exile of the people to Babylon (2 Kings 25). Postexilic historiography retells the story down to the exile (1–2 Chronicles) and further narrates the life of the former Judean community under the Persians (Ezra and Nehemiah).

Guided by this overall outline, archaeology and texts outside the Bible traditionally served to illustrate the biblical narrative and to fill in the blanks. A good
example of a history book about ancient Israel that uses the Bible for its basic historical outline would be John Bright's *History of Israel* (1959). The earlier parts of
the biblical narrative, in particular the patriarchs and matriarchs as well as the Israelite enslavement in Egypt and the exodus, would be considered historical
events to be situated in the Middle Bronze Age (ca. 2000–1550 B.C.E.) and Late
Bronze Age (ca. 1550–1200 B.C.E.). Archaeology would provide information that
would seemingly bolster the accuracy of the biblical account. For example, the
Israelite connection to the Hapiru (or Habiru) mentioned in Mesopotamian
sources was long a preeminent question in biblical studies, as the word *hap/biru*
seemed rather close to the word "Hebrew." Similarly, the Israelite migration to
Egypt was thought to be linked to western Asiatic immigrants mentioned in Egyptian texts. In these instances, extrabiblical information served to buttress the biblical narrative. Especially in older American and Israeli scholarly treatments, the
Bible was treated accordingly as historically accurate, though some possible anachronisms might be conceded (for example, Abraham and Sarah traveling on
camels in Genesis 12:16 and 24:10-23, or the Philistines mentioned in Genesis 26).

When it came to Joshua–Kings, the biblical narrative provided not only source
material for a historical picture, but also the basis for delineating the periods of
Israel's past. The books of Joshua and Judges were essentially regarded as com-
mensurate with the Iron I period for ancient Israel (ca. 1200–1000 B.C.E.), and
1–2 Kings constituted the primary source for the period of the monarchy (ca. 1000–
586 B.C.E.). The beginning of the exile (ca. 586–538 B.C.E.) was based on the
final chapters of 2 Kings 25 and on other sources. The end of the exile was founded
on "Second Isaiah" (Isaiah 40–55), in particular Isaiah 44:28 and 45:1, with their
references to Cyrus the Persian, and on extrabiblical sources, for example, the
Cyrus Cylinder (*ANET,* 315–16). Scholarly descriptions of life during the Persian
period (540–333 B.C.E.) in Judah, in this period called Yehud, would draw largely
on the books of Ezra and Nehemiah, with some blanks filled in by some of the
prophets. As new texts and archaeological discoveries continued to emerge, they
were seen to confirm the framework provided by the Bible.

This way of approaching biblical history long dominated scholarly research
in the United States, but since the 1970s it has come under increasing attack.
First there was seen to be a lack of "historical-looking" information in Genesis–
Deuteronomy, known in Jewish tradition as the Torah and as the Pentateuch in
Christian tradition. Furthermore, the problem of the temporal gap between the
events related by this biblical work and its composition has left substantial doubt in
the minds of many scholars as to its historical value. Although the events allegedly
related by Genesis through Deuteronomy were situated by scholars in the Middle

and Late Bronze Age, biblical scholars have long dated these works as we presently have them to the period of the monarchy and exile. This dating is based convincingly on the grammar of the prose portions of the Torah, which compare most closely to Samuel and Kings. Hebrew grammar in ancient Israel developed over time, and just as English compositions, such as Beowulf, the Canterbury Tales, Shakespeare's plays, and T. S. Eliot's poems can be identified linguistically as belonging to different periods of the English language, so too biblical books or their parts date to different phases of Biblical Hebrew. The oldest stage of Biblical Hebrew is represented in the archaic poetry of Genesis 49 and Judges 5; standard preexilic Hebrew is reflected in most prose of Genesis–Kings; and postexilic Hebrew is exemplified by Chronicles, Ezra, and Nehemiah. Accordingly, the Torah looks like a largely monarchic period production.

Scholars have also identified a number of different sources underlying the Torah. This theory, known as the "Documentary Hypothesis" or the "four-source theory," was long resisted by many Jewish and Christian scholars, but in the last few decades it has become broadly accepted, though with significant modifications. One sign of this development is the state of the current debate. At present, the vast majority of critical scholars, including Jewish biblical scholars, accept the notion that the Torah is composed of multiple works, though not necessarily four separate sources as such. The most accessible discussions of this hypothesis are by Richard Elliott Friedman (1989, and especially 2003, which lays out the whole Torah in translation with the various sources marked by color and highlighting; see also the important book of Carr 1996).

The first source is customarily labeled the Yahwist ("J," from the German "Jahwist"), based on the divine name Yahweh (substituted by "the LORD" in most translations) in narrative up to the call of Moses. The second is the Elohist ("E," based on the divine name Elohim, translated as "God"). Differentiated largely according to these different divine names as well as narrative doublets, "J" and "E" had been considered independent narratives covering events down to the Israelites' arrival at Sinai and the wilderness travels afterward. Based on the place-names mentioned in "J," this source was thought to have been composed in Judah, the southern kingdom, probably during the monarchy. By the same logic, the "E" source was considered a northern or Israelite composition also dating to the monarchy. That "J" dates to the monarchy can be seen in its stories about Esau, said to be the ancestor of the Edomites, who were neighbors of Judah. As Friedman has observed, the "J" story of Genesis 25:23 and 27:40 refers to Judah's dominion over Edom until the reign of the Judean king Jehoram (ca. 848–842 B.C.E.). Genesis 25:23 presents Israel's domination of Esau and 27:40 predicts Edom's independence. Only a monarchic setting would be appropriate for such these references. That "E" also reflects a setting also during this period can be seen in how its story of the golden calf in Exodus 32 seems to be less a historical account of the Late Bronze Age than a monarchic period polemic against the royal calf cult of Jeroboam I. What we see in Exodus 32:4, 8 is a reaction against Jeroboam's shrines in 1 Kings 12:28, as both passages refer to the northern cultic tradition that "these are your gods which brought you out of the land of Egypt" (see Toews 1993). Based on this kind of detective work, the written composition of the "J" and "E" works has been dated to the monarchy period. For a long time, scholars favored dates in the tenth and ninth centuries, respectively. However, their dates have been a matter of debate. Some contemporary scholars have lowered their dates by at least a century. Furthermore, "J" and "E" may not be independent works. It is possible that one may have been a series of supplements to the other.

Deuteronomic texts (or the "D" source) are represented first and foremost by the book of Deuteronomy. In addition, other Deuteronomic texts to be found in other books of the Torah were largely identified by the vocabulary and style in Deuteronomy; these include passages such as the Passover instructions in Exodus 12:24-27. Generally speaking, most Deuteronomic texts seem to belong to the seventh–sixth centuries based largely on parallels between Deuteronomy and a number of Neo-Assyrian treaties as well as other texts (see Levinson 1997).

Priestly material (or "P") is the most extensive "source" in the Torah. It includes stories throughout the Torah, beginning with Genesis 1:1—2:3 and ending in the priestly addition in Deuteronomy 34:7-9. It also involved a huge corpus of laws, or better labeled by Chaim Cohen (personal communication) as "priestly instructional literature," including instructions for, and construction of, the tabernacle in Exodus 25–31, 35–40; the instructions in Leviticus, often divided into two works: Leviticus 1–16, mainly for the priesthood, and Leviticus 17–26, "the Holiness Code," designed to serve as the priestly equivalent for the people; and much of the opening chapters of Numbers 1–10. Priestly hands are also thought to lie behind the final compilation of the Torah. Given the wide range of priestly material, it seems better not to regard it as a single source, but as various materials from priestly tradition dating from around the eighth century, though possibly earlier, through the Persian period (ca. 540–333)(see Knohl 1995, 2003). In addition, two legal compositions, which may or may not be associated with the other works, have been identified. One is the famous Ten Commandments, thought by some scholars to be early, despite priestly additions in the Exodus 20 version and Deuteronomic touches in the Deuteronomy 5 version; the other is "the Covenant Code" in Exodus 21–23.

Many scholars still support the idea of four separate sources, although their dates continue to be debated. Some holding this view retain the older idea of four "sources" as such, while others offer a more complicated version of this theory and combine sources with some ongoing revisions within the sources. Still other scholars instead see the Torah (Pentateuch) as a "rolling corpus" composed first of either the Yahwist or the Elohist—themselves incorporating earlier traditions— supplemented by the other, to which the priestly and Deuteronomic materials were subsequently added, further supplemented by priestly editorial revisions.

Most scholars locate these works and their associated editorial activity during the late monarchy and the exile, although a small number of academics date the essential composition of the Torah even later, to the Persian or even Hellenistic period. While some late scribal changes and additions in the Torah may belong to this period, the linguistic evidence for the vast bulk of the Torah militates against this late date. Theories abound in the present debate, but what is not debated is the composite nature of the Torah and the dating of its written composition in the period of the monarchy and afterward. As a result, if one wants to view the biblical presentation of the past as a linear history, then one has to deal with the problem that the events associated with the biblical patriarchs predate the composition of Genesis by many hundreds of years, and the events of the rest of the Torah by several hundred.

A comparable difficulty affects how we understand the so-called historical books of Joshua, Judges, 1–2 Samuel, and 1–2 Kings. Although the writing of these works stands closer in time to the events they purport to present, these works have also passed through multiple levels of composition, each reflecting interpretations of the past layered on top of one another. These works seemed to have come together under the influence of an Israelite writer or a series of authors operating in the late monarchy and exile and afterward and influenced by Deuteronomy, or, more broadly, by the tradition represented by this book (as surveyed by Schniedewind 1996; see also Barrick 2002, Knoppers 2001, and the essays in Römer and de Pury 2000). The biblical books from Joshua through 2 Kings have therefore been labeled "the Deuteronomistic History," as its later layers show the perspective also in evidence in Deuteronomy, its basic text thought to be a seventh- or sixth-century work with later additions (such as Deuteronomy 1:1—4:43, with its references to exile among the nations). It is arguable that the earliest versions of the "Deuteronomistic History" may have drawn on and incorporated some prior written sources, for example, the poem in Judges 5, and some material from the histories of the kings of the northern and southern kingdoms, and some form of the Elijah cycle in 1 Kings 17–19. Even so, these prior texts were likely modified in light of later circumstances when they were incorporated into the Deuteronomistic History, and there also remained many gaps in the knowledge of Israel's past. In other words, the oldest edition proposed for this Deuteronomistic History, whether in part or in whole, has been dated to the time of Hezekiah (see Barrick 2002 for a critical discussion, as well as Schnieckwind 2004). Working with this date for the Deuteronomistic History, a substantial gap still stands between most *oral tradition*

events narrated in Joshua, Judges, 1–2 Samuel, and 1 Kings 1 through most of 2 Kings on the one hand, and, on the other hand, the date when these works were composed overall.

The history of the textual composition of all these so-called historical books may indeed have varied quite a bit, prior to their larger amalgamation into the Deuteronomistic History. Moreover, it would seem from the critical analysis of these works that they passed not from one early stage of oral tradition to one later written phase, but through several stages, with oral and written versions potentially influencing one another (see Schniedewind 2004). Getting at the "history" in these so-called historical works is no simple task. Certainly, it would be mistaken to understand these works as history, if by "history" one means a presentation of the past with any critical reflection on the nature and quality of the sources used. As Machinist has observed (2003, in a discussion of the book of Nehemiah), biblical presentations of the past make no effort to produce what was the practice of ancient Greek historians such as Herodotus or Thucydides (much less modern historians), namely, a presentation of the past that shows an effort either to determine the nature of the evidence for what is narrated or to judge what is authentic or verifiable.

Despite these problems, many scholars—perhaps operating under the influence of their own religious traditions—would affirm the accuracy of biblical events even as they recognize the texts' later date of composition in their present form. To fill in the temporal gap, some have appealed to the notion that oral compositions of the Torah and the Deuteronomistic History would have been handed down over the centuries, with their linguistic features being updated along the way. For example, linguistic updating of this type is indicated in the case of some biblical doublets such as Psalm 18 = 2 Samuel 22. In the absence of such doublets, however, such a long duration is impossible to confirm. Such activity may be accounted for by differences not between earlier oral versions and later written versions, but between written versions of different dates in addition to earlier and contemporary oral versions. As a result, the jury is still out over the plausibility of identifying such oral tradition generally for the biblical representations of Israel's past, with widely varying opinions being voiced. No one doubts the importance of oral tradition and some earlier written texts in ancient Israel, but it is unclear how well and to what extent these fill many of the temporal gaps we are considering. Even if such long traditions could be sustained and some earlier written works can be uncovered, this would not necessarily support the general historical reliability of such traditions or works, as they would have been subject in different generations to revisions, with their later concerns and horizons overwriting older ones. These would be historical to some degree, yet they would have also been added to and modified in light of later circumstances. Untangling the older historical traditions and material from the later additions can be exceedingly difficult at times, and scholars widely disagree over which is which.

It is evident from the monarchic-period grammar and other features in the Torah and the Deuteronomistic History that what they preserve is not so much "history" as foundational narratives about Israel's identity as it was being discussed and debated over the period of the monarchy and later. In the Torah, readers glimpse not so much an original word-for-word historical account of events from the Bronze Age, but monarchic-period and later memories about Israel in narrative form as well as prescriptions about what Israel should be. In other words, the Torah is teaching, which is in fact the very meaning of the word. The Deuteronomistic History shows a moralistic effort in explaining the past, in particular the reason why Israel has the land (divine choice and conquest in Joshua), why Israel needed a monarchy (Israel's apostasy described in Judges), how Israel came to have a monarchy (by divine concession in 1–2 Samuel), how an initially glorious monarchy failed (thanks to divine patronage followed by moral failures in 1–2 Kings); in short, why Israel was defeated, its king imprisoned, its Temple destroyed, and its people exiled in 586 B.C.E. The goal of explaining Israel's past has deeply informed its presentation, both in its selection and in its perspectives. The "biblical history" constructed in the Torah and the Deuteronomistic History represents Israel's national foundational story hostage to the conditions of the people's present and their hopes for the future.

In view of these goals of the Torah and the Deuteronomistic History, "biblical history" or the Bible as history has been consequently demoted in the contemporary historical task. Without being dismissed as historically useless, the Bible no longer holds a privileged place in dictating the norms for reconstructing Israel's past. Especially in some quarters in the United States until the early 1970s, there was also a sense that the Bible's representation of the past is historical unless shown otherwise; it was given the benefit of the doubt. For any given event or development, biblical evidence—like any other source about the past—is to be scrutinized for its historical reliability. For historians, confirmation or verification of any witness, wherever possible, is the preferred mode of operating. The biblical witness is considered and weighed along with archaeological evidence and extrabiblical texts after these have separately been assessed for their historical value.

As a reaction against using the Bible as a historical source, it has been common to hail archaeological discoveries and extrabiblical texts as antidotes that allow scholars to "get behind the Bible." Yet these sources of information, though not mediated by thousands of years of religious tradition, are mediated by the process of archaeological preservation and discovery as well as subsequent interpretation. Archaeologists argue over the number of occupational phases at various sites, not to mention the possible dates of these phases or evidence for them.

mediation

The interpretation of items discovered at these different levels is also a matter of discussion and debate. Moreover, like many biblical scholars, many archaeologists enter this field inspired by their religious training in the Bible, and their horizons for interpreting the past via archaeological discoveries may be shaped either by religious convictions or by subsequent rejection of religious faith. This does not mean that such discoveries are necessarily suspect, but it does mean that elucidating archaeological discoveries, like reading the Bible, involves a substantial amount of interpretation. No one enters the enterprise of biblical studies (or any area of study) without interpretive horizons.

Another major change over the past few decades involves the very subject of history. In interpreting biblical texts in conjunction with archaeological discoveries, the task of reconstructing history has moved from an emphasis on specific events and important personages to a broader reconstruction of cultural history that acknowledges a wide variety of social, economic, religious, and intellectual factors. Under the influence of broader historical studies (for example, the *Annales* school), microhistory, and feminist and cultural studies, the study of the ancient world has shifted toward the larger context of ancient life, its societal structures and environmental conditions.

Any description of the biblical past operates at three levels: the events themselves and their larger cultural context in the past; the texts that describe and interpret those events and that context, as well as the other artifacts that reflect that context; and the modern historical inquiry that attempts to sort through the texts and other evidence in order to get at that past. Each of these three levels entails difficulties. The total past reality is not recoverable, and even if it were, its understanding would remain highly debated. The sources available in the Bible are largely snapshots of the past, with later narrators superimposing their own interpretations of Israel's past on these older pictures. These narratives have been supplemented and interpreted by yet later narrators and other snapshots so that any earlier material or our sense of them is highly interpreted at best and badly distorted at worst. The authors at all of these stages were not writing disinterested history; the texts often reflect their authors' present concerns. Indeed, what seem to be historical narratives are themselves responses to the challenges of the times when their composition took place. The large historical-looking works of the Bible contain several levels or stages of composition, and these various stages are themselves responses to different challenges, whether it was the Assyrian conquest of the northern kingdom of Israel in 722 B.C.E., the Babylonian conquests of the southern kingdom of Judah in 597 and 586, the exile of Judean leadership to Babylonia first in 597 and then again in 586, or the often impoverished conditions of life and subservience under the Persian Empire after 540. Finally, we modern interpreters also have our horizons shaped in rather particular ways, and our own individual interests are often at work. Furthermore, we are unable to perceive very well our own roles in distorting our data.

Given this situation, my effort at sketching "biblical backdrop" in this chapter presents biblical writings both as products of their authors' times and as older historical realities arguably standing behind and informing these texts, as understood in light of the current available ancient sources and archaeological remains and cognizant of contemporary biases and limitations in reconstructing history. In chapter 4 I discuss at greater length the question of biblical writings as products of their authors' own times, in other words, how biblical works constitute the collective memory of their authors. In what follows in this first chapter, I offer some remarks along these lines, but the focus for now remains directed at the question of biblical works as sources for history. For readers interested in a critical study of Israelite history, the best single-volume work available in English is Gösta W. Ahlström's *The History of Ancient Palestine from the Palaeolithic Period to Alexander's Conquest*. For Israel's history, I also highly recommend the works by Baruch Halpern and Nadav Na'aman. For some good reflections of history and history writing in the biblical world, I would suggest also the works by Marc Brettler, Peter Machinist, and Marc van de Mieroop. For overviews of Israelite religion, one may consult the books by Rainer Albertz and Ziony Zevit. For archaeology and the study of ancient Israel, I would recommend the works by Elizabeth Bloch-Smith, Avraham Faust, Amihai Mazar, and Nadav Na'aman. (These authors' works are listed in the bibliography in the back of this book.)

What readers will see in many of these studies is a picking apart of the Bible's works for historical purposes correlated with archaeological and textual information from outside the Bible. The resulting picture hardly looks like the Bible's own outline of Israel's history. The "biblical backdrop" really combines Israel's later memory of its past with actual events and conditions of that past. How the Israelites remembered and passed on their stories expressed as much about themselves as the events they attempted to relate. We might say, then, that the Bible shows a mixture of Israel's past and Israel's collective memories about that past.

I would like to give one illustration of what I mean. The description of the Jerusalem Temple in 1 Kings 6–8 refers to actual historical facts, but parts of these chapters also date from different times and they reflect different views of the Temple from various periods. Based on parallels from the archaeological record, it would seem that the types of artifacts, pictorial representations on the Temple's walls, and its overall architecture described in 1 Kings 6–7 reflect a tenth- or ninth-century background, in short, the time when the Temple was first built. As demonstrated by Elizabeth Bloch-Smith, the Temple itself is an expression of divine residence in the royal chapel—an indication of divine blessings on the king, the people, and the land. Divine warriorship is reflected in the mention in 1 Kings

7:23-26 of the superhuman-sized bronze sea (about 7.5 feet high), which symbolizes the divine victory over the sea. Divine blessing is represented in the names of
the pillars of the Temple, called Yachin and Boaz in 1 Kings 7:21, best understood
as a request for blessing: "May he [God] establish [his people/king/house] in
strength" (compare the blessing in Psalm 29:11: "May the LORD grant strength to
his people, may the LORD bestow well-being on his people"). Divine kingship is
reflected in the back room as a divine throne room. As Torje Stordalen (2000),
Philip King and Lawrence Stager (2001), and others have observed, the Temple
also reflects the home of the god on his holy mountain-garden, marked by the
palm trees and cherubim on the walls (1 Kings 6:35).

   This is not the only view of the Temple preserved in the text. The dedication
prayer of Solomon in 1 Kings 8 shows an awareness of exile, as in verses 46-48:

> When they sin against You (for there is no one who does not sin), and You are
> angry with them and You deliver them to an enemy, and their captors carry them
> captive to enemy land, whether far or near, and then they turn in their heart in the
> land where they have been taken captive, and they turn and make supplication to
> You in the land of their captors... and they pray to You in the direction of their
> land that You gave to their fathers, the city that You chose and the House that I
> built to your name....

This passage seems to reflect captivity to lands both near and far, in other words,
exile to a number of different nations, a condition of Judeans during the Persian
period (ca. 540–333). In this part of Solomon's prayer in 1 Kings 8, the Temple is
presented not so much as a house of sacrifice, one of the main functions of ancient temples, but as a house of prayer (vv. 27-30).

   A number of features in this chapter recall Deuteronomy. For example,
1 Kings 8:9 mentions the tablets of stone, which Moses had placed inside the ark
at Mount Horeb, which is also Deuteronomy's word for Sinai. Also based on the
other features of this prayer shared with Deuteronomy (provided in great detail
by Cogan 2001), scholars now generally argue that this prayer is exilic or postexilic. In the memory of 1 Kings 8, the Temple is no longer an expression so much
of divine warriorship, blessing, and kingship—in short, power and presence. Instead, it is the commemoration place of God's covenant with Moses at Mount
Horeb; it is also the site not of sacrifice but of prayer. This God to be prayed to is
not in the Temple as in the older view; instead, the Temple serves as a "relay station"
for prayers that come from anywhere on earth to the God who is in the "heavenly
abode" (1 Kings 8:30).

   In between the original construction of the Temple and the later Deuteronomistic (exilic or postexilic) view are other memories of the Temple. Within the
non-Deuteronomistic material in 1 Kings 6–7, some features suggest that the text

itself, as opposed to what it refers to, may have been written down in the eighth century. Because these features have largely gone unnoticed, some specifics need to be mentioned at this point. The first set of features involves Akkadian loan words into the Hebrew of 1 Kings 6–7. Relevant examples would include the verb "covered" *('achaz)* in 1 Kings 6:10 (rendered "joined" in the NRSV). This word's sense "covered" is regarded as a "loan-meaning" from Akkadian into Hebrew (noted by Mankowski 2001 and Cogan 2001). Another possible case concerns the phrase "solid gold" *(zahab sagur)* found in 1 Kings 6:20; 7:49, 50 (sometimes translated as "pure gold" as in NRSV). This looks like a loan-phrase from Akkadian *huratsu sagiru*. Given the exceptional meaning "solid" for the Hebrew word *sagur* in 1 Kings 6–7, and given its considerable attestation in Akkadian, the term in Hebrew is evidently some sort of loan from Akkadian. For the purposes of dating, these linguistic features are not firm in themselves. They allow room anywhere from the eighth through the sixth centuries B.C.E. (and perhaps wider). They are valuable for our discussion because they caution us against placing the composition of the building account, as we presently have it, in Solomon's own time in the tenth century. One might try to get around this problem by hypothesizing a rewriting of the text from Solomon's time down to the eighth century B.C.E. That way, one could claim that 1 Kings 6–7 was based on an older "book of deeds" of Solomon (1 Kings 11:41). However, a proposed rewriting of this sort cannot be confirmed.

As corollary support for at least an eighth-century date for the enshrinement of older traditions in 1 Kings 3–11, one might appeal to the lists of officials in Solomon's administration given in 1 Kings 4. These are generally free of ideologically laden additions, and they have suffered some secondary displacement (see 9:23). Both factors would suggest the presence of the lists in the record prior to the present Deuteronomistic arrangement of 1 Kings 3–11, and they may point to some amount of historical material (as discussed by Fox 2000). In sum, the older composition of 1 Kings 6–7 in its current form would not date to either the tenth or ninth century in view of the apparent Akkadian influence, which would not come into play until the eighth century.

A more crucial consideration favoring the eighth-century date for the written composition of the pre-Deuteronomistic material in 1 Kings 6–7 has been put forward by Cogan (2001). If the author of 1 Kings 6–7 had written this text in the time frame of the exilic period, then the changes in the Jerusalem Temple plan made by King Ahaz (as described in 2 Kings 16:17-18) would have been reflected into the account of 1 Kings 6–7. The historical implication is at once simple and significant. The pre-Deuteronomistic text of 1 Kings 6–7 was apparently composed prior to Ahaz's change in the Temple arrangement. In sum, given our present information, a time prior to Ahaz appears suitable for the basic composition of the pre-Deuteronomistic sections of 1 Kings 6–7. It would seem that in emphasizing the Temple's gold, the eighth-century author wanted to stress its wealth. We may guess also that this composition offers up a nostalgic memory for the old Temple and for the old Solomonic monarchy.

So far we have a tenth- or ninth-century Temple plan reflected not in the composition of our text, but in the architecture and the items described by it. We also have an eighth-century composition of 1 Kings 6–7 reflected by some Akkadian loan items as well as the retention of the older Temple plan that was changed by the eighth-century king Ahaz. Then we have an exilic or postexilic composition that reflects Deuteronomistic views. These three levels show different memories of Solomon's Temple: the Temple as an expression of divine power and presence; the Temple as a site of royal wealth and perhaps nostalgia for the old Temple and the "good old days" under Solomon; and the Temple as the site of Mosaic teaching and prayer. These are three very different memories of the Temple, and they are not the only memories or levels of memory inserted into the Temple account. Scholars have detected others as well. In sum, the Temple account mixes historical details and memories. 1 Kings 6–8 attracted from different periods various memories of the Temple that also expressed hopes for Israel's future. In its current form, the Temple account is now an echo chamber of the past views of the Temple. It is this mix of actual events and different memories of them that informs the Bible's representation of the past.

The following description of the biblical backdrop or biblical representation of Israel's past focuses on the Bible's historiographical works, namely, the Torah and the Deuteronomistic History as well as 1–2 Chronicles and Ezra–Nehemiah. Within these texts, we see the biblical backdrop (or what we might call the historical setting of ancient Israel) mixed with memories of the past. We also find expressions of the crises faced by Israel over its history, and sometimes it is these that have altered Israel's memory about its past and therefore its representation of its past in the Bible. In short, later crises generated new memories of Israel's earlier periods. Both Israel's history and its responses to its historical challenges meet in the Bible's memories of the past.

The Mythic Period of Moses

What would have passed in older scholarly descriptions of Israel (for example, Bright 1959) as the moments of its earliest history would have been the stories of the patriarchs in Genesis and the exodus from Egypt. Over the past few decades, this view has badly eroded, if only for a lack of texts inside the Bible or outside it that offer a contemporary or near-contemporary witness to the events in question. In the Bible as we have it, the books of Genesis and Exodus, indeed the five books of the Torah (Pentateuch) overall, generally date to no earlier than the monarchy. As noted above, it is not professionally responsible for historians to give more credence to the historical value of the Bible simply because it is the Bible. However, this is not the end of the matter. While it has remained problematic to grant any historical substance to the patriarchal stories as such, this is not quite the case with the exodus. It is true that the exodus story shows signs of monarchic (and later) construction. The language of the Hebrew in Exodus is hardly premonarchic, and occasionally allusions in the book betray its monarchic context (as in Exodus 32:4, 8, compared with 1 Kings 12:28, which we will discuss later). However, beyond the matter of assembling and assessing information, historians may consider circumstantial evidence as well, and in the account of the exodus there are some circumstantial considerations. These have been debated, and many scholars would reject their value for historical purposes; other scholars accept one or more of them as having historical value indicating that there was some sort of departure from Egypt by some antecedents of the Israelites. It is true that several unpersuasive and grandiose claims continue to be made with little warrant, but there are lesser claims that may be viewed as having some plausibility.

Three features suggest a possible historical kernel behind the biblical account of the exodus. First, the names of Moses, Aaron, Phinehas, and others in their line are an important consideration in this discussion, because these names are not Hebrew but Egyptian. So these names may suggest an Egyptian background for at least some Israelites. The biblical tradition is further interesting, since it ascribes a Hebrew etymology for the name of Moses (Exodus 2:10), provided by an Egyptian no less. It shows that the Egyptian background of these biblical names had been forgotten. One might argue instead that Moses and others in his line received Egyptian names in order to lend an Egyptian flavor to the story. If this were true, then the Egyptian background of these names would be significant for the biblical writers, but then they would not have provided a Hebrew explanation for the name of Moses. Indeed, it is less plausible that some writer would make up Egyptian names for their Israelite legendary heroes to give an Egyptian ring to the story, only to provide a Hebrew etymology for such names. Instead, it is more likely that the Egyptian names of Moses and Aaron point to some early memory of Israel in Egypt. In other words, the line of Moses and Aaron could have descended from part of a group that had contact with Egypt.

Second, it seems to many historians that no ancient group would have made up a foundational tradition that presents its ancestors as slaves; more glorious origins would have been more likely. The Bible does offer a number of other foundational stories, often with supernatural conflict (Psalm 74:12-17) or other superhuman features (Genesis 32). So, in view of the Bible's sense of origins in texts such as these, we may doubt that some writer artificially created a story locating Israel's origins in slavery.

Third, specimens of what have been taken to be some of the older poems in the Bible recall the exodus (Exodus 15; Numbers 23–24). What suggests their historical value to my mind is their fundamentally different presentations of the god responsible for the exodus. The old poems of Numbers 23–24, which vary in date from the eleventh century through the early monarchy, use the divine name El more times than Yahweh for the God of Israel. This usage suggests an alternative Israelite view in the region on the eastern side of the Jordan River (Transjordan). This understanding stands in contrast to what became the conventional idea in the period of the monarchy that Yahweh was the god of the exodus. These poems specify that it was El who brought Israel out of Egypt (Numbers 23:22; 24:8). In contrast, the allegedly old poem in Exodus 15 associates this event with Yahweh.

This difference in perspective, El versus Yahweh as the god of the exodus, within what are thought by many biblical scholars to be among Israel's oldest literary specimens, may be viewed as evidence for different traditions lying behind the poems in Exodus 15 and Numbers 23–24. To my mind, the variety in these old biblical traditions over the deity of the exodus points to a substantial period of tradition lying behind what seem to be some of Israel's earliest texts. The point may be added that Israel was already some sort of social entity by about 1208, the time of the reference to Israel in a stela praising Pharaoh Merneptah's victories. So Israel must have had some traditions predating 1208. Although there is no further means available to confirm the exodus tradition, it is possible that it existed among some Israelites already by this time. In short, the exodus seems to belong to Israel's earliest traditions, and its historicity in some form cannot be rejected or assumed to be false at the outset.

At the same time, it is true that the exodus may not have taken place in all the exalted ways recalled in the later strands of the prose narrative of Exodus 1–14, but that hardly precludes the possibility that some elements of historicity may lie behind the text of Exodus. Many scholars are utterly dismissive, even contemptuous, of attempts to search for a historical kernel of the exodus. Affirmations of the historical veracity of the exodus are sometimes regarded as intellectually feeble efforts inspired by misplaced religious sensibilities. The points that I have mentioned in favor of seeing some sort of exodus are disputed, yet they cannot be dismissed out of hand.

More to the point, neither skeptics nor the religiously devoted can "prove" their view, largely because of the gaps in the textual and archaeological record.

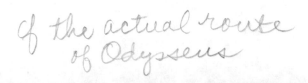
of the actual route
of Odysseus

Like old shards of ancient memory preserved in Genesis, the narrative of Exodus through Numbers may contain older traditions that were shaped to later Israelite concerns. That some of these do not conform to the ideas of monarchic Israel and later would suggest some historical basis for them; how much older these are and how precisely they conform to some sort of ancient historical reality are questions that lie beyond our reach. However, the evidence as it stands permits the historical possibility that the groups known to have moved by land routes between Egypt and the Levant may have included some ancestors of the Israelites (though hardly the large numbers reported in the Bible). In the land, this early Israelite people evidently constituted a patriarchal society with a subsistence economy based on agriculture and animal husbandry, which in turn supported and required trade and various crafts and technologies. The picture of this society becomes clearer when we get to the sources for the premonarchic period, sometimes labeled the "period of the judges."

The Period of the Judges (ca. 1200–1000?)

On the stage of world history, Israel does not appear until the end of the thirteenth century. Outside the Bible, as already mentioned, Israel is first attested in a victory stela of Pharaoh Merneptah, as a people living in the highlands of the southern Levant (ca. 1208 B.C.E.). Merneptah brags: "Israel is laid waste, his seed is not" (*ANET,* 378). Unlike other names in the stela marked with the special sign for a land or place, the name of Israel is marked with the special sign for a people. Many scholars take this point in time as Israel's earliest known historical indicator as a people. Based on archaeological information and older sections of the book of Judges, we get a sense of the general conditions of the people residing in the highlands. During this period, patriarchal clans lived in the highland territory between the Mediterranean coast and the Jordan River valley. Their agricultural harvests over the course of the spring and early fall matched the timing of dry weather, while the rainy season running from fall through early spring permitted agricultural activities of plowing, planting, and tending the crops, as reflected in a tenth-century inscription known as the Gezer Calendar (*ANET,* 320). For a description of Israelite life at this time (as well as later periods), I highly recommend King and Stager (2001).

The archaeological and textual evidence also supports the view favored since the 1980s that Israelite culture was largely based on the local "Canaanite" (or West Semitic) culture. Contrary to the biblical presentation, the Israelites did not entirely come into the land from outside. On the basis of shared traits such as pottery and burial types, language, and other cultural features, scholars have come to the conclusion that the "Israel" of the highlands in the premonarchic period largely developed out of the local culture. (For this view, see Smith 1990, 2002a; and for a highly sophisticated study from an anthropological and archaeological perspective, see the groundbreaking article by Bloch-Smith 2003.) This view, however, does not preclude the plausibility of the biblical memory of Israelites as outsiders to the land. Indeed, the very complexity of the biblical traditions of Israel as outsiders to the land may suggest some ancient memories of foreign origins. While it would be impossible to prove the historical veracity of the traditions, they show variety as well as apparent contradiction and harmonization. The biblical traditions preserve the memory of both the exodus traditions of Israel from Egypt and the tradition of Israel coming from Aram (Deuteronomy 26:5: "my father was a wandering [or better, 'refugee'] Aramean"). This variation may itself be a witness to some ancient memory that some elements of early Israel derived from outside the land.

As we find throughout the ancient Near East, the religion of ancient Israel was built on the family unit. Amply demonstrated in a first-rate treatment by van der Toorn (1996), family religion was both the model and the setting for religious practice and belief. Home shrines, perhaps located in doorways and gates as well as the recesses of houses, served as the focal point for religious expression to deities and deceased relatives: both belonged to the category of divinity *(elohim)*. Altars, as well as other religious symbols, such as the sacred pole or tree called the asherah (possibly representing the goddess known by the same name), might be constructed outside the home for family (or clan) religious practice (for an example, see Judges 6). Religious celebration marking the various life-cycle events of birth, marriage, and death were all family affairs, which marked lines of continuity through the generations (see the important book of Bloch-Smith 1992). It is clear that many practices associated specifically with the various phases of women's lives are not a central concern to the biblical authors, and what we know specifically of Israelite women is often relatively incidental. One exception is an annual ritual of adolescent girls involving lamentation that marked their transition from childhood to womanhood (Judges 11:40; see Day 1989).

At the next order of social complexity of clans, the so-called high places *(bamot)* served as the religious meeting place for local sacrifice. This ritual could be led by a local patriarchal figure, "a man of God," as in the case of Samuel, who presides at a sacrifice at a high place (1 Samuel 9). How typical this was we cannot say. At yet a third order of social complexity, most shrines were located either at the center of tribal units or at their boundaries; in the premonarchic period, these would include Bethel, Shechem, Shiloh, Gilgal, and Dan, all major sites in the central and northern highlands. Such shrines were the destination of annual pilgrimage, primarily the fall festival of the fruit harvest later associated with the Feast of Sukkot (Booths). This was an occasion for communal sacrifice as well as personal piety, as shown in the beautiful story of Hannah in 1 Samuel 1–2. Social celebration was an integral component as well; note the dance of the women at Shiloh during the fall festival (Judges 21). Each shrine housed a priestly line with its "patriarch," and each maintained a tradition of its foundation, such as the association with Jacob at Bethel (Genesis 35) and the prestige of Moses claimed by the priesthood at Shiloh (Judges 18:30). At these levels of social complexity, ancient Israel in this period was not "a people of the Book," but a society largely working in oral modes of religious memory and communal celebration.

Early Traditions in Joshua and Judges

Underlying the narrative presentation of Joshua and its monarchic and exilic concerns may be a number of older traditions. The references to the ark, which disappears shortly after David's establishment of Jerusalem, may echo its older place in Israelite religion. The conquest stories of Joshua 1–12 sometimes look more like an elaborated version of a local migration story, with tribal scouts looking over the land followed by migration to that territory. Just such a story appears in Judges 18, with many of the components of the conquest narrative. It has been noted that the genre of land allotment as elaborated in Joshua 13–21 is quite old, with examples dating back to the time that Joshua purports to relate; accordingly, some scholars believe that the traditions of Joshua are old. Specific local land claims and their associated stories of origins may also reflect older local traditions (as shown by Rofé 2000). Yet the narrative form of this genre of land allotment, especially with the great length it displays in Joshua, does not seem old, and its language seems to belong to monarchic-period Hebrew. All told, there are relatively few older features in Joshua. As we will see in the next section, the book of Joshua presents us with a paradox of biblical history writing: as a work apparently put together during the time of Josiah (640–609), Joshua may derive from the final decades in the land, though it purports to relate Israel's earliest time in the land.

In contrast, Judges contains more early traditions, in addition to monarchic and postmonarchic material. A work that reflects different stages of Israel's traditions, the book presents Israel's "judges" in sequence from chapter 3 through chapter 16. The book as a whole takes its name from these "judges," but the word *shofetim* in Hebrew is better understood as "chieftains" (as in NJPS) or "leaders," based on related words (of the same root) in Akkadian and Ugaritic. To be sure, one of these leaders shows judicial functions, namely, Deborah (4:4-5). In her case, her judicial function seems to be tied to her role as a prophet, which is mentioned

in the same context. For the most part, however, these leaders are not legal functionaries. Instead, it is their military feats that are generally on display. The title is
ultimately a reflection of premonarchic realities; it is best attested outside the
Bible in the Middle and Late Bronze Age sites of Mari and Ugarit. Moreover, as
Hess (2003) has observed, many of the proper names in the book of Judges best
fit the setting of the late second millennium. These sorts of features at least suggest the antiquity of some of the traditions in the book.

Despite some old features in Judges, few texts in the book actually date to the
early period. Fortunately, later transmission has preserved an old poem in Judges 5.
This poem is written in the oldest Hebrew in the Bible, and it would suggest that
this particular account of the victory led by Deborah was not a creation of the
monarchic era. Showing through the poem are the general circumstances of premonarchic Israelite society. The antiquity of the poem could be reflected in its
omission of Judah, which is known archaeologically as the last region to develop
(in sharp contrast to Judah's preeminence during the monarchy). The broader
portrait in the poem also looks old (Stager 1988; King and Stager 2001; Schloen
1993): clans engaged in local occupations and living in distinctive topographic
zones (vv. 14-18), in unwalled villages (*perazon* in v. 7); local conflict over trade
(v. 6), and other tribal friction (vv. 16-17), yet friendly relations with Amalek, a
people remembered in later biblical and Jewish tradition as Israel's bitter enemy
(v. 14); and victories enshrined in song (v. 11), attributed to the warrior/storm-
god of Israel said to be from Edom (vv. 4-5).

Judges 5 provides a further old cultural practice: tribal militia leaving their
hair uncut as part of war preparation (verse 2). Known later as the nazirite vow, it
was a mark of either a temporary vow made for service by oneself (Numbers 6)
or a lifelong vow made by one's parents (Samson in Judges 13 and 16; Samuel in 1
Samuel 11; cf. Ezekiel 44:20; Mishnah *Nazir*). The older usage in Judges 5:2 (cf.
Deuteronomy 32:42) is different, since it is specifically military in nature. The
noun "locks" (NRSV, NJPS) designates fighting men, and would seem to mean
literally "longhairs," reflecting the older custom of leaving the hair uncut for the
duration of a military campaign. (This idea partly informs the way the hairy
fighter Samson is portrayed in Judges 14–16.) This military background has been
traced back to Late Bronze Age Ugarit, but it falls out of usage in the Bible except
in older poems, and only in Judges 5 is the word used suitably in a military context. From all these details in this chapter, we get a snapshot of early Israel.

Early elements embedded in Judges are not confined to the poem of Judges 5.
From other passages, we get some sense of home religion. A layman drafts his
own son to serve as a household priest (17:5). An image made of Yahweh is kept in
a household shrine room (17:3-4). There are images of household gods known as
teraphim (17:5; 18:14, 18), also called gods (18:24). Evidence of the same idea of

teraphim occurs in Genesis 31 where Laban's "gods" (verse 30) stolen by Jacob and Rachel are identified as teraphim (verses 34-35; called "household gods" in NRSV). The range of deities in premonarchic Israel hardly suggests the later monotheism of Israel. For instance, Gideon is said to have a second name, Jerubbaal, interpreted in Judges 6:32 as "Let Baal contend with him." The name suggests that the parents of the son acknowledge the worship of Baal as a legitimate religious practice, and the story acknowledges that the father is a worshiper of Baal. We also know of Baal-names in this period from inscriptions (discussed by Hess 2003). The larger context of Judges was created by a later historian (often called by scholars the Deuteronomistic Historian, based on similarities of language and ideas found in Deuteronomy); this historian saw the Baal family altar as idolatry associated with other peoples. This idea does not inform the actual narrative, however, and this passage inadvertently provides an ancient witness to the idea that in premonarchic Israel, Baal worship was considered a legitimate practice. The sacred post, the asherah, is also mentioned in this context (6:25); it too was considered acceptable among Israelites despite its later condemnation (for example, Deuteronomy 16:21). Other chapters in Judges allude to early religious practices and ideas perhaps lost in later Israel: the making of an ephod (8:27); a temple at Shechem for Baal-berit (9:4), perhaps a title of Baal or the god El (called El-berit in 9:46); and the angel's ascent in fire (13:20).

All in all, early Israel enjoyed a wide variety of religious practices as well as a range (perhaps not a great one) of various deities, which in the later perspective of Deuteronomy and other biblical works were viewed as idolatrous; premonarchic Israel, however, knew nothing of this religious standard. The book of Judges also reflects a society where leadership roles may have been less differentiated compared to monarchic Israel. Deborah is an example of this combination of societal roles. Her role as judge seems tied in Judges 4:4-5 to her capacity as prophet. Similarly, it would seem that women could emerge in leadership roles; once again Deborah would be the clearest example. In Judges 5 she functions as a military leader. In the premonarchic period, leadership exercised by men could likewise be less differentiated, as reflected by the different roles of Samuel. Men evidently dominated leadership roles, but apparently women were not entirely excluded.

Premonarchic Israel in Genesis?

The book of Judges is not the only potential source of information about premonarchic Israel. It is possible that premonarchic features that continued into the monarchic era would have been preserved in other biblical books. For example, Genesis presents the old idea of the patriarchal god of the family. Attentive to the human concerns of children and crops, this type of god conforms to what is elsewhere known in the ancient Near East as the household god, or, as he is understood in the Bible, "the god of the father" (Genesis 26:24; 28:13; 31:5, 42, etc.; cf. Exodus 15:2). In Genesis this god is also El the Most High, the creator-god (Genesis 14:19-20, 22); El Shadday (17:1; 35:11), the latter term translated as "Almighty" in the versions; El, "the Everlasting God" (21:33); and "El, the god of Israel" (33:20). The god El is known also from Middle and Late Bronze Age texts (in particular, the Ugaritic texts of the Late Bronze Age), and the resemblance between Abraham's god and the old patriarchal god El has suggested to many scholars that this biblical portrait of the deity is to be traced back at least to premonarchic Israel. Indeed, the name Israel seems to point to El as its original deity, not Yahweh (hence Isra-el rather than Isra-yahu or the like, as Theodore Lewis remarked in a personal communication). The biblical tradition identifies El Shadday as another name for Yahweh (see Exodus 6:2-3), but here cultural amnesia as much as cultural memory seems to be at work. For just as biblical traditions preserved a memory of El as the old god of Israel, the same traditions seem to have forgotten that El was not the same god as Yahweh. (This point is discussed further in chapter 4 below.) The gods El and Yahweh are sometimes identified with one another, sometimes not; they are also identified by different titles and associated with various traditions at several cult sites. The later identification of these divinities as a single figure seems to represent Israel's initial step toward what will later develop into Israel's monotheism during the late monarchy and exile. The notion that one god embodies the main roles associated with several deities begins a process of understanding God as one.

Early Israel probably knew a variety of goddesses, especially Asherah, and here the ancient poem in Genesis 49 may preserve the oldest Israelite witness to this goddess. Attested in the Ugaritic texts as El's consort, Asherah seems to be El's consort in early Israel: the reference to "Breasts and Womb" in Genesis 49:26 following El Shadday in Genesis 49:25-26 appears to be a title of hers. Perhaps as part of Israel's secondary identification of El with Yahweh, Asherah was considered Yahweh's consort. Later their association would be reduced, with the loss of the goddess's cult and with her symbol becoming generically incorporated into the god's own group of symbols; subsequently, even this accommodation would be criticized. In general, early Israel seems to have known a wide variety of divine figures. Indeed, as Alan Cooper and Bernard Goldstein (1992) have observed, various lesser divinities populated the imaginations of earliest Israel, for example, deceased ancestors and various sorts of demons and angels, themselves better understood as minor deities who serve as messengers for more powerful deities. With the story of Jacob adopting the name Israel in Genesis 32 ("for you have striven with gods and men," v. 28), later Israel would preserve a memory that early Israel knew various sorts of divinities. Later Israel would recall that early Israel revered these sorts of divinities, but the recollection was recast often as Israel imitating the idolatry of its neighbors. The older reality that these divinities were at home in early Israel was largely forgotten.

The Origins of the God of Israel

An important cultural memory of early Israel involves its recollections of the Edomites, Midianites, and other groups located to the south of Judah. The Edomites in particular receive a great deal of attention in Genesis 36. From this rather neutral presentation, it would seem that in the premonarchic and early monarchic periods the Edomites and Israelites (or some of them) enjoyed friendly contacts (Deuteronomy 23:7 calls the Edomite "your brother" or "kinsman"). The older state of positive relations appears embedded in the archaic level of Israelite poetry (Judges 5:4; cf. Deuteronomy 33:2; Habakkuk 3:3). These passages attest to the old belief that Israel's god, Yahweh, came from Edom, the general area in the deep south also called in these poems Midian, Teiman, Paran, and Seir: "O LORD, when You came forth from Seir, Advanced from the country of Edom" (Judges 5: 4 NJPS). This verse seems to reflect this older tradition about the origins of Yahweh's god, namely, that this god derived not originally with Israel but with Edom (as noted by van der Toorn 1996, Lang 2002, and others). It seems unlikely that such a formulation would be created in a period of hostilities. Behind the formulation in Judges 5:4 may lie a relationship between the Edomites and Israelites involving trade (see Schloen 1993). As a result, the Edomites shared the worship of this god with the highland Israelites in the Early Iron Age (ca. 1150 B.C.E.).

The monarchic story of the twin sons Jacob and Esau may also reflect a tradition of the close bond between the Edomites and the Israelites. Cast as the younger brother supplanting the older brother, Israel took over a god of Edom, and in claiming that Israel was chosen by Yahweh, Israel was also staking out that deity as its own, and over time it forgot that this god ever belonged to Edom; Yahweh is the god of Israel. Genesis 36 additionally reflects substantial knowledge about the Edomites. Early trade with Israel's other southern neighbors, the Midianites, and the Ishmaelites (Genesis 37), and even the much-hated Amalekites rendered "in the valley" in NRSV (Judges 5:14), is also reflected in various levels of the tradition. Later hostilities between Israel and these groups may reflect the monarchy pushing out trade competitors. As we will see in chapter 4 below, cultural memories about several early Israelite features were submerged beneath the weight of the nationalist concerns of the monarchy and the attendant royal institutions of the priesthood and the temple. Early stories may have been passed down, and some of them may have been incorporated into later collections, themselves subsequently lost or used for even larger collections shaped by later national concerns. As a result, Genesis and Judges would preserve an incomplete recollection of early Israel's religion and culture, yet the basic presentation of the family of Israel in these two biblical books, with its variety of religious practices and experiences of divinity, would ring true for their audience during the monarchic period.

The Period of the Monarchy (ca. 1000–586)

As we enter the period of Israel's monarchy, more historical-looking material is available both inside and outside the Bible. In addition to many biblical works that contain monarchic-period collections (such as 1–2 Samuel and 1–2 Kings), many writings from outside the Bible provide information about this period of Israel's history, especially beginning in the ninth century (about halfway through 1 Kings). The society of ancient Israel did not change tremendously. Family lineages remain the basis for social organization, despite massive assaults on family units beginning in the eighth century. The rural landscape of ancient Israel, as shown in essays in a book with this very title (edited by Maier et al. 2003), maintained the extended family as the basic social unit (for a discussion of Israelite cities in this period, see Faust 1999 and the literature that he cites). The patriarchal model of society prevailed, extending to the level of the royal household and its administration.

One area of change involved leadership roles, which arguably became more formalized and stratified in the context of monarchy institutions. Where Levitical priests were normal during the premonarchic period, the period of the monarchy witnessed greater competition and hierarchy among the priestly lines. Leadership roles occasionally open to women in the premonarchic period (exemplified by Deborah) seemed to have almost exclusively closed off as options for women, at least in monarchic institutions. Instead, their leadership roles seemed to be restricted to divination (1 Samuel 28) and prophecy (for example, Huldah in 2 Kings 22; cf. the female prophets of Ezekiel 13:17), an older role known for women (Miriam, Deborah). Women also continued in their occasional role as sages (the wise woman of Tekoa in 2 Samuel 14) and as singers and communicators of battle (Psalm 68:11 [v. 12 in Hebrew and NJPS]).

Genesis and Ruth as Pictures of Israel during the Monarchy

The picture of "biblical history" in Genesis reads less like history and more like a family story extending across generations. Genesis uses episodes of family life to convey a picture of Israel's identity and place within the world of monarchy. Genesis is concerned not only with describing the nature of Israel, but also with defining its social or ethnic boundaries by delineating its relations to other groups in geographical terms (what Hendel 2002b insightfully calls the "ethnoscape" conveyed in Genesis). The family story situates Jacob-Israel's origins within an earlier family structure of his grandfather Abraham, thereby explaining who belongs

inside this family structure and who is excluded. The boundaries of familial identity are constructed according to three categories: Israelites, namely, the descendants of Jacob-Israel; non-Israelites with some familial relations to the Israelites;
and unrelated non-Israelites. This last group includes different peoples largely
identified by land: the Egyptians (in Genesis 12); the "people of the land," the
Canaanites (12:5-6; coupled with the Perizzites in 13:7, and listed with other peoples in 15:19-21; cf. 23:2, 19; 24:3), and the Hittites (23:3-18); and the Philistines
(chap. 21, especially v. 34).

Between these polar opposites are non-Israelites related to Israel by various
degrees. The closest are the Edomites, represented as descendants of Jacob's brother,
Esau (25:30; 27:40; 36:8, 9, 43). Edom would eventually shake off the domination
of Israel. (Apparently alluded to in Genesis 27:40, this development is mentioned
in 2 Kings 8, during the reign of King Jehoram, ca. 848–842 B.C.E.) Accordingly,
we may see in the Jacob–Esau traditions a reflection of relations between the
Israelites and Edomites during the monarchic period, which, as shown in other
texts, knew the Edomites' close relationship to the Israelites (Deuteronomy 23:7).
The state of hostility would intensify, especially with the Edomite participation in
Jerusalem's destruction in 586 B.C.E. (Psalm 137; cf. Ezekiel 35). A step removed
with respect to Abraham is the Aramean line of his brother Nahor, his grand-
daughter Rebekah, and her brother Laban (Genesis 24:24-27 and 25:20; cf. Laban's
speaking Aramaic in 31:47). As Rebekah marries into the family, the Arameans
(or at least, the members of this line) are considered that much closer to the
Israelites. As noted above, this sense of familial tie to the Arameans seems to be
reflected also in the biblical memory in Deuteronomy 26:5: "My father was a wandering [or better, 'refugee'] Aramean." Next closest are various southern peoples
(including Midian) produced by Abraham and his wife Keturah (Genesis 25:1-6).
Finally, the Moabites and Ammonites are construed as the offspring produced by
Abraham's nephew, Lot, and his two daughters (19:30-38). It is apparent that Genesis reflects Israel's perception of its relations to other ethnic groups during the
period of the monarchy, especially given the references to the Philistines.

It is within the context of these relations that we may view the story of Ruth.
Ruth is a most beloved of biblical works, in particular for its portrayal of the deep
trust and love of Ruth for Naomi, one a Judean and the other a Moabite. Situated
in the time of the "judges" ("chieftains," 1:1), the work dates at the earliest to the
monarchy. The two women cope with the trauma of losing the one man related
to them both; against societal expectation, mother-in-law and daughter-in-law
remain together to deal with the circumstances. In the patriarchal, agricultural
world evoked by Ruth, such a loss put the two widows at life-threatening risk, especially in a time of famine. Together the women take their lives into their own
hands, culminating in Ruth's courtship of Boaz (cf. Jeremiah 31:22 NJPS: "the

LORD has created something new on earth: a woman courts a man"). This marriage brings a new future of children for Ruth and grandchildren for Naomi, remembered as ancestors of King David. An inspiring piece of literary artifice, the book evidently reflects the traditional agricultural, village life well known to monarchic Judah, including the general societal roles of men and women and the occasionally porous lines of marriage with close neighbors. Indeed, Israelite society was hardly homogeneous during the monarchy. Various ethnic groups seemed to have coexisted within Judah, and the Judeans included different groups such as the Rechabites (2 Kings 10:15-17; Jeremiah 35). With a sense of the general societal setting during the monarchy, we may turn to its political backdrop, as represented in the books of Samuel and Kings.

1–2 *Samuel: Transition to Monarchy*

The books of Samuel continue the narrative of Judges. Like the preceding works of the Bible, 1–2 Samuel revolve around the lives of famous men, in this case, Samuel, Saul, and David. These books trace the difficult road from tribal leadership to monarchy. Samuel is the focus of 1 Samuel 1–8, until Saul is introduced in 1 Samuel 9. From this point on, Samuel plays an important role as a barometer of Saul's success and failure until the king's death in the final chapter of 1 Samuel. In contrast to Saul's life of misfortune is the ever-successful David, who enters the narrative in 1 Samuel 16 just after Samuel leaves Saul for the last time.

Up to the famous episode of David and Bathsheba, David's life is presented as one success after another. David's path to power is smoothed by his marriage to Saul's daughter, Michal (1 Samuel 18), and by his friendship with Saul's son, Jonathan (1 Samuel 19–20). The kingship of Saul and David is a study in contrasts, and it is this perspective that informs the biblical presentation of the two kings. Saul's kingship is marred by loss of divine support, Samuel's displeasure, and defeat at the hands of the Philistines, whereas David's kingship is marked by unflagging divine favor, Samuel's blessing, and the Philistines' defeat at his hands. As a result, 1–2 Samuel has been read largely as a polemic against Saul that served as pro-Davidic propaganda. The Bathsheba incident (2 Samuel 11–12) would seem to be out of place for this reason; some scholars regard it as an anti-Davidic polemic secondarily inserted by critics of the Davidic dynasty. Pro-Saul narratives have not been entirely excluded; even after his death it is evident that pro-Saul sentiment continued and confronted the Davidic monarchy (2 Samuel 16; see the discussion of Esther below). Overall, the text tends to focus on the great men in its organization of the past, but the text also admits of a wider social clash, a civil war between "the house of Saul and the house of David" (2 Samuel 3).

The polemical nature of the text does not guarantee its antiquity, since concerns over Saul and David would continue long after their own reigns. By the same token, the political machinery in David's court would have quickly set to work to justify him as Saul's successor, since he was not a son of Saul and therefore not in line to succeed him. The books of Samuel may reflect the rewritings of older stories that exalt David at Saul's expense. In other cases, it is possible to peek through the story's veneer to see how a positive tradition once associated originally with Saul has been secondarily attached even to the figure of Samuel. The story of Hannah in 1 Samuel 1 uses the root letters of the consonants of Saul's name in the verses "you have made" in v. 17, in "I have asked" in v. 20, "I asked" in v. 27, and "I lend him" in v. 28 (NRSV). This use of the root letters (sh, ', l) in these words has led many commentators to see this chapter as tied originally to the figure of Saul, and only secondarily applied to Samuel. If correct, it would imply that the story of Hannah originally celebrated the birth of Saul, not Samuel. In any case, in his own time Saul was surely celebrated more than the Bible now shows.

The demotion of Saul and the exaltation of David are so great that one may sense that 1–2 Samuel involves more than simple polemic. One may read between the lines of the narrative, as many commentators have, and suspect that David was not particularly scrupulous in his pursuit of power (see the important books by McKenzie 2000 and Halpern 2001). The stories of David's early life are overzealous in the presentation of this heroic youth in service to the king (1 Samuel 17, the Goliath story) and in his reverence for him at his death (2 Samuel 1). They scarcely mask David's playing the Philistines and Israelites off one another (1 Samuel 21, 27–29). Indeed, it is difficult to avoid the impression that David betrays both sides. His relationships with Saul's children appear motivated more by proximity to kingship than love (see 1 Samuel 18–20; 2 Samuel 9). The stories are devoted to showing an alternatively angry and repenting Saul in pursuit of the innocent David (1 Samuel 19, 23–24, 26). The narrative also takes great pains to explain David's whereabouts away from the battlefield where Saul dies (1 Samuel 30–2 Samuel 1). Following Saul's death, David's supporters have the impression that he wants Saul's descendants and supporters killed, yet the stories manage to place the king far from the scene of the crimes; he even appears conciliatory toward his opposition (2 Samuel 3–4). In David's founding of Jerusalem and his desire for a temple for Yahweh, the narrative makes him seem additionally pious (2 Samuel 5–7; cf. 2 Samuel 12:20 for the tradition that David already had some sort of "house of the LORD"). However, founding a new capital and establishing a temple for the patron god are equally an expression of the king's new power. In the words of the subtitle of a comprehensive book by the brilliant Baruch Halpern (2001), David was "Messiah, Murderer, Traitor, King." Such was David's path to the throne.

David's later military successes are described in fawning terms, even if they may be in the main defensible from the historian's perspective. At present, issues of chronology raised by archaeologists and critical questioning by biblical scholars have eroded the overly glorious view of David that he receives in later religious tradition. Given the relative power vacuum around Israel at the time of his kingship, however, it is not surprising that he was successful, even if the text exaggerates at times. This is not to take away from the achievement: David's military abilities may be legendary, but the legend is likely founded on historical victories over his Philistine neighbors to the west and perhaps some victories against his neighbors to the north and east (as Na'aman 2002 has suggested, some of these may have been enhanced secondarily). There is no reason to question the historical existence of David, as has been the craze among some academics. A reference to "the house of David" in an Aramaic inscription excavated at Dan shows what the Israelites knew: the figure of David was associated with the founding of a dynasty.

In current scholarship, the extent of the "united monarchy" under David and Solomon has been debated, with a number of critics suggesting that their reigns were hardly as wondrous as implied by biblical authors. Instead, these kings are seen by such critics as little more than rulers of a relatively minor kingdom. Following suit, many of the building projects known from the archaeological record associated with Solomon have been disputed as well. This debate is a complex one, involving disagreements about overall chronology as well as arguments over chronological sequences at a various archaeological sites (see Finkelstein 2003, Mazar 2003, and Stager 2003). However this dispute is resolved, the relative weakness of Israel's neighbors during this period might make one think that the initiation of the monarchy by David and Solomon marked a decisive turn in Israel's history. By the same token, royal polemic and apologetics often seem as much on display as the historical facts, and this monarchy was perhaps not nearly as grand as it was once thought.

1–2 Kings

The books of Kings survey Israel's history from the end of David's life through the "exile" in 586. After the description of Solomon's reign in 1 Kings 1–11, 1 Kings 12–2 Kings 25 is framed according to the reigns of the kings of the northern kingdom (Israel) and the southern kingdom (Judah). The story begins with Solomon's reign in 1 Kings 1–11, which draws on a number of traditions. Some sections, like the lists of officials (1 Kings 4:2-6), look as if they may come from royal administration. Others, such as the legends associated with Solomon's wisdom (for example, the story of the baby and the two prostitutes in chap. 3, and the Queen of Sheba in chap. 10), bear the appearance of popular tales attached to the narrative as deemed appropriate by later scribes. For example, the Queen of Sheba story, perhaps based on trade to the Arabian Peninsula and beyond, follows the end of chapter 10, with its mention of trade launched at the head of the Gulf of Aqaba. Even legendary material provides important cultural information, in this case regarding the ideal of royal wisdom as well as international horizons attributed to this king's reign, even though the text sometimes waxes more grandiose than historical reality (for example, 1 Kings 4:21-25, 29-34). Solomon's achievements are notable in the economic and diplomatic spheres, although his reign marks a retreat from David's military successes against neighbors on Israel's eastern flank.

On the domestic side, Solomon's capacity as royal administrator is signaled by a more developed bureaucratic apparatus as well as by building projects. Among these projects, Solomon's signal achievement for the biblical authors was the Jerusalem Temple (1 Kings 6–9). Though not the largest structure masterminded by the king, the Temple dominates the narrative. As noted earlier in this chapter, archaeological parallels indicate that the type of temple and the accompanying paraphernalia best suit a date in the tenth or ninth century (as discussed in Bloch-Smith 1994). Parallels from texts and artifacts speak to the Jerusalem Temple's ideological function as the palace of the divine king, who receives offerings from his loyal subjects as he takes up his throne in the back room, or better, his throne room. The accession of the divine king is accompanied by divine victory over the cosmic Sea, signaled by the presence of the huge "bronze sea" in the courtyard area in front of the Temple. As noted earlier in this chapter, the Temple complex reflects a pattern of victory followed by accession to the throne by the divine warrior-king, the very progression marked by texts such as Psalm 29.

The temple is a spatial icon of Israelite hopes for divine presence and blessing as well as support for the Solomonic dynasty. It would also appear from the iconography within the temple, with its cherubim and trees, that the Temple was regarded as a divine home, conceptually related to the garden of Eden. Like the garden in Genesis 2–3 and Ezekiel 28, this one is guarded by the figure of the cherub, and like Ezekiel 28, the house of God represented by Solomon's Temple is imagined to be located on the holy mountain of God. In addition, at least for the priesthood, this temple—like any temple—would be regarded as cultically pure and holy. The throne room of the divine palace was understood as the "holy of holies." These symbolic meanings were encoded in the Temple's very construction. It served several functions—political, social, economic, and religious.

The Division of Judah and Israel

After Solomon's death, his domain divided into the northern kingdom of Israel and the southern kingdom of Judah; apparently his reign was not without its domestic stresses and difficulties. Indeed, the division of the north and the south points to the fundamental regionalism of Solomon's kingdom. Jeroboam, a former official of Solomon, became the new king of the northern kingdom. His monarchic operation is remembered as sinful later in the books of Kings, as he furnished his shrines at the old religious sites of Dan and Bethel with what has been called "the golden calf," thanks to the story given this name in Exodus 32 (as discussed by many scholars such as Toews 1993). Jeroboam established Dan and Bethel as royal sanctuaries at the opposite ends of his kingdom over the northern tribe, in part as countersites to Jerusalem. According to 1 Kings 12:27-28, Jeroboam established these royal shrines in order to detract northerners from continuing their pilgrimages to the Jerusalem temple. The "houses on high places" (NRSV) or "cult places" (NJPS), which Jeroboam is said to make in 1 Kings 12:31, evidently included the site of Dan. Excavations there led by Avraham Biran (1994, 1999, 2001) have uncovered a massive raised platform, a square enclosure with steps and an altar, a room with an altar, iron shovels and jars with ash, two other altars, and various installations; these were accompanied by a number of items related to religious worship, such as incense stands, oil lamps, jars with snake decoration, and a female figurine (a consort for Yahweh?).

According to 1 Kings 12:31-32, Jeroboam appointed priests who were not members of the tribe of Levi. The passage appears polemical, perhaps deriving from a competing shrine where Levites served as priests, such as Shiloh. As suggested by the character of both the sites and the priestly lines, Jeroboam I used traditional practices to develop a new national identity for the northern kingdom in order to compete with the Temple in Jerusalem. As argued by van der Toorn (1996) and by Cooper and Goldstein (1992), Jeroboam also developed Passover into a national holiday to express a northern perspective on its split from the south: freedom from Egypt became the model for the north's liberation from the southern monarchy.

Later polemic against Jeroboam's use of the exodus story in this way can be seen from the similar wordings found in 1 Kings 12:28 and the "golden calf" story in Exodus 32: "Behold *(hinneh)* your gods *(eloheka)*, O Israel, which brought [plural verb] you from the land of Egypt" (1 Kings 12:28); and "These *(elleh)* are your gods *(eloheka)*, O Israel, which brought [plural verb] you up from the land of Egypt" (Exodus 32:4, 8; cf. 1 Samuel 4:8; Hosea 8:6; Nehemiah 9:18). Aaron's words in Exodus 32:5 ("tomorrow shall be a festival to the LORD!" [NRSV]) show that the idolatry involved was the making of this image for Yahweh. The "golden calf" story seems, then, not to be a polemic against the calf as the symbol of a non-Israelite god (such as Baal), but a polemic against representing Yahweh with a calf. (Later it would be remembered as idolatry to a foreign god, for example, in Tobit 1:15, in the Vaticanus and Alexandrinus texts of the Septuagint.) Shrines had different representations associated in various ways with Yahweh (cf. cherubim and the ark at Shiloh and Jerusalem), and it may be that Exodus 32 constitutes the polemic of a priesthood at one of these places aimed against Jeroboam's royal establishment. In short, polemic turned alternative Israelite traditions of representing Yahweh into false worship or idolatry.

Images were probably originally considered suitable for Yahweh in the monarchic period; for example, there was a divine image at the shrine of Shiloh, according to Judges 17–18 (especially 18:20, 30, 31, called "the idol" in the NRSV), and the description of the shrine there presupposes that Yahweh was the god involved (note the references to Yahweh ["the LORD"] in connection with the the "idol" in 17:2-3). According to the story (18:30), this was the situation until the fall of the northern kingdom in the late eighth century. Later, images become viewed as a means of other deities infiltrating Israelite religion, and for traditions that apparently tended not to use images for Yahweh himself (such as the Jerusalem Temple), images were interpreted then as belonging only to other gods, hence as idolatry. Although Jeroboam surely did not think of his calves as idols, the author of the "golden calf" story did.

With this account of Jeroboam's calf iconography as reflected in the golden calf story, we find a foundational statement about the origins of northern idolatry, for this is one of "the sins of Jeroboam" (1 Kings 14:16; see also 15:26, 30, 34; 16:26, 31; 22:53; 2 Kings 13:2, 6, 11; 14:24; 15:9, 24, 28), later viewed in the historiography of 2 Kings as the basis for the fall of the northern kingdom (2 Kings 17:16). In short, the golden calf story in Exodus 32 and the memory of Jeroboam in 1–2 Kings convey a theory of idolatry based on a reading of Israel's monarchic past: the name of Jeroboam explains Israel's idolatry during the monarchy. In other words, Jeroboam's reign provides an etiology of idolatry in the memory of Judah's royal chroniclers.

From Jeroboam on, the history of the kings of Israel and Judah initially revolved around conflict among a number of regional states. Israel and Judah remained rivals, although episodes of alliance also take place. In the ninth century, the dynasty of Ahab would forge an unprecedented relationship with the Phoenician kingdom of Tyre. This alliance inspired royal patronage for religious devotion to the Tyrian patron god, Baal. With Assyria looming on the horizon, more attention was paid to Israel's relations with the various coalitions arrayed to meet this threat (see Holloway 2002 for a fine book about Assyrian power and ideology). For the coalition forces mustered against the army of Shalmaneser III at the famous battle of Qarqar of 853, Ahab was said to have provided ten thousand foot soldiers (*ANET*, 278–79). Afterward, occasional vassalage was incurred by the northern kingdom. In its encounters with Assyria first in the reign of Shalmaneser III (853, 841) and later in the reign of Adad-nirari III (in 796), Israel could escape

Assyrian conquest by paying tribute. Shalmaneser mentions the "tribute of Jehu, son of Omri" (*ANET*, 281; see similarly Adad-nirari, in *ANET*, 281–82).

Regional alliances and conflicts continued, but the nature of regional conflict shifted dramatically in the eighth century with Assyrian power moving westward. Despite such international difficulties, the northern monarchy managed quite well. Omri's dynasty was perhaps the most powerful in the north's history. The northern kingdom would be known in Assyrian records as "the house of Omri" (*ANET*, 284, 285). Omri's dynasty also created a new capital at Samaria, which archaeological research has shown to have been substantial both in its public works and in its wealth, displayed through its carved ivories decorated with gold foil and lapis lazuli (see the valuable study by Tappy 1992–2001). This wealth matched its regional hegemony. The king of Moab recounted his country's past: "As for Omri, king of Israel, he humbled Moab for many years" (*ANET*, 320). The last flowering of northern wealth took place during the reign of Jeroboam II (786–746), as reflected in the Samaria Ostraca. Dating to the ninth, tenth, and fifteenth years of the king, these inscriptions record receipts for oil and wine. Despite economic good times, the fall of the north to Assyria was only years away. The campaigns of Tiglath-pileser III to the west from 743 to 732 marked the end for Israel as an independent political force. Assyria would conquer first in 732 and again in 722, with the number of deported inhabitants reported in Assyrian annals put at 27,290 (*ANET*, 284).

From that time on, the north became part of the Assyrian Empire. Sargon II reports that he installed an officer over the north (*ANET*, 284.) Probably already by 732, the situation in the north seems to have stimulated a massive exodus to the south. It is known from archaeology that the city of Jerusalem doubled in size in this period, and such a flow of refugees southward would help to explain the presence of northern works among the books of the Bible (for example, Hosea, a number of Psalms, perhaps Exodus 21–23 and part of Deuteronomy) as well as books inspired by some of these works (perhaps Jeremiah). The administrative practice of the Assyrian Empire issued in deportations of Israelites to Assyria and of other Assyrian vassal groups in Mesopotamia to Israel (*ANET*, 284; 2 Kings 17 ; Na'aman and Zadok 2000). These deportations may have transpired over several decades. Assyrian records also mention a deportation of Arab tribesmen to the province of Samaria in 715. Ezra 4 relates later deportations to the north from Assyria. Despite major shifts in population to and from the north, it did not mean the end of hope for its restoration (Jeremiah 31; Ezekiel 37). Expectation for the north's resurrection would not be groundless, as the late seventh century would witness Assyria's demise.

The books of Kings offer unqualified praise for two kings who reign after the fall of the north, Hezekiah and Josiah. Early in his monarchy (ca. 715?–687?),

Hezekiah extended Judah's hegemony over the Philistines on its western flank (2 Kings 18:8; see also *ANET,* 287–88). He was particularly noted for surviving the Assyrian invasion of 701 (2 Kings 18–19), for which he had prepared, with works to protect Jerusalem's water supply (2 Kings 20:20; 2 Chronicles 32:2-4, 30; *ANET,* 321) and to fortify its walls (2 Chronicles 32:5; see Vaughn 1999). Despite the Assyrian conquest of Judah's cities, Jerusalem itself was ultimately spared. However, the Assyrian damage was severe. Sennacherib boasts of his conquest of forty-six walled cities in Judah, with 200,150 persons claimed to be taken captive (*ANET,* 288; for a variety of views about the historical events surrounding this invasion, see Grabbe 2003). It is important to note that in terms of the human cost, Sennacherib's campaign represents the beginning of Judah's exile to Mesopotamia. This high number of people reported to have been taken as slaves may be only an estimate or an exaggeration (or perhaps both), but for a striking contrast, note the number of 27,290 persons said to have been taken from the north (*ANET,* 284) or the 4,600 captives attributed to the combined conquests of Jerusalem in 597 and 587 (Jeremiah 52:28-30). With the first visual presentation of Judeans taken into captivity, Sennacherib's palace was adorned with scenes of the Assyrian capture of the southern Judean city of Lachish (cf. 2 Kings 18:14; 19:8). Despite the massive losses, the book of Kings recalls Jerusalem's survival during this campaign as a great miracle, a defeat inflicted on the Assyrians by divine intervention (2 Kings 19:35). The south would remain a vassal to Assyria, until its withdrawal from the west in the late 620s; conflicts within Mesopotamia brought down the Assyrian Empire in 612.

Manasseh, the major Judean king between Hezekiah and Josiah, enjoyed a particularly long reign of forty-five years (ca. 687–642) during the Assyrian imperium in the west. According to 2 Kings 21, Manasseh is associated with idolatry, but 2 Chronicles 33:11-13 adds an account of his repentance. The differing assessments of this king would continue for centuries: in the pseudepigraphical composition known as the "Prayer of Manasseh" he is recalled as a model of repentance, while rabbinic texts such as Mishnah *Sanhedrin* 10:2 and Babylonian Talmud *Sanhedrin* 102b debate his piety. Whether he repented later or not, Manasseh perhaps was devoted to practices considered by some to be idolatrous, but those practices were largely traditional ones not regarded as idolatrous by most Judeans at that time; the view of these practices as idolatrous would become normative only later. According to 2 Kings 21:3-7, these practices included: local shrines outside Jerusalem; devotion to the religious symbol of the sacred tree called the asherah, possibly associated with the goddess by the same name and arguably regarded as the spouse of God; worship of "the Baal," possibly a cover terms for male deities other than the traditional God of Israel; worship of astral deities, probably considered traditional as the heavenly hosts of God (as in 1 Kings 22:19 and Zephaniah 1:5); various forms of divination and necromancy; and occasional child sacrifice, probably practiced only under the severest duress, to judge from biblical and extra-biblical sources. Later condemnations by the prophet and priest Ezekiel (chapters 8–10) would suggest that these practices had a number of critics in later monar-chic Judah, but also that these were rather well-accepted, traditional practices. Their rejection by Hezekiah and Josiah should not be viewed simply as high-minded religious reforms, but as political-religious acts of centralization designed to help withstand political pressures of their times. The author(s) of 2 Kings agreed with these kings' "reforms" and accordingly heaped praise on them.

Josiah (640–609) enjoyed the particular good fortune of coming to the throne at a time of Assyrian weakness. With Assyria's hold shaken by 620, Josiah was able to exercise some regional hegemony over the territory to his north and west. Josiah's so-called religious reforms were marked by the putative discovery of a previously unknown scroll of the religious teaching (2 Kings 22). With Josiah, the praise is particularly enthusiastic in the book of 2 Kings 22–23, and perhaps the author of these chapters, who may be a redactor of 1–2 Kings down through 2 Kings 23, was especially partial to this king. His death at Megiddo (2 Kings 23: 29-30; 2 Chronicles 35:20-24) ended Judah's hope.

Afterward the kingdom spiraled toward its demise at the hands of the Baby-lonian king, Nabu-kadurri-usur, also known as Nebuchadnezzar (*ANET*, 564; for an interesting study of this king, see Sack 2004). By biblical accounts, execution, mutilation, destruction, deportation, famine, and even cannibalism marked the Babylonian siege and capture of Jerusalem, the Temple, and the population (2 Kings 24–25; Lamentations, especially 2:20; 4:10; cf. Ezekiel 5:10; Psalm 74:4-8). In this final moment of monarchic Jerusalem, the aid provided by troops consist-ing of Judah's neighbors (2 Kings 24:2; Ezekiel 25; Lamentations 4:21-22; cf. Psalm 137:7-9) would be recalled with particular bitterness.

The "Exile" (ca. 586–538)

The time from 586 through 538 has often been regarded as a separate period in the history of Israel. Certainly, the Bible's presentation of these years in 1–2 Kings and in the postexilic books of Ezra and Nehemiah highlights the Babylonian conquest of Jerusalem in 587–586 and the Persian authorization for the return of Judean captives to their home in 538. The Bible stresses the Babylonian captivity (2 Kings 24–25, especially 24:14-16). It is also evident, however, that the history is not monolithic. The beginning of the "exile" was not a single point in time, but a process over a decade beginning with a deportation in 597 (and, as noted in the preceding section, perhaps beginning already in 701, with Sennacherib's claim of deportation of over two hundred thousand people). Indeed, in the biblical record, the deportation of 597 is recalled as three times more severe by way of number of captives taken than the later deportation following the destruction of the Temple in 586 (Jeremiah 52:28-30). Clearly, the deportation of 597, which included the priest and prophet Ezekiel, was a traumatic one (note also the plaintive notes sounded by the Lachish letters in the context of this Babylonian invasion, *ANET,* 322).

The fall of Jerusalem did not translate into a single, wholesale movement of Judah's population to Babylon (see Albertz 2003). The Bible places the number of people exiled to Babylon at 4,600 (Jeremiah 52:30), which was hardly the total number of Judeans at the time. Instead, the decade from 597 to 586 was marked by the spread of Judah's population over several geographical areas. The Bible indicates that many Judeans fled to Egypt (2 Kings 25:26; Jeremiah 43–44, 52). Some Judeans had already left for Moab, Ammon, and Edom (Jeremiah 40:11). Moreover, many Judeans, perhaps even the bulk of the population, remained as virtual serfs working the land under the Babylonian Empire (2 Kings 24:14; 25:22-24; cf. 2 Kings 25:26). For those who remained in the land there was no "exile," but an onerous and precarious colonial existence. The archaeological evidence suggests the continuation of some rural settlements, albeit at a reduced level (this issue is discussed in the articles in Lipschits and Blenkinsopp 2003, especially the piece written by Lipschits and the article on the sixth century by Faust).

If the lament of Psalm 74 is any indication, some sort of communal religious life continued amid the city's ruins. Lamentations 5 also describes conditions shortly after the events of 586, with basic subsistence representing a major difficulty (cf. Ezekiel 12:19). Where Psalm 74 laments the loss of religious order marked by prophecy and the Temple, Lamentations 5 mourns the loss of social order, including hangings and rape. Decades later, the tradition of lamenting the major dates surrounding Jerusalem's fall is mentioned for the first time (Zechariah 8:19); it is possible that this tradition is older, perhaps dating to the decades following the city's demise.

In contrast, life in Babylonia was not entirely oppressive. In 560 King Jehoiachin was released from prison and provided with support (2 Kings 25:27-30). According to Babylonian records, rations were ordered for the king and his sons (*ANET,* 308), and this development may signal a change in the fortunes of the community more broadly. Jeremiah 29 suggests that the captives in Babylon would develop substantial community, even prosper, with the Judeans encouraged to seek the well-being of their new homeland. The later religious polemics of Isaiah 44 suggest that some Judeans were attracted to Babylonian images of their deities, and Isaiah 46 presupposes that Judeans witnessed, or at least had knowledge of, public aspects of Babylonian religion. Accordingly, the biblical category of "the exile" in Babylon for this period in Judah's history applies only to those Judeans who went to Babylon. It was not the experience of Judeans who remained in the land or moved to places other than Babylonia, and the biblical term in fact functioned in "postexilic" literature as a means of distinguishing this sector of the Judean population when it asserted its privileges upon returning to what would be called Yehud under the Persian Empire after 538.

The Persian Period (ca. 540–333)

This period marks a major shift in life for Judeans. Even as successive groups of Judeans returned home, new communities of Judeans were being established in the Persian Empire. Where one independent center at home had played the only significant role in Israel's history down to the fall of Jerusalem, now various communities of Judeans were growing at different rates in various locales in Mesopotamia and Persia. At this point, the small Persian province of Yehud, as Judah was now called, became one center instead of the only center. As a result, a new dynamic between Judean communities abroad and the community of Yehud would play a central role in molding the identity of the people.

Life in Yehud after 538

The Persian period is marked by a lack of warfare in the area, and the Persian administration was regarded as relatively benign. Yehud's political status as a province within the larger system of Persian satrapies nonetheless required its paying taxes to the empire, which increased its financial burden (see Nehemiah 5:15). Progress toward economic recovery for the small community of Yehud seems to have been slow. For all the lack of criticism against Persian authorities in the Bible, life under the empire was not an easy one for most people. Some Judeans had to sell themselves or their children into slavery in order to pay off debts (Nehemiah 5). Still, some Judean families prospered in Persian period Yehud (Nehemiah 6:17).

Two books that purport to derive from Solomon, the Song of Songs and Qohelet (Ecclesiastes), were likely composed or completed during the Persian period for the interest and entertainment of the wealthy, educated elite of Yehud (it is possible that Qohelet was composed a little later, in the early Hellenistic period). Despite their attribution to King Solomon, the two works show signs of Persian period composition, for example, the Persian loanword into Biblical Hebrew, *pardes*, "park, orchard," in Qohelet 2:5 and Song of Songs 4:13 (the same word is also related to the English word "paradise"). Qohelet may be regarded as the reflections of a Persian-period sage belonging to Yehud's upper class. Even if the work is regarded as a sort of royal fiction, it likely drew on conditions known to the work's learned audience in the Persian period. This ideal figure can own slaves and land-

holdings (see chapter 3 below). The Song of Songs dramatizes an intense courtship in the setting of village and countryside, evoking traditional agricultural life.
From the picture in these two books, we see a socially stratified and largely agricultural society within Yehud. The very production of this literature further suggests a ruling, educated elite that celebrates Solomon as a model for its interest in
love poetry and wisdom.

For the backdrop of political events, we may begin with the book of Ezra,
which picks up at the end of "the exile" in 538 B.C.E., an end attributed to Cyrus
the Persian. Ezra provides three snapshots focused on religious developments in
this period, one from 538 (chaps. 1–4), a second from 520 (chaps. 5–6), and a
third of unknown date (chaps. 7–10). The first concerns the initial restoration of
exiles from Babylon to the province of Yehud (Ezra 1–2). The leadership is headed
up in Ezra 2:2 by Zerubbabel and Jeshua; one is of royal descent, the other a
priest. The genealogy of Ezra 2 provides an inventory of the men said to return
from Babylonia, and its categories delineate a religious organization and hierarchy of priests, Levites, singers, gatekeepers, and temple servants. Clearly, the
author tells the story of social authority, not a broad historical narrative of how
the people returned, reestablished their homes and economic livelihoods, as well
as other nonreligious matters. Chapter 2 includes concerns about genealogies
that were partially unknown, with a possible question about marriage to non-
Israelites; such men are excluded from priesthood.

The leadership turns to the task of constructing the Temple, and the narrative
dramatizes efforts to carry out this plan in the face of opposition (Ezra 3–4). The
description of events shows Jeshua and Zerubbabel, a priestly royal leadership,
together at work (3:2). The description also presents a priestly religious practice
of daily burnt offerings following "the teaching of Moses" (3:2-6). This is to include the proper celebration of the holidays (Booths, also called Sukkot, in 3:4;
Passover-Unleavened Bread in 6:19-22). It is to be noted that sacrifices were con-
ducted, although the Temple had not yet been rebuilt.

Shortly after the Temple's foundations are laid with great celebration (Ezra 3:
10-13), work is suspended (Ezra 4). Adversaries of Judah and Benjamin, said to be
"the people of the land" who had remained in the land (4:4), wish to join in the
building. Later, these adversaries are said to appeal to Persian authorities and succeed in stopping the construction project. Work on the Temple's reconstruction re-
sumed only in the second year of King Darius, around 520 (4:24), in part inspired by
the prophets Haggai and Zechariah (5:1). The oracles of these two "minor
prophets" are preserved in the books named after them, and from them we can see
how the Temple and the leadership of the people were their preeminent concerns.
Work on the Temple proceeds, initially without Persian authorization (Ezra 5), but
then authorization (originally related in chapter 1) is discovered in the Persian

archives and then confirmed (chapter 6). Evidently, the author of Ezra is concerned with proper relations with the Persian authorities. The end of chapter 6 relates the completion of the Temple, marked by the entire community celebrating. To this picture in Ezra the books of Haggai and Zechariah add a sense of cosmic anticipation that accompanied the rebuilding of the Temple and a hope that the Persian Empire might even fall, as the transition to Darius I's reign raised expectations in Yehud and elsewhere. The Persian Empire would become only stronger during Darius's reign, but this brief transition brought to the surface the sorts of world-shaking, apocalyptic hopes felt within the small community of Yehud.

Within the account of Ezra's mission, we can see broad social dynamics and issues of community definition at work. When the first group left Babylonia, it left intact a community of Judeans there. That community enjoyed an ongoing structure of leadership. The Babylonian community provides the leadership that enters the story at Ezra 7 in the form of the man for whom the book is named, Ezra. This figure reflects the structure of religious authority, as he is a priest of Aaronide descent said to be a scribe expert in the Mosaic traditions. The story of Ezra also betrays the shifting situation of the "sons of Levi" within the community structure. Ezra 8 relates that the priestly line of Phinehas (son of Aaron) was first in rank in the company of Ezra, while no Levites were found. Ezra says that he makes an effort to find Levites, and successful in this effort, these are to serve as temple servants. The story reflects the gradual demise of the Levites within the priestly ranks, a trend that predates the fall of Jerusalem but appears more advanced at this point in time. The Levites are no longer called priests, in contrast to the book of Deuteronomy, especially Deuteronomy 33:8-11. Instead, they are given employment that supports activities in and around the Temple apart from the socially esteemed sacrificial duties of the priests.

Some of the same aspects of life in Yehud appear in the book of Nehemiah. Nehemiah relates his travels from Shushan in Persia to Jerusalem perhaps around the year 445. A Judean official in the royal court appointed to be the new governor of Yehud (2:6; 5:14), he receives Persian approval to obtain materials and to rebuild Jerusalem's walls and gates. This project proceeds despite opposition from the neighboring governors of Samaria, Ammon, and others, and despite general impoverishment in Yehud (chaps. 2–6). Nehemiah served as the Persian political appointee, while Eliashib the high priest (3:1) was Yehud's religious leader. Nehemiah 6:17-18 is particularly revealing, as it indicates political alliances between wealthy Judean families and the powerful Transjordanian figure Tobiah (also a Judean), one of the officials opposed to Nehemiah's construction work in Jerusalem. Nehemiah 13:28 indicates that later the daughter of Sanballat, a governor of Samaria and another official opposed to Nehemiah, married a grandson of the high priest, Eliashib. In Nehemiah 8:8, the Levites are represented as having the important roles of reading and interpreting "the law of God" to the people.

The course of Yehud's internal politics continued to be marked by conflict and shifting alliances among the powerful. In the fourth century, Nikaso, a daughter of Sanballat III, then governor of Samaria, married Manasseh, brother of the high priest Yaddua (Josephus, *Antiquities* 11.297–303; Schiffman 1998, 92–93). Conflict over Manasseh's marriage led first to his departure from Jerusalem and then to his acceptance of Sanballat's offer to serve as high priest for a new temple to be constructed on Mount Gerizim, apparently completed in the early years of Alexander the Great. According to Josephus, many Judean priests followed him. This event seems to represent a major turning point leading to the split between Jerusalem and Samaria, or, as it would be known later, between the Jews and the Samaritans, as reflected centuries later in the New Testament story of the Good Samaritan (Luke 10).

The Samaritans, like their priestly peers in Jerusalem, produced written works, including the Samaritan Pentateuch, an important textual witness to the Torah, the first five books of the Bible (the Pentateuch in Christian tradition). Each of these two communities of Judeans was on its way toward becoming "a people of the Book." Within the postexilic community, the "Book" becomes a central feature of ritual. According Nehemiah 8, Ezra leads a communal reading of the Torah, which leads in turn to a celebration of the Feast of Booths. This practice of communal reading draws on the past to inform ritual in the present. In this particular instance, we see the ritual use of the past not simply to legitimize the present, but to draw out its fuller meaning in the view of the Yehudian leadership: the Feast of Booths remembered from the wilderness in the Torah becomes the Feast of Booths in Jerusalem. Days of communal recollection and lamentation (mentioned in passing in Zechariah 8:19) cite the major dates surrounding the fall of Jerusalem as days of lamentation. The overall picture is a rich communal life organized hierarchically (with no women in view) oriented to Temple and Torah: in developing rituals in texts and texts for ritual, these twin foci were the context for re-forming the Judean community as "Israel."

Judean Life outside Yehud

Judean communities in Egypt and Babylonia continued long after Judeans returned to Yehud. In Egypt, Judeans formed communities as the result of trade and mercenary opportunities. The book of Jeremiah (44:1) suggests a number of Judean enclaves at various sites along the Nile. Papyri from the southern town of Elephantine (or Syene) provide evidence for Judeans in Egypt. These texts point to a Judean mercenary enclave toward the end of the fifth century. These texts also show this community's sense of religious heritage in its desire to keep the feast of unleavened bread (*ANET,* 491) and to maintain a temple (called an "altar-house") dedicated to YHW (a variant of the divine name Yahweh). Built prior to the Persian conquest of 525 B.C.E., the temple of this Judean community was destroyed by Egyptian soldiers, and the fifth-century papyri record the colonists' wish to rebuild it (*ANET,* 492). They appeal to authorities primarily in Jerusalem, but they also mention their appeal to the sons of Sanballat, a reflection of Samaria's authority for the Judean colonists. From the same corpus of texts, it is also evident that Anat-Yahu, as well as Anat-Bethel, Eshem-Bethel, and Herem-Bethel, were recognized as divinities of some sort by the Judean colonists. (Whether these were distinct as goddesses or various forms of the gods Yahu and Bethel is debated, as reflected in van der Toorn 1992.) In addition, local Egyptian deities were recognized on occasion.

The Babylonian community of Judeans remained a major center of Judean life outside Yehud. When groups of Judeans left Babylonia, they left intact a community of Judeans there. The biblical accounts of the Judean returnees indicate that many Judeans remained in Babylon. Communication between different centers of Jewish life apparently continued (Nehemiah 1). The larger Mesopotamian community provides the leadership that enters the biblical story in the form of Ezra and Nehemiah. The first of these two figures reflects the structure of Judean religious authority, as he is a priest of Aaronide descent said to be an expert scribe in the Mosaic traditions. Nehemiah was a product of Persian court training. In a sense, Nehemiah and Ezra are emblematic of the Judean leadership from Mesopotamia.

Evidence for the further spread of Judean communities in Mesopotamia comes from a number of different sources. Biblical figures in addition to Nehemiah, such as Daniel and Esther (both discussed at greater length in chapter 2 below), reflect the migration of Judeans from the Mesopotamian heartland to major Persian centers such as Susa (Shushan). Some Judeans, like Nehemiah, evidently rose to high positions within the Persian administration. Moreover, the production of literature such as Daniel and Esther points to a certain ethnic identity in foreign lands. More specifically, these stories both entertain the Judean audience and affirm its identity. They also show how local traditions begin under Diaspora conditions. The Feast of Purim mandated by the book of Esther is not mentioned until 2 Maccabees 15:36. It seems to be unknown to Ben Sira (ca. 190), and so some have argued that the work did not make its way westward from Mesopotamia until the Hellenistic period. It may have remained unknown to the Judean community in Alexandria until the first century C.E., and it is the only work that became a book in the Bible that was not discovered among the Dead Sea Scrolls. This slow development in the Feast of Purim indicates the possibility of regional celebrations that communities of Judeans in different locales could occasionally develop in order to meet communal concerns and needs. Or, as we see in the Dead Sea Scrolls, they could add new dimensions to older festival traditions (see, for example, the Temple Scroll [11QT^a, cols. 19–21]).

Texts from outside the Bible also dramatize some aspects of Judean life in Mesopotamia and Persia. Mesopotamian documents from the Murashu business firm dating to the fifth century include references to Judeans (see Bregstein 1993). The business was active in generating cash and credit in the area around Nippur, with occasional business trips made to Susa and Babylon. The bearers of the eighty or so Judean names within the firm lived in many villages around Nippur, not in a Judean enclave. These Judeans were not major players in the Murashu firm, but were smallholders, low-level officials, or witnesses. They rarely did business on the Sabbath or feast days, yet, like many Judeans who had returned to Yehud, they gave Babylonian names to their children.

With the demise of the Persian Empire and the major shifts that would transpire during the following Hellenistic period, Jerusalem would eventually restore its own lines of authority, even as Judean life outside Yehud continued to spread through the western Mediterranean basin, up through Asia Minor (Turkey), and further afield in Mesopotamia and beyond. From its origins in the Late Bronze Age to the end of the Persian period, Israel had experienced radically different societal transformations. The many challenges that faced Israel through these centuries—including its very ability to identify itself as a single people called Israel through the almost thousand years of its "biblical history" (roughly speaking, 1150–332 B.C.E.)—are the subject of the next chapter.

Challenges to Israel during the Biblical Period

2

Zion says: "The LORD has forsaken me, My LORD has forgotten me."
—Isaiah 49:14

The challenges posed to the Israelites over the centuries varied as the circumstances of life changed. In many respects, the biblical texts show us the effects of cultural changes, as they made their impact on ancient Israelite society and as it responded to those changes. Many of the challenges developed out of the dynamics of Israel's physical environment. Others emerged from Israel's own domestic struggles, while still further challenges were posed by the various international settings that exercised influence over the life of Israel or where many Israelites eventually lived. As one of its fundamental responses to all these challenges, the very identity of Israel shifted over the course of the centuries. As I will note at various points in this chapter, the very definition of "Israelite" went through several transformations, thanks to the many changes taking place in Israel's different political, social, and religious landscapes.

Premonarchic Challenges

Early Israel faced several basic challenges. The foremost among them involved the struggle for survival. A subsistence society was easily threatened by drought and famine. Dependent on the rains from off the Mediterranean during the wet season from October through March, Israelites lived a precarious existence from one year to the next.

Israel's topography offered further challenges. In contrast to the valleys and the coast held by other peoples, highland Israel could be literally a harder row to hoe. The rocky soil of the highlands put Israel at a distinct disadvantage. Furthermore, its location away from the major trade routes on the coast would favor Israel's neighbors economically; in terms of importance, Israel's inland trade lines were secondary or tertiary routes. Often cited in this regard is the superior development of metal technology among the coastal Philistines, reflected in the simplified recollection of 1 Samuel 13:19: "No smith was to be found in all the land of Israel." Indeed, the archaeological record shows considerable metallurgical activity at Israelite sites in this period (see Bloch-Smith 2003). What Israelite and Philistine archaeological sites distinguish, according to Bloch-Smith, is the Philistines' relative advantages in producing metal weaponry. Their location on the coast gave them greater access to both ore imports from Cyprus and new types of weapons developed in the Aegean. Their coastal location also gave them control of metal trade to the inland area of Israel. The Philistines developed more elaborate bronze workshops as well.

A further challenge to Israel posed by topography was the Jezreel Valley, which cut across the highlands and could under certain conditions cut tribal units off from one another. The Jordan River likewise divided the Transjordanian tribes from their Cisjordanian counterparts. The distances between various tribes, with their own local topographical conditions and means of support, were an impediment to intertribal relations.

These environmental conditions in turn generated further difficulties. Given its topographical and economic disadvantages, Israel would be relatively easy prey to its neighbors. The book of Judges reports external threats from neighbors. Israel's response to such threats involved tribal militias ready to assemble on an occasional basis to meet temporary threats. The story of Judges 5 is a fine instance of geographically more proximate tribes meeting the call to respond to a non-Israelite threat, in this case apparently to trade through the central highlands, while tribes located further away from the threat do not answer the call. According to the book of Judges, intertribal violence could also be problematic (for example, Judges 12), and internal violence could spiral into greater acts of tribal warfare (see chaps. 19–21). When the violence threatened the existence of a tribal unit, some sort of social balance could be sought, sometimes at great social cost (in Judges 21, in particular to women).

Shifts in tribal status apparently underlie changes in different listings of tribes from the late premonarchic period through the monarchy. Reuben enjoyed the traditional first place (Deuteronomy 33), but in southern circles this tribe would be criticized for the sake of Judah's promotion (Genesis 49). Indeed, Reuben would be entirely supplanted by Judah in southern circles, as reflected in the order of tribal allotments in Numbers 34 and Joshua 15–21 and by tribal stories in the book of Judges. A parallel trajectory issuing in the supremacy of Joseph and Benjamin also took place in northern circles (compare Genesis 48; cf. Psalm 68:27).

In the eyes of later Israelites as well as later readers of the Bible, some features of early Israel seemed like severe challenges. Its polytheism, its tolerance for images

of deities, its failure to follow religious laws, and its lack of unity were all condemned by monarchic and postmonarchic critics, as seen by later Deuteronomistic levels of the book of Judges. However, during the premonarchic period
these challenges were experienced by Israelites themselves in rather different terms.
The problem was not polytheism, but competition between different deities supported at different shrines. The problem was not images as such, but competition
among forms of religious symbols, an issue that went hand in hand with struggles involving competing shrines and lines of priesthood along with their main
deities. In other words, the crises of this period perceived by later Israel looking
back on it often did not match the crises as experienced by premonarchic Israelites
themselves.

These challenges raise a further question: What is an Israelite? Biblical tradition
in general apparently answered this question relatively simply as one belonging to
the twelve tribes, but it is not apparent that this identity was so obvious in this
early period. It is evident, as we noted in chapter 1, that Israel was some sort of
social unit, a people, to judge from the Merneptah stela. However, what did this
Israel actually consist of? For example, the tribal call in Judges 5 omits Judah, and
one might read the presentation in Judges 20 as contrasting the Benjaminites
with the Israelites. It is also evident that Israel was a developing polity of tribal
units in the central highlands. Some tribes of the northern highlands did not answer the call in Judges 5; so perhaps their relations to other Israelite units were
somewhat tenuous, and the southern tribes were perhaps not even considered
"Israel" at this point. It is also evident that within these tribal units considered to
be Israel lived others not considered Israelites as such. In short, we see an Israel
whose tribal identity was probably based on clan and family identity; cross-tribal
or pan-tribal identity operated for specific military purposes and perhaps for
cultic and cultural purposes as well, which required intertribal cooperation. As
long as economic and political conditions did not seriously threaten this situation, it could continue. The rise of the monarchy was in fact a response to a massive challenge to these conditions.

The Challenges of the United Monarchy: Saul, David, Solomon

As we saw in chapter 1, Israel on the eve of the monarchy was a highly local society
organized around the units of family and clans. All aspects of life—social, religious, economic, political—functioned within this highly local social organization and structure. Supraclan activity seems to have taken place primarily in two
contexts: defense against external threats (such as disruption of trade in Judges 5 and
the Philistines in 1 Samuel), and internal communal activity (such as celebration

at shrines including Shiloh, Shechem, and Bethel). The repeated external threat of the Philistines seems to have generated the need for ongoing military apparatus, and this need in turn generated the apparatus of a monarchy. The monarchy was viewed as a sociopolitical level built on the structure of family, clans, and tribes, and indeed David's clan was among the most powerful within the tribe of Judah. The impetus for this new kingship evidently came from the ongoing outside threat not easily met by the instrument of tribal militia.

Saul and David deployed different strategies to face this challenge. Saul's response was traditional, largely operating with the old military structure of tribal militia. Saul worked out of his own tribal land as a power base in Benjamin and remained largely dependent on other tribes to join his efforts. At the end of his reign, it is apparent that "all Israel" constitutes only "Gilead, the Ashurites, Jezreel, Ephraim, and Benjamin" (2 Samuel 2:9). From this list, it is evident that Saul's rule did not include the far northern tribes or Judah. Saul's military resources were accordingly limited. Saul also chose to meet the Philistines head-on (as well as other enemies, according to 1 Samuel 14:47-48), and in the face of the Philistines' superior resources and technology, Saul eventually met his death in battle (1 Samuel 31).

David's path to power was considerably different (see McKenzie 2000 and Halpern 2001). He began his climb first through military success in Saul's army. In his bid to establish legitimacy, David married Saul's daughter Michal (1 Samuel 18). He also became best friends with Saul's son Jonathan. As a result, he became integrated into the royal family. Moreover, his marriages (2 Samuel 5:13-14) perhaps forged new bonds with important families. (David's later marriages would mark further bonds with important families further afield in Israel, as some of his wives came from peripheral areas of his growing kingdom; see 1 Samuel 25:43; 2 Samuel 3:2-5; and note also his marriage to Bathsheba in 2 Samuel 11.) From his developing tribal base of Judah (2 Samuel 2:10-11), David first played the Philistines and the Israelites off one another (1 Samuel 21, 23, 29). Even before David became king, he developed his own army (1 Samuel 22), loyal to him and ready to operate as needed.

At this point, David looks less like a king and more like a tribal leader with his own personal army. His success in battle as well as the legitimacy he gained through royal marriage made him seem the obvious successor to Saul; the tribes fell in line behind him (2 Samuel 5). Through his army and his marriages, David developed military and social advantages that Saul never had. Clearly, David's approach was more promising over the long run. Although it took considerable time and effort to do so, David ultimately prevailed over the Philistines (2 Samuel 5 and 8). His military capability turned from defense against his neighbors on the west to hegemony over them (2 Samuel 8, 10, and 12; these accounts may have been amplified because of later wars in this area).

The competition between Saul and David issued in a further challenge: civil war at the inception of the monarchy. The Bible largely presents Saul and David as a succession of Israel's first two kings, but this presentation may obscure the crisis of civil war. Prior to David's kingship, Saul's supporters disputed Davidic claims to the throne (2 Samuel 2–4), and they remained contested through his reign (2 Samuel 16). The debate over David's legitimacy apparently did not end with his eclipse of Saul and his descendants. The list of twelve generations of Saul's descendants in 1 Chronicles 8:33-40 suggests ongoing support of his line. In the book of Esther (2:5), Mordecai's genealogy echoes Saul's background and thereby preserves another later recollection of support for his line (see Brettler 1995).

The local structure of Israel's society posed a challenge to the establishment of the monarchy. David built on his own tribal base of Judah and added to it the territory that his predecessor had ruled. Apart from David's increased hegemony extending to the northern tribes, the patrilocal structure of Israel's society tended to work against national interests, except in cases of military action. Therefore, the monarchy required mechanisms to develop ongoing means for its operation and legitimacy. The monarchy initially responded in several ways to these challenges. David's reign was marked not only by his establishment of his own standing army, but also by his choice of Jerusalem as a capital city (2 Samuel 5). Jerusalem would serve as the new home for the ark (2 Samuel 6), a brilliant strategy by David, who dressed his innovation of a capital city with the traditional symbol of the people's wars. In short, a symbol acknowledged across tribal lines was incorporated within the new institution of the monarchy.

It has also been thought that another brilliant aspect in selecting Jerusalem as capital involved its location. Since prior to David's conquest of Jerusalem it was situated on non-Israelite land, the choice is often thought to have been motivated by Jerusalem's location between what would later be the two kingdoms of Israel (the northern kingdom) and Judah (the southern kingdom). This is not exactly right, since Jerusalem is not centrally located between the north and south. Perhaps David chose the site because it was central to Judah, compared to his own home in Bethlehem. In general terms, Jerusalem would serve as a point between the northern and southern tribes. By location, it would not be disputed by any specific tribe, and it would link the two major parts of this new monarchic polity.

David began to develop mechanisms for rule, especially in the military and the priesthood (2 Samuel 8:16-18). Religion could be placed at the service of the king not only through this symbolism of the ark, but also through personnel. David's selection of two priests has been thought to have been one that balanced southern and northern constituencies. At the end of his reign, David had established the incipient basis for Israel as it would be classically remembered, as the twelve tribes. Prior to the monarchy, the label "Israel" applied to the northern tribes. With David's new royal state of Israel, this label functioned to link together Judah with Israel under the nominal rubric of Israel but under the actual political leadership of Judah. With a Judean as the head of this royal polity, the term "Israel" served to exalt Judah and to help establish its political claims vis-à-vis Israel. Now Israel, in the service of Judean royal ideology, slightly shifted in its significance to include Judah. This would be only the first of many such alterations that the term "Israel" would take over the course of Israel's past. In this period, the label "Israel" would serve David well. In the end, it seems that David ruled a tribal state as Saul had, but with some real differences. One was the scale of their tribal kingdoms and another was the balance of power between each king and the tribes.

Though not the military leader his father was, Solomon responded to the challenges of his own day in ways that his father never envisioned. Instead of military success, Solomon extended the diplomatic successes of his father. Both father and son enjoyed treaty relations with Tyre (2 Samuel 5:11; 1 Kings 5), but Solomon took the next step in opening a new trade network at the northern end of the Gulf of Aqaba (1 Kings 9:26-28). According to 1 Kings 10:11, it would appear that this enterprise was a joint undertaking with Tyre. Combined with trade relations with Tyre and perhaps other points on the Mediterranean, the establishment of a port on the Gulf of Aqaba (the attribution to Ezion-Geber is disputed by archaeologists) would have put the young kingdom at the crossroads of regional travel between the coast of the Mediterranean and the Gulf of Aqaba. Even if Tyre had the upper hand in this arrangement, Israel was no longer simply a backwater of the highlands; instead, it was integrated into the larger regional economy, as reflected in the legendary story of the Queen of Sheba and the mention of trade in 1 Kings 10. Furthermore, Solomon used the strategy of marriage to forge international links. He is reported in 1 Kings 3 to have married a daughter of Pharaoh; and 1 Kings 11, written by a later critic of Solomon's reign, stresses his international marriages as a whole. By these strategies, Solomon helped to turn Israel into a significant regional economic player.

On the domestic front, Solomon used his formidable skills to build up a bureaucracy that could further integrate local and national levels of administration. The list of officials and the establishment of prefects throughout Israel in 1 Kings 4 suggest both a developing central administration and its projection into tribal holdings. According to 1 Kings 4, Solomon also married off two of his daughters to these regional officials, strengthening the bond of loyalty between them and their king. This step was enhanced by his domestic construction projects at key sites in Israel (1 Kings 9:15-19, 24). As another part of Solomon's domestic agenda, his construction of the Jerusalem Temple (1 Kings 5–7) may be regarded as a further answer to the domestic challenge facing the monarchy. The Jerusalem

Temple would help to develop national identity by focusing the devotion of Israelite society on the national god. As noted in chapter 1, the Temple told the story of the Deity through its structure and symbols; and by its location and its royal patronage, it expressed divine support for the monarchy. It also served to focus on the military and royal aspects of the Deity. In short, religion and politics served together in the Temple complex to support the monarchy.

The effects of the Temple were felt further through the economic activity that it seems to have generated, not only through tithes made to the Temple but also by the additional economic activity of trade that would have transpired during pilgrimages made to Jerusalem. Furthermore, the Jerusalem Temple became the home of worship that integrated themes of the close relations, even identity, between the divine and human kings. What has been called "royal ideology" (represented by later "royal psalms" such as Psalms 2, 18, 72, and 89) generated a worldview that put the monarchy at the center of the religious and political world of Israel. In sum, the Jerusalem Temple rerouted clan religious and economic activity from local shrines with their religious traditions and identities to the one national shrine under the divine and human kings, now closely associated with one another by a royal religious viewpoint that identified the monarchy at the top of the social and political pyramid.

Despite his many achievements, Solomon did not continue all of his father's successes. Externally, he was never the military force his father was, and he was able to compensate only somewhat for this lack through diplomatic and economic means. Internally, his management of the priesthood in Jerusalem was not successful. Whether or not Abiathar was demoted as a result of his support for Adonijah, Solomon ousted Abiathar from the priestly leadership post that he had held under David (1 Kings 2:35). As a result, this line of the priesthood lost its royal support, which in turn generated resentments. Priestly competition and criticism would remain a standard feature of the religious landscape of monarchic Israel, and it would anticipate even greater tensions and conflicts that would afflict the priesthood right through the Hellenistic period (ca. 333–160) and the Roman destruction of the Second Temple in 70 C.E. One may say that the challenges to the priesthood as an institution were rarely met in ancient Israel, and indeed they contributed to its demise under the Romans.

The Challenges of the Divided Monarchy

Political and Religious Challenges

According to 1 Kings 12, the aftermath of Solomon's death led to the split of the northern and southern tribes. It probably indicates that the phenomenon of

Judahite rule over the northern tribes of Israel was achieved by force and persuasion; the united monarchy of David and Solomon was hardly the natural state of
affairs. The reversion to a divided monarchy was in fact a return to the earlier situation prior to David's kingship. With the split of Solomon's kingdom into north
(Israel) and south (Judah), the script for creating a new royal polity was replayed
in the northern kingdom. For Jeroboam, the new king of the north, establishing
royal shrines at Dan and Bethel was not designed simply to establish a new royal
identity for the northern kingdom over and against nonroyal shrines, but to create a new royal and religious identity vis-à-vis Jerusalem. Like David and Solomon,
Jeroboam used traditional symbols to make his innovations more at home. As
noted in chapter 1, he adopted a preroyal tradition of the exodus and identified
his cult symbols of the calf of this tradition with the iconography of his own
royal shrines (1 Kings 12:28). In this way, he addressed the ongoing challenge of
Jerusalem as a royal-religious site. The rivalry between the two kingdoms would
remain a hallmark of Israel's history down through the fall of the northern kingdom beginning in 732 and completed in 722.

Jeroboam and his successors had additional challenges to face. Compared to the
southern kingdom, the northern kingdom had its population spread out over a
larger territory with greater topographical variation, and as a whole it was exposed
to more outside threats. Moreover, Israel suffered through eight changes of dynasty
over approximately two hundred years, with two major changes of dynasties (of
Ahab and Jehu) in the ninth century. In contrast, Judah was smaller, more isolated, and socially united largely under the tribe of Judah. As a result, the Davidic
dynasty based in the south would continue for over four hundred years.

For the north, the house of Ahab marked a basic change not only of dynasty
but also of religious policy. Readers of the Bible often think that the religious
issue at stake with the prophet Elijah squaring off against the prophets of Baal on
Mount Carmel (1 Kings 18) involved preserving Israel's monotheism. More precisely, the religious crisis was a political challenge to Yahweh as the state god of
the northern kingdom. Elijah does not ask the people to reject all deities; instead,
he asks them to choose between Yahweh and Baal, whom the people tolerated up
to this time. As long as Yahweh remained the divine king of Israel, other deities
regarded as lesser divinities in the court of the divine king could be tolerated.

Indeed, it is quite possible that Yahweh and Baal could have been identified or
at least tolerated together, as suggested by the personal names from Samaria with
both Yahweh and Baal. Among many Israelites, the two gods might have even
enjoyed what Jan Assmann (1997, 3, 28, 44–54) has called "translatability": equiv-
alence made between two deities by different groups in cultural and political contact with one another. Or, assuming that Yahweh and El were already identified in
this region by this period (which seems likelier), Baal could have been a second-

level god subordinate to Yahweh-El (see chapter 3). Yet once King Ahab sought to elevate Baal to the status of a state-supported god, evidently under the influence of his Phoenician-born wife, Jezebel, a minority of Israelites experienced a crisis of religious definition. It seemed that Baal was being supported by the northern monarchy as equal in status to Yahweh-El within a political structure that assumed one patron god for the royal dynasty. This crisis was not a general one of monotheism versus polytheism, although Elijah's championing of Yahweh as Israel's God would later serve as the model for later proclamations of Israel's monotheism; this is part of the reason why 1–2 Kings incorporates the Elijah traditions.

The World Theology of the Monarchy

There is a great deal about religious practices in this period that is little known, including the range of Israel's deities. One account of the final conquest of the north by the Assyrian king Sargon II includes a reference to "the gods of their confidence" that his army captured. Taken at face value, it would indicate that the northern monarchy supported at least a number of deities, probably under the authority of the national god; perhaps it fostered a broader group of gods. The same may be said of Judah, given the later tour of the Temple in Ezekiel 8–10. These biblical chapters, if they may be accepted at face value, suggest that in God's house there was room for a number of divinities.

By the eighth century (if not earlier), Israel modified the old, traditional theology of the polytheistic family, headed by the elderly El and dominated by Yahweh, in turn supported by a household of deities both major and minor. In a passage such as 1 Kings 22 (especially v. 19), we now see the presentation of Yahweh presiding over the heavenly court of divinities, called the "host of heaven." On the eve of Assyrian power in the west, Israel had developed a religious worldview that exalted Yahweh as its national god and subordinated to Yahweh various figures of the divine household that included members of his divine retinue (Resheph and Deber mentioned by name in Habakkuk 3:5 [NRSV "pestilence" and "plague"]) as well as his divine servants, including messengers (angels). This chief god, the divine patron of the northern and southern kingdoms, was attributed the standard roles of divine leadership. We may suppose that this family of deities included a limited number of goddesses, quite possibly Astarte and Asherah, who perhaps by this point was the consort of Yahweh. This reconstruction offered by many scholars is based in part on eighth-century inscriptions from Kuntillet Ajrud and Khirbet el-Qom, which offer blessings "by Yahweh . . . and by his asherah" (see the essays in Becking et al. 2001, in Dietrich and Klopfenstein 1994, as well as Olyan 1988, Hadley 2000, and Zevit 2001). Whether the latter is a symbol or the name of

Asherah

the goddess seems to matter little to scholars who view the reference to "asherah" as either the goddess or her symbol. Other scholars are reticent to see the goddess or her separate symbol even here, since the blessing is "to Yahweh . . . and to his asherah." In other words, the asherah refers to a symbol, belonging by this time to the god and not the goddess. Even so, the symbol likely did refer earlier to the goddess by the same name, and it is possible that this remained the case in various locations at the same time.

Surrounded by several polities of similar scale or power, Israel recognized that all the nations had their own national gods, while Israel had its own. It would seem that in this "world theology," Israel could tolerate and explain the notion of other nations with their own national gods. All of these national gods were thought to belong to a single divine family headed by a figure known as El Elyon. This world theology was particularly political: each nation has a patron god who supports and protects the human king and his subjects. From the political emphasis in this world theology, it was apparently attractive to the monarchy as a way of expressing its place in the world. It is even possible that this world theology in the form that it developed in Israel arose only with the monarchy, although its basic structure and elements are evident already from the Ugaritic texts. What is remarkable about the early form of this world theology is not only that it recognized other gods, but that it continued the older notion of El Elyon as the head of this divine arrangement of the world, under which Israel is subsumed. As we will see in chapter 3, this is the picture presupposed by both Psalm 82 and Deuteronomy 32:8-9. In general, the picture of Yahweh as divine warrior-king and patriarch presupposed a certain tolerance for, and perhaps cultic devotion to, other deities within his divine household, even if they were considered subordinate to him.

As one of the hallmarks of biblical religion, monotheism is usually considered to be a standard feature of Israel from its inception, only to be undermined by Israelites attracted to the gods of the other nations. As this discussion would suggest, however, prior to the eighth century a traditional family of deities was headed by Yahweh as the divine patriarch. This divine family was viewed as parallel to the royal family. So we are a considerable way off from Israelite monotheism. Even the presentation of Moses hardly projects a forceful monotheism, but a monolatry cognizant of other deities. We can see this viewpoint presupposed by the Ten Commandments' prohibition against of other gods "besides Me" or "before Me" (al-panay; Exodus 20:3; Deuteronomy 5:7). Parenthetically, this phrase seems to refer to other gods not to be worshiped in Yahweh's cultic presence, which would explain the use of panay, "face" (used elsewhere for cultic presence, for example, in Psalm 42:2). This viewpoint of multiple deities under Yahweh also underlies the praise offered in Exodus 15:11: "Who is like You among

monolatry

the gods *(elim),* O Yahweh?" Compare the divine beings, *bene elim,* under Yahweh (NRSV "the Lord") in Psalm 29:1. There are other gods for Israel, but Yahweh is to be its undisputed patron god.

This viewpoint seems to represent the standard religious perspective of ancient Israel down to the eighth century, and it may have been very early in some parts of Israel. For example, the Song of Deborah (Judges 5) would suggest the possibility of this viewpoint already in the central highlands of premonarchic Israel. By the ninth century, the patron god had become the head god, but only in the seventh and sixth centuries did the head god become tantamount to the godhead. The world theology would nicely express Israel's identity within the immediate context of its neighboring states, in particular the Transjordanian states, the Phoenician city-states, and perhaps the Aramean states. Clearly and interestingly, the exception of the greater powers of Egypt and Mesopotamia suggests that the scope of this world theology did not address the wider world beyond Israel's neighboring states. Otherwise, the picture of each state with its own patron god within the larger family headed by El Elyon made good sense of Israel's place in its immediate Levantine world down to the eighth century.

Along with this world theology, in both royal and popular practice Israel continued its old devotion to deceased ancestors, such as communication with them and meals offered to them. Later, in texts dating to the eighth century and afterward, these practices would be condemned (Leviticus 19:31; 20:6, 27; Deuteronomy 18:9-14; 26:14; 1 Samuel 28; 2 Kings 21:6). Moreover, a number of other traditional practices were only later regarded as idolatrous. These would include worship at local sites called "high places" *(bamot)* and child sacrifice made in times of crisis. Until the eighth century and perhaps later, these practices were generally considered compatible with the worship of Yahweh. Even child sacrifice, arguably the most vile of Israelite practices, was acceptable down to the sixth century, as shown by the repeated denials in Jeremiah and Ezekiel that Yahweh ever commanded it (Jeremiah 7:31; 19:5-6; 32:35; Ezekiel 20:25-26; see Hahn and Bergsma 2004). We may view ongoing adherence to traditional practices as an effort of Israel's clans to meet the challenges of the times, including the loss of family lands and other disruptions to family identity. The monarchy supported or tolerated a range of beliefs and practices.

Prophetic Critiques

It is in the context of eighth-century social and political shifts that Amos and Hosea prophesied. The two prophets appear on the scene in the final decades of the northern kingdom, which fell in 732–722. During the prosperous years of Jeroboam II (786–746), Amos decried oppression of the poor (4:1) as well as additional taxes placed on them (5:11), and he condemned the activity of what we might call the upper class (6:1-6). By combining these observations, Amos offered a fundamental sort of analysis that combines social, economic, and religious factors: the wealthier of ancient Israel able to purchase land from poor people (who evidently sell their land in order to pay taxes) supported the sacrificial system maintained in the name of God (for example, 2:6-9). As a result, Amos condemns ill-gotten gain and proclaims, "let justice well up like water, righteousness like an unfailing stream" (5:24). Indeed, Amos may have been speaking against his own social or class interests, as suggested by Steiner (2003).

Palestinians

Amos observed the social crisis that the loss of family lands entailed, specifically the erosion of traditional identity based on families and their ties to their ancestral lands. In many modern Western societies, personal identity is partially and loosely tied to land by comparison to the ancient Israelites. For them, land was family identity: land, family lines, and home religion together formed the fabric of identity. Amos cries out against the basic loss of family land during eighth-century Israel, yet the decimation of family lineages would continue, as later conquests by the Assyrians first in the north in 722 and then in the south in 701 would sever the ties of most families from their ancestral lands.

In contrast, Hosea dramatizes religious threats of idolatry (Hosea 3) as well as political upheavals (Hosea 7). The latter generally suggests the situation between the end of Jeroboam II and the end of the northern Kingdom of Israel. Despite the highly elusive (and allusive) language of Hosea, the book's critiques against other deities as other "baals" are to be taken seriously; yet it remains difficult to determine the precise religious situation that the prophet was addressing (for a recent discussion, see Nocquet 2004). As noted above, the Assyrian king Sargon II includes a reference to "the gods of their confidence" that his army captured in his campaign against the northern kingdom. At a minimum, there was some sort of northern ditheism consisting of a god and a goddess and lower-level divinities as well. We could also imagine for Israel a world theology described above; how much more polytheism may have been involved in Hosea's time is difficult to determine. In any case, the book of Hosea offers a religious analysis that links idolatry and political destruction together as cause and effect directed by God. This linkage will become the cornerstone of Israelite interpretation of the demise of the northern and southern kingdoms.

The Crisis of the Syro-Ephraimite War (734–732)

As a last effort to resist the Assyrian advance westward, the northern kingdom under King Pekah joined forces with the Aramean kingdom of Rezin based in Damascus (2 Kings 21). In turn, these two kingdoms attempted to induce Judah to join their coalition. However, the kingdom of Judah, ruled at this time by King Ahaz, rejected their offer, and they in turn decided to force Judah into this coalition by attacking Jerusalem. Second Kings 21 reports that Ahaz paid the Assyrians for their help, further making Judah into an Assyrian vassal.

During this crisis, the prophet Isaiah called on King Ahaz to trust in God, and not to fear Aram and Israel (Isaiah 7–8). The king's own son would be a sign of divine support against the two kings, who in turn will soon feel the wrath of the Assyrian Empire. The Assyrian king Tiglath-pileser did come to Judah's aid against Aram and Israel, setting in motion the process of Israel's fall. Although the help was perceived in the prophetic view as divinely granted, it was one mediated by Assyrian power. This view of history would serve Judah later when it would attempt to make sense out of its own demise in 586.

The Fall of the Northern Kingdom (732–722) and the Response of Deuteronomy

Largely unrecognized by readers of the Bible, the fall of the northern kingdom and its tribes was the single greatest crisis in Israelite identity up to this time. The Assyrian devastation of the northern kingdom created a flood of Israelite refugees south to Judah. The northern tribes lost a central piece in their identity, for they were a society that defined identity according to ancestral land. The impact of the Assyrian conquest of the north is reflected in the Bible in many ways. One involves the ongoing use of the terms "Israel" and "Israelites" within works (now in the Bible) either produced or transmitted in Judah. In other words, Judah became the "repository" of Israelite identity despite the loss of Israelite land. With this development, we see a major shift in the Israelite identity. No longer referring primarily to an independent political polity of the northern kingdom, "Israel" also did not refer simply to a conquered kingdom. It functioned at this point as the name for the identity of northerners displaced to the southern kingdom of Judah, as well as a marker or label of northern traditions that would be absorbed in Judah. As a result, the label "Israel" also became identified with Judah itself.

Furthermore, the south absorbed a number of northern works, which contained religious visions that would challenge Israel's traditional religious practices and beliefs. The greatest of these may be Deuteronomy's extensive presentation of the covenant as a treaty between Israel and Yahweh as its sovereign king. (Deuteronomy hardly invented this idea, but makes it fundamental to its presentation of the covenant.) Perhaps as a denial of the earthly power of Assyria, which commonly used treaties to keep its vassals in line, Deuteronomy deploys the treaty format to express Israel's single-minded devotion and utter subservience to its only king: preamble of relationship of parties to the treaty, chapters 1–11; terms of the treaty, chapters 12–26; curses and blessings to the treaty, chapters 27–30; witness to the treaty, chapter 32.

Deuteronomy criticizes the traditional practices mentioned earlier (other gods, the asherah, high places, child sacrifice, divination, tithes given for offerings to the deceased); only worship of Yahweh is acceptable. It would seem that in Deuteronomy the radical changes in the wake of the north's demise issued in a radical vision of oneness: one god, with one divine teaching to one people who meet in only one place of worship. This monotheism represents a profound response to the external threat of Mesopotamian empires and the internal challenge of social deterioration (for the latter, see especially the series of important articles in Halpern 1987, 1991, 1993, 1996). The looming threat of Assyria undermined the world theology traditional to ancient Israel. The world theology was premised on the relative correlation of the divine and human kings: as long as human kings were in power, it was a sign of divine power and protection. By ancient Near Eastern standards, however, the demise of a nation could also signal the impotence of its patron god. The rise of the Assyrian Empire in the west undermined this worldview. For, if the north fell, it could seem that the patron god of the north might be correspondingly powerless. An alternative Near Eastern response, namely, that the patron god was punishing the north, was favored by many in the south to explain the north's demise. To meet the challenge of Assyria as an empire, there was a reconceptualization of Israel's worldview, which I will examine in the next chapter.

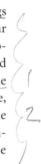

As a result of this change in worldview, Deuteronomy offered a corresponding critique of the exalted view of kingship in Israel. Within royal circles, divine support of kings had been viewed prior to the Assyrian threat as an unconditional "eternal covenant" (as expressed in 2 Samuel 23:1-7, in particular v. 5, although it has been argued that this text or some its elements may be later). God's cosmic power resided in the kings (Psalm 89:25), and their rule, ideally speaking, extended over the whole world (Psalm 2:8-11). Kingship could approach the status of divinity. The king in Isaiah 9:6 receives the title "Mighty God," and Psalm 45:6 proclaims that "your divine throne [or: your throne, O divine one (namely, the king)], is forever and ever." On the day of his coronation, the new monarch gains a new status as God's "son" (Psalm 2:7; cf. Psalm 89:26), who issues from the (divine?) womb (Psalm 110:3).

Lang (2002) has proposed that in the Judean coronation ritual the king was thought to ascend ritually to heaven, where, after his new birth as the son of God, he would join the company of the other "sons of God" seated at the right hand of God and receive divine power; thus the king is invited by divine oracle, spoken perhaps by a priest: "Sit at my right hand" (Psalm 110:1). The view of kingship in

Deuteronomy differs markedly. Rather than being a virtual divinity unconditionally supported by the divine king, the human king was to be a student of Torah (Deuteronomy 17:18-20), whose reign would be judged according to its standards (see Knoppers 2001). The fall of the north would cast a shadow over all institutions and ways of thinking. A view of matters that probably began under the influence of prophets like Hosea, this Deuteronomic critique of the monarchic worldview would make headway in royal circles during the reign of Hezekiah.

Hezekiah and Josiah

Hezekiah was particularly heralded for holding off the Assyrian invasion of 701 B.C.E. (2 Kings 18–19). The most difficult political challenge of the time, it looked as if Judah would go the way of Israel, which had fallen to the Assyrians only twenty-one years earlier. However, Hezekiah had prepared for this invasion (Vaughan 1999). As discussed in chapter 1, his waterworks in Jerusalem are noted in passing in the Kings account of his reign (2 Kings 20:20), while the Chronicles account stresses this achievement as well the monarch's efforts to fortify Jerusalem (2 Chronicles 32:3-4). The Siloam tunnel inscription also celebrates the digging of an underground channel 1,200 cubits (over 1,700 feet) long to divert water into the city. The Assyrian conquest of Judah resulted in a good deal of its population taken into slavery and the destruction of numerous towns and the siege of Jerusalem. During the siege of Jerusalem, however, the Assyrian army departed to address problems at home. The book of 2 Kings recalls this change in fortunes as the greatest of miracles, a defeat inflicted on the Assyrians by divine intervention (2 Kings 19:35).

In the description of the reigns of the northern and southern monarchs in 1–2 Kings, Hezekiah was one of two royals without peer. Hezekiah was viewed as not only particularly successful but also strongly pious. More specifically, he is presented as the first king to accept the new vision of Deuteronomy. It is not clear whether this embrace on Hezekiah's part reflected his great piety or a political savvy (or both) that saw in Deuteronomy's plan of centralization a realization of Judah's needs with Assyria looming. Many scholars believe that an initial edition of 1–2 Kings did take place under Hezekiah (see Schniedewind 2004, 77–81 for a summary, as well as the incisive work of Barrick 2002). In view of the recent fall of the north to Assyria, the departure of the Assyrian army from Judah may have been a particularly compelling impetus for seeing Hezekiah as the high point of Judean monarchs. In the alleged first edition of 1–2 Kings under Hezekiah, the history of the south would have culminated with the glorious reign of this king. We may see not only the particular account in 2 Kings 18–19 as a celebration of Hezekiah, but the entire historical work in its first edition as a celebration of this king's success.

The glorification of Hezekiah was not restricted to depicting the climax of kingship under his reign. It also may extend to the beginning of the historical work from Joshua through 2 Kings. In the book of Joshua, we see some signs that Joshua served as a model for Hezekiah's royal program (Schniedewind 2004, 80). It is apparent from verbal parallels between Joshua 1 and 2 Kings 18 that the authors of Joshua, perhaps in the time of King Hezekiah, imagined their king to be similar to Joshua: both dedicated to the divine teachings as mediated by Moses; God is with both of them wherever they go; and they were successful (Joshua 1:7-9, 17; 2 Kings 18:5-7). In each instance, the description of leadership serves as preface to conquests, in the case of Joshua described by the work named for him, and in the case of Hezekiah only in a summary verse (2 Kings 18:8) that, despite its brevity, bespeaks a hope for a restored nation.

Joshua in particular emulates the Deuteronomic ideal of kingship (Deuteronomy 17:18-20): to be a constant student of Torah (Joshua 1:8). What we see in Joshua, then, is not simply a recounting of the land's initial conquest, but a late-monarchic expression of hope for the reestablishment of the kingdom back to what was thought to be its earlier boundaries. With Hezekiah's time witnessing the fall of the northern kingdom in 722, Joshua now appears to be a book that reflects the reduction of ancient Israel, not its initial glorious conquest. Joshua may echo not only the success of Hezekiah, but also the depth of northern loss rather than territorial gain. Joshua's stress on the twelve tribes may also express hope against the real loss of tribal land for the northern ten tribes in 722, and possibly for the southern two in 586. Perhaps as a way to respond to the trauma of the north's fall, biblical writing in this case allowed a people to gain in textual form what may have been otherwise lost in experience. Joshua expresses through past narrative what Jeremiah 31 and 33 would communicate in future oracles: hope for a restored united monarchy lived under the ideals of the teaching of God.

Even greater than the praise of Hezekiah is the praise of Josiah in 2 Kings 22–23. Like Hezekiah, Josiah is credited with religious reforms as well as other actions that seem to implement the religious program set out by the book of Deuteronomy. Second Kings may have ended with Hezekiah originally, but many scholars think it was updated to glorify Josiah. As an illustration of the Deuteronomistic edition of the historical books in the time of Josiah, its ending may have been 2 Kings 23:25, as this verse both echoes both Deuteronomy 6:5 and the ending in Deuteronomy 34 (with its similar characterization of Moses in v. 10). Josiah is presented as the embodiment of a king devoted to the standards of Torah. Second Kings focuses on the history of the north as a history of sin, ending with its destruction; the history of the south would have culminated with the glorious climax of Hezekiah in the first edition of Kings and then with Josiah in a revised version. Yet this moment of royal glory was fleeting. Josiah's death at Megiddo in 609 marked a terrible setback for a Judean state that was prospering during this phase of Mesopotamian weakness. The king's death in fact signaled the beginning of the Judean monarchy's demise, a challenge that would not be met again until the Maccabees of the second century B.C.E.

Responses to the Fall of Judah and Jerusalem (586)

The destruction of Jerusalem and the Temple, as well as the captivity of the elite population, inspired numerous literary creations (nicely surveyed by Albertz 2003). Literature would capture in words what had been suffered and lost in experience. Most responses focused on trying to understand what had happened: in these presentations, the relationship between God and Israel was interpreted in different ways.

Lamentations

The first and most basic response to the terrible fall of Jerusalem was lamentation, a ritual expression of national death. The biblical book of Lamentations thrusts its audience into what was recalled as the greatest trauma of Israel's history, the destruction of Jerusalem in 586 B.C.E. Lamentations expresses the raw pain suffered by Israel, its utter sense of national calamity, in five laments (a genre best known from Israel's worship, especially the book of Psalms). Chapter 1 opens with the first letter of the Hebrew alphabet (*aleph*) and runs through the last letter of the Hebrew alphabet (*taw*) in personifying Jerusalem as a princess sitting in lament like a widow for the deceased (1:1). This use of the acrostic form (alphabetic letters at the head of each verse) to structure the lament is perhaps to suggest a notion of completeness, that the topic of destruction is covered, as we might say in English, "from A to Z." Told in a third-person voice, the first lament likens Jerusalem to a widow who prays to God for help, as enemies have brought this destruction upon her, and acknowledges her wickedness as the cause for her plight. The second chapter also uses the format of the alphabetic acrostic to describe the destruction of Jerusalem. Yet here God is the agent of suffering, marked by mothers and children languishing from starvation, with infants victim to their cannibalism. Torah and prophecy, king and priest are gone; all marks of religious identity as well as the land as the site of ancestral identity are lost.

Chapter 3 also takes the form of an alphabetic acrostic, this time for an individual lament that provides another viewpoint on Jerusalem's fall. The individual, the "I," perhaps standing for each Judean who is suffering, expresses the demise of Jerusalem as God's personal destruction. The lament turns to an expression of hope and trust at verse 21, and here Lamentations begins to explore the reality that the destroying God is ultimately also the God of Israel's help. Both of these sides of God reflect divine concern for Israel's ultimate well-being. The individual voice of chapter 3 describes his nearing death; here individual death serves as a symbol for the people's collective death. Moreover, this individual plea conveys the suffering felt by each member of the people. It is not simply one collective suffering, but the sufferings of many people together. The lament returns to a plea against the nations who have participated in the destruction, thereby distinguishing for the future what the nations are doing from what God may do on Judah's behalf.

The alphabetic acrostic lament in Lamentations 4 offers a third-person description of Jerusalem's suffering. Again raised is the awful specter of children begging for food and mothers cooking their young for food. The lament ends with a theory about Israel's loss, that a time is to be served as expiation for sin.

The final chapter is a lament offered in the voice of the communal "we" that acknowledges both its sin and its tremendous loss, and ends with a prayer that God take back the people even as divine anger continues against them.

The Exile as Punishment by Israel's Goddess: Jeremiah 44

The view of divine punishment in Lamentations was also accepted by Jeremiah and his interlocutors in Jeremiah 44. In this chapter Jeremiah receives a divine oracle to be addressed to Judeans living in Egypt. The oracle (vv. 2-14) declares Yahweh's condemnation of the Judean worship of other gods, which is given as the reason for the punishment. However, the audience of this prophetic speech does not accept Jeremiah's explanation. Instead, they attribute their divine punishment to the Queen of Heaven (vv. 16-19). They claim that it was traditional to make offerings to her, that this practice had been performed by their own ancestors as well as Judah's kings. As long as they continued their ritual devotion to the Queen of Heaven, they prospered. It was only when the cult of the Queen of Heaven was discontinued that they were consumed by the sword and famine. In other words, the Queen of Heaven is the divinity who punished them, not Yahweh. The very same religious practice devoted to this goddess, along with its family setting, is also condemned in Jeremiah 7:18. (The identity of this goddess is disputed, but, as I will note in chapter 3, the word for her cakes in 7:18 and 44:19 looks like an Akkadian loanword, suggesting the cult of the goddess Ishtar or a syncretized form of her with a traditional West Semitic goddess, perhaps Astarte [see Ackerman 1992].) In 44:20-23 Jeremiah responds by claiming that it was this very devotion that led to Yahweh's punishment of Judah. It is not difficult to see in Jeremiah 44, in particular in Jeremiah's further announcement of condemnation of these Judeans (vv. 26-28), a justification for the fate of the Judeans in Egypt; they will not play a role later in the postexilic community of Yehud.

What is interesting to note is that Jeremiah does not condemn his Judean audience in Egypt for not worshiping Yahweh. In view of what is known generally of ancient religion, it would seem that such a goddess would probably have been regarded as the spouse of the chief god, in this case Yahweh; he would have been "the King of Heaven." Just as Yahweh-El was king, so a local goddess, perhaps Astarte, identified with Ishtar, could have been queen. The issue does not seem to have been a failure to worship Yahweh, but a failure to worship Yahweh in the form that the prophet regarded as normative. Most readers of the Bible assume that such goddess worship could not have been normative for ancient Israel, but clearly the people in Jeremiah 7 and 44 regarded it as acceptable, and in fact inscriptions from the sites of Kuntillet Ajrud and Khirbet el-Qom have suggested to many scholars that such a ditheism of God and his consort may have been quite common in this period (see the essays of Becking et al. 2001, as well as Olyan 1988, Hadley 2000, and Zevit 2001). Most biblical responses to the exile essentially concur with Lamentations and Jeremiah, but it should hardly be assumed that the biblical responses represented the norm for Judeans in general; it does represent the norm for the Babylonian leadership of Yehud, leadership that championed and preserved this response found in these biblical works. The most sustained of these responses was generated in the books of Kings.

History as Explanation: 1–2 Kings

The various historians of Joshua–2 Kings wrote a further explanation for the fall of the south and the exile of its leadership to Babylon about 586. This series of books influenced by Deuteronomy in varying degrees (hence the name, "the Deuteronomistic History," given by scholars) is not simply a straightforward representation of biblical history from Joshua through the end of Kings. Indeed, it appears that the Deuteronomistic influence in these historical books varied tremendously, suggesting that they were produced at different times (see Knoppers 2001). The exilic author(s) took the preexilic edition of the books of Kings, first collected and arranged during the reign of Hezekiah and then revised in the monarchy of Josiah, and added the final sections of 2 Kings 24–25. This exilic transmitter of this work did not produce a wholesale reedition of 1–2 Kings, but added a number of touches. The ending of the book skips from 586 B.C.E. (down to 2 Kings 25:26) to events around the year 562. Omitting the Babylonian incursion of 582 mentioned in Jeremiah 52:30, 2 Kings 25 concludes with King Jehoiachin released from prison and supported for the duration of his days (a historical point confirmed by Babylonian records). The lesson intended to be imparted by this ending is unclear. Perhaps for the author(s) of the final addition, the history of the Judeans remained open at this point in time. A sense of hope for the royal family and the people hovers in the air, yet it remains unresolved.

While the force of the ending remains unclear, the larger purpose of the work is abundantly clear. In its final form, 1–2 Kings was constructed to answer the single most serious challenge to Israel's existence: Why did the conquest of Judah happen? In a world where political demise could signal the powerlessness or the disinterest of a patron god, the fall of Jerusalem created a crisis of national identity; the accompanying loss of another major marker of identity, the land, exacerbated this crisis. To explain the divine role in the exile, the Deuteronomistic author(s) of Joshua–2 Kings used various sources to create a story of Israelite sin and divine wrath, a religious interpretation of the past well known in Israel's worship. (For example, Psalm 78 attributes the fall of the north to its sin, and Psalm 106 would interpret the exile as the divine answer to Judah's failings.)

The overall end product is a history with a religious purpose, namely, to explain the reason for the conquest of the northern kingdom in 722 and the destruction of Jerusalem and the Temple, as well as the exile to Babylonia, in 586. The moral assessments of the various kings in 1–2 Kings show the implicit educational purpose of the work, a view that was explicitly recognized later in the Dead Sea Scrolls. One Dead Sea Scroll text encourages the leader of another group to "remember the kings of Israel and reflect on their deeds, how whoever among them who respected the Law was delivered from afflictions" (4Q398, fragments 11-13, lines 6-7 = 4QMMT C, lines 18-24). The books of Kings stood as a lesson for their postexilic audiences for centuries. All in all, the textual record of Israel's monarchy provided an opportunity for an ongoing process of reading and interpreting past events long after the past had faded.

Prophetic Responses to the Fall of the South

Unlike 1–2 Kings, the Major Prophets would offer answers that do not reduce the fall of Jerusalem to a question of crime and punishment. As witnesses to the Babylonian conquests of the southern kingdom, first in 597 and then in 587, Jeremiah and Ezekiel suggest that the Israelites badly mistreated God, and God was pushed away by them. In Jeremiah the language of love expresses the soul of the divine dilemma (Jeremiah 2–3). After Israel's abuse of God, what can God do? Rejected, God will punish them with great anger (12:7-8):

> I have abandoned My house,
> I have deserted My inheritance,
> I have given the beloved of my life
>   into the hands of her enemies.
> My inheritance acted toward me
>   like a lion in the forest;
> she raised her voice against me.
>   Therefore I hate her.

In other words, as God says a little later, "You have rejected me" (15:6). In these divine speeches, the aggressor is not simply God with divine punishment, but it is Judah first with its sin. Emblematic of this larger situation are Jeremiah's own circumstances. Just as Israel hurts God, so too Jeremiah's own family seeks his life (12:6; cf. 11:19; 18:18, 23; 20:10), and, as a result, the prophet prays for their destruction (11:20).

The prophet's own career symbolizes the breakdown of the people's relationship with God. Jeremiah laments the deterioration of his prophetic role, to speak to the people for God and to God for the people. God will no longer listen to the prophet as expected (11:14; 14:11; 14:19 — 15:1), and the people will not listen to the prophet (13:11). In his role as prophet, Jeremiah questions God's justice and calls for the destruction of the people he is supposed to serve (12:1-3; 17:18):

> *You would be just, O LORD,*
> > *If I contend against You,*
> > > *still I would speak charges against you.*
> *Why does the way of the wicked prosper?*
> > *Why are all the treacherous at ease?*
> *You planted them, so they have taken root,*
> > *they grow, so they yield fruit.*
> *You are near in their mouths,*
> > *yet far from their hearts.*
> *But You, O LORD, have known me, examined me,*
> > *you tested my heart—it is with You.*
> *Drive them like sheep to the slaughter,*
> > *set them apart for the day of slaying!*

Prophet becomes anti-prophet. Unable to help the people, Jeremiah suffers: "Why is my pain unceasing, my wound incurable?" (15:18). In turn, he experiences his own prophetic mission as divine deceit: "You are really toward me like someone deceitful, like waters that are unreliable" (15:18). All parties speak, aggrieved and suffering, but none of them hears the others. In the end, everyone suffers.

Ezekiel's explanation for the exile is couched in terms of Israel's purity, suiting his background as a priest. The divine presence in the Temple is threatened by religious impurity, dramatized by the tour of the Temple's precincts that the prophet is given by an angelic being in Ezekiel 8–11. The Temple has become an arena of idolatry of various sorts: some type of unacceptable image in 8:3, 5; other unacceptable images on a wall in 8:10; worship of the Mesopotamian god Tammuz in 8:14; and in 8:16 worship of the sun, elsewhere a separate deity (see Ackerman 1992). This invasion of unholiness drives the holy presence of God out of the Temple (8:6). The divine response to this Temple impurity unveils another side of priestly imagination. With a mystical sense of the divine, the priestly narrative of

Ezekiel presents an otherworldly vision of the heavenly chariot. In chapter 11 the divine presence marked by the chariot lifts off and departs, heading east toward Babylon, into exile. In short, God goes into exile in advance of the people still in Jerusalem; only then can Israel's enemies conquer Jerusalem and send them into exile. In short, the prophets explain to the people what they have done to God and how they have hurt themselves as a result.

These prophetic explanations do not simply address the past, but they offer a vision of the future as well. Each Major Prophet sounds a miraculous note. For Isaiah 40–55, the return from the exile will involve a divine corps of engineers who will level every valley and hill for the Judeans' path home. There is more: all will see the divine glory accompanying this return (Isaiah 40:3-5). Echoing the image of love lost, Jeremiah presents God declaring his eternal love for Israel (31:3), and promising a renewed covenant whose teaching will be written in their very hearts (31:33). Reversing the departure of the divine presence from Jerusalem, Ezekiel promises a divine re-creation of the exiled people. The famous vision of "the valley of the dry bones" (Ezekiel 37) heralds the people's re-creation, with the divine spirit infusing them (37:14). New glory, new heart, and new spirit are all miraculous answers proportionate to the despair of exilic loss. Each of the Major Prophets responded to what was the dominant view among the people in exile, that God abandoned them (Isaiah 49:14) and that they were as good as dead (Ezekiel 37:11, as nicely observed by Olyan 2003; compare the language in Lamentations 3:54).

Readers of the Bible may think of all this as metaphorical language, decorative of the people's experience. But the case was the opposite: just as Israel (the northern kingdom) had suffered annihilation in 722, Judah experienced national death with the exile. Miraculous hope, hope against hope, was offered in response. With the return of Judeans from Babylonia thanks to the Persians (ca. 538), the beginning of such miraculous hope would be seen to enter into historical reality.

The impact of this history on the three Major Prophets reaches into their very organization as books. All three are arranged largely into sections of oracles of judgment against the people (Isaiah 1–12; Jeremiah 1–29; Ezekiel 1–24), oracles of judgment against the nations (Isaiah 13–39; Jeremiah 46–51; Ezekiel 25–32), and oracles of consolation for the people and their restoration (Isaiah 40–66; Jeremiah 30–34; Ezekiel 33–48). We might say that this larger arrangement of these works tells the story from the people's perspective in or after the exile: the people sinned and therefore were punished; the nations served as the instrument of this punishment, but their role has come to an end and they will be punished in turn for their excesses; and so a remnant of Judah is about to be restored. Isaiah 40–55 addresses a people poised to return, thanks to the divinely supported victories of Cyrus the Persian (44:28; 45:1), while Isaiah 56–66 presents a struggling community back in Yehud. With Ezekiel 40–48, we find a priestly plan that will allow the holy divine presence to dwell once again in Israel's midst. In the end, Isaiah 40–66 and Ezekiel 33–48, as well as the smaller section in Jeremiah 31–34, are about salvation; they offer visions of hope against loss. The end of exile for the Judeans in Babylonia is in view.

Job: A Wisdom Response to Exile?

Set in an unnamed time and a land far away, Job does not refer explicitly to Israel's history. The prose framework of the book introduces the story of a proverbial hero known from long ago (Ezekiel 14:14, 20); Job thrives, then suffers unexplainable loss. As Job is joined by three friends, the book moves from prose folktale to a series of nine poetic dialogues. In these Job and his three friends (and later a fourth interlocutor named Elihu) probe the reasons for Job's loss. In a final scene, facing the divine presence, Job ultimately finds the meaning of his situation beyond his understanding and yet now has some understanding that relies on his own experience of God, not what he had heard about God (Job 42). In the cosmic topics raised by Job 38–41, the universe and God in particular are shown to be irreducible to human systems of good and evil.

In chapter 3 we will see how God answers Job from "the whirlwind" (38:1), which is not the type of storm that the deity customarily appears in (see Fitzgerald 2002, 136–39). God usually appears not in the dry wind but in a storm that provides rain, showing God's beneficence for Israel's agricultural society (as in Psalm 29). The uncharacteristic sort of divine appearance at the end of Job signals that God and the good that the Deity provides to humanity cannot be bounded by human systems or human efforts to understand them. It has often been thought that the book of Job as we have it was inspired by Israel's historical circumstances, as it may have been arranged and expanded as a response to the challenge of the Judean "exile" (ca. 586–538). Whether it was inspired by the exile or not, the book of Job dramatizes the problem of suffering and a crisis over the lack of intelligibility about the world.

The Exile Continued

With their references to exile among the nations and not simply to one nation, parts of Deuteronomy's introduction and the final section look as if they were composed later in the exile (4:27; 28:64; 30:3). At this point, it would seem that Deuteronomy was put within the exilic priestly edition of the Torah as a sort of appendix that balances Genesis. All told, the construction of Genesis through Deuteronomy provided Israel with a plan of life that notably is not dependent on institutions of monarchy or temple or on living in the land. If we locate the last parts of priestly editorial activity to the exile (586–538 B.C.E.) and later, the Torah offers a response to the exile's crippling effects on Israelite identity. Being an Israelite in monarchic times would have meant what Genesis evokes, namely, life in the land. Yet Exodus through Deuteronomy shows a nontraditional, innovative religious vision: a people without land, though hoping for it; their god dwelling at times in a portable shrine rather than all the time in a temple; and religious leadership largely without a human king.

In short, the central text of the Jewish Scriptures is a charter that does not define Israelite identity as much as redefine it. At the end of this chapter, we will examine how the Torah, in its completed arrangement, constituted a profound response to postexilic life: what was remembered as the earliest moment of Israel's religious identity at Sinai continued to be added to as a way for Israel to deal with later problems of religious identity and practice.

Persian Period Challenges

Life at Home

The final four books of the Hebrew Scriptures, Ezra, Nehemiah, 1 and 2 Chronicles, portray critical issues facing the people at home in Yehud during the Persian period (538–333 B.C.E.). The people faced the initial difficulties of securing their day-to-day needs, as well as opposition by neighbors and taxation from Persian authorities. In addition, the people faced a series of major religious challenges. The struggle to reestablish public works, including the Temple, was daunting, in the face of opposition from neighbors and economic problems. The nature of the community itself was debated, with returned exiles competing with those who had remained in the land during the exile. Priestly leadership within the community was also a source of conflict; the sons of Zadok asserted their preeminence (Ezekiel 40:46; 44:15; 48:11) over the wider lineage of the sons of Aaron (as preferred by the priestly authors of the Torah, for example, in Exodus 28; compare Leviticus 1:5), and against the even wider priesthood of the sons of Levi (Deuteronomy 17:18; Jeremiah 33:18; note also Isaiah 66:21). Finally, there were ongoing issues of proper worship, with accusations made against religious practices continuing from the preexilic period (Isaiah 57 and 63); many, if not most, of these seem to be domestic religious practices, including devotion to deceased ancestors (see Ackerman 1992). The very definition and identity of the deity was itself an ongoing process with immense consequences for social order and identity. How do the authors of Ezra, Nehemiah, and 1–2 Chronicles reflect and address these challenges?

In Ezra 4, adversaries of Judah and Benjamin, said to be "the people of the land" who had remained in the land (v. 4), wish to join the Judean returnees from Babylon in rebuilding the Temple (v. 2). According to the story, the people in the land are presented as foreigners, who are not truly Israelites (vv. 2, 10). Scholars have seriously questioned whether this presentation is historically accurate. With this conflict, we witness a shift in the definition of who is an Israelite. The remnants of the northern tribes whose descendants did not go into exile in Babylonia are excluded by definition. The status of the northerners was not clear at this point and seems to be a matter of ongoing discussion. Although the little biblical evidence that we have seems to regard northerners generally as non-Israelites, it is equally evident from extrabiblical sources that the Jerusalem priesthood enjoyed good relations with the religious leadership of the Israelite community that had survived in the north, known later as the Samaritans. Josephus (*Antiquities* 11.297–303) records a tradition of intermarriage between the leading priestly families in Jerusalem and Samaria (discussed in chapter 1). At this point in the south, Israelite identity was denied by the author(s) of Ezra to the northerners.

A further exclusion is directed against Judeans left in the land during the "exile." The returnees are regarded as the true Israelites. It is they and not those who had remained in the land who are said to constitute "Judah, Benjamin, and the Levitical priests." In Ezra 6:16 we hear of "the Israelites, the priests, the Levites, and all the other exiles." In this presentation, "Israel" is constituted as those who had gone into exile and had now returned. Elsewhere there is the same community debate between the returnees from Babylon and those left in the land (Jeremiah 24; 27:11; and 40:4, discussed by Seitz 1985 and Sharpe 2003). In the book of Ezra, what we see at work is a defining of the community, with northerners presumed to be outsiders and Judeans left in the land being tainted in turn as northerners.

In short, Ezra's community polemic informs the definition of who is an Israelite. On the one hand, "Israel" refers to the narrow group of the postexilic community of the old two southern tribes of Judah and Benjamin headed by the priesthood represented by Levi. On the other hand, "Israel" would continue to refer in an ideal manner to the wider twelve tribes. "Israel" served to designate the descendants of the twelve tribes that had gone into exile to Babylon, over against all others who had not. In this way, the postexilic leadership in Yehud could restrict the label "Israel." This ideological use of "Israel" would enjoy considerable longevity, as the same usage appears in the Dead Sea Scrolls. For example, the War Scroll (1QM, col. 1) can refer to "Levi, Benjamin, and Judah" as the representation of Israel, while the Temple Scroll (11QT, cols. 19, 24-25, 39-41) details the twelve tribes by name to present the future restoration of the people.

Ezra 9–10 relates a further challenge to the people's definition, and that is the question of intermarriage. The priestly lineage already required clarification, since the priesthood had been defined by descent long before the fall of Jerusalem.

Chapter 9 raises the issue as a crisis afflicting all levels of Yehudian society. Again it is unclear that the issue is simply a matter of avoiding marriage to the groups mentioned in 9:1; these are the same as the groups said to be defeated by the Israelites when they originally conquered the land (compare Joshua 3:10; 12:8). This standard seems to represent an effort to clarify descent at the margins of Yehudian society, perhaps aimed in particular at the descendants of Judeans who had remained in the land during the exile. The social dynamic at work is not entirely clear in this story, but the leadership of Ezra makes an effort to clarify the ambiguities in the people's identity, perhaps by applying the priestly approach to the people's lineages more broadly. We might say that Israel was in this sense conformed to the idea of "a kingdom of priests and a holy people" (Exodus 19:6).

Some of the same issues of postexilic life in Yehud appear in the book of Nehemiah. Nehemiah's building project proceeds despite opposition from Sanballat and Tobiah, the neighboring governors of Samaria and Ammon, as well as impoverishment in Yehud (chaps. 2–6). Within this context of external struggle, we see Nehemiah in conflict with the Yehudian Tobiah, who is married to a priestly family and who had been given chambers in the Temple complex by the high priest, Eliashib. Nehemiah promulgates a concept of Israel that eliminates Tobiah. What is particularly interesting is the method said to be used. According to Nehemiah 13:1-3, the book of Moses is read, specifically Deuteronomy 23:3-4, which forbids Ammonites and Moabites from entering the congregation of Yahweh, and this is applied directly by Nehemiah to Tobiah. The Judean Tobiah is regarded by Nehemiah as an Ammonite (he is called "the Ammonite servant" in Nehemiah 2:19), who then is denied his room in the Temple. The two dynamics at work here — scriptural application and community definition — are correlated by a process of interpretation and political circumstances. Scripture was becoming one of the means available to meet political challenges within the community. The census of the people taken in chapter 7 likewise suggests an effort to retain clarity about the lines of authority and inclusion within the population of Yehud. Nehemiah 8 shows Ezra and the Levites leading a communal reading of Torah, another indicator of the role that Scripture has come to play in shaping the communal identity of Yehud. The ritual confession in chapter 9 shows the place of the Levites in leading communal psalms (9:5), as Ezra recalls the people's ancient traditions in order to illuminate their situation and to reaffirm a new covenant for community regulations (chap. 10).

These final chapters of Nehemiah witness to a temporary resolution of the struggles within the priesthood. The efforts of the sons of Zadok to assume priestly pride of place seem not to have been successful. Instead, the sons of Aaron (which included the Zadokites) emerged as the dominant class of priestly sacrificial leaders. Tensions within the very highest ranks seem to run through the priesthood's history down to the destruction of the Temple in 70 C.E.; it was a challenge that was in effect not resolved with success. Instead, it helped to generate several priestly schisms. These included the Judean–Samaritan priestly split toward the end of the Persian period as well as the founding of the Dead Sea Scroll community in the mid-second century B.C.E.

The priestly differences did not afflict only the priesthood's very highest echelons. The Levites, who had enjoyed the priestly prerogative of offering sacrifices during the preexilic period, were excluded from sacrificial duties, with their accompanying income. In a postexilic context, they worked as temple guards and singers. Their role as temple singers can be seen in some of the prose labels at the beginning of the Psalms that mention the sons of Korah and Asaph (Psalms 42–50, 73–85). The Asaphites are also mentioned as singers in Ezra 2:41. These same names appear in the history of the monarchy, as reported by 1 Chronicles 16. It is possible that these Levitical groups had already moved into this role during the preexilic period, while other Levitical groups offered sacrifice like other priestly lines. Indeed, 1 Chronicles 16 traces the Levitical role of temple music and song to the time of the inauguration of the First Temple. In the postexilic Temple, however, the Levites were excluded from sacrificial privileges. There are some reasons for believing that the Levites, with their roles of reading and interpreting Scripture (Nehemiah 8:7-8), also served as the scribal arm of the priesthood.

There are some signs that the Levites were the transmitters of what would become the three parts of the Jewish Bible: Torah, Prophets, and Writings. What the Levites lost in priestly rank and privilege, they gained in the ultimately more important task of textual transmission. Anticipating later developments, we may note that the destruction of the Temple in 70 C.E. inverted the relative importance of the roles served by the priests and the Levites: what the Levites transmitted in the form of biblical writings proved to provide the basis for later Jewish religious life, while the priestly sacrificial duties lasted largely only as memories in those texts.

Finally, beneath the surface of the biblical presentation of Israel's Persian period past is the issue of the identity and configuration of Israel's divinity. Many scholars have assumed that with the exile, Israel essentially becomes monotheistic. Although this monotheism may have been the dominant view of the postexilic leadership, it is not clear that this was the norm in Yehud or among Judeans outside the land (at least in Egypt). The biblical texts, generated largely by this leadership, were hardly concerned with presenting a balanced sociological and historical description of the religious beliefs of the general populace; they were concerned instead with proper behavior. So polemics against allegedly heterodox worship (for example, in Isaiah 57:3-13 and 65:1-7) should be taken seriously as an indicator of possible polytheism among the Yehudian population. Some of the practices mentioned in these two passages seem to be traditional family devotion, including reverence of deceased ancestors and worship at local sites (sometimes called *bamot,* usually translated "high places"; see Ezekiel 20:29 for an interesting folk explanation associating the word with the Hebrew verb to "go" [NRSV]); it is possible that traditional goddess worship, perhaps under the larger rubric of Yahwistic ditheism, also was involved. The challenge that family religion represented to the religious leadership of Yehud was met by the leaders' efforts to outlaw it and condemn it as "pagan." From the historical perspective, there was a certain religious inversion, so that the historically more traditional broader band of Yahwistic beliefs and practices becomes branded as "pagan" by those who favored a less traditional, more restrictive worship of Yahweh alone.

With Haggai and Zechariah, we move to the postexilic situation of Yehud under the Persian Empire around 520 B.C.E. At this time, the old Davidic house continued to embody hopes for restoration. Persian governors were appointed from the Davidic house, and their leadership likely continued as a focal point for a sense of well-being and continuity with Israel's monarchic past. At this moment of transition, the governor of Yehud was Zerubbabel, a royal scion, who was joined in the religious leadership by Jeshua, the chief priest. In the larger situation in the Persian Empire, Darius was consolidating his power. Inside Yehud, the community was working to rebuild the Temple, inspired by the divine encouragement voiced by two prophets, Haggai and Zechariah. The rebuilding of the Temple, combined with the precarious hold that Darius may have seemed to have on his western provinces, inspired in Haggai and Zechariah the hope that Zerubbabel, as a royal scion, might be God's chosen instrument for Judean restoration, perhaps even freedom (Haggai 2:1-5; Zechariah 4). Without a trace, he disappeared from the scene. Instead, the priesthood, led by Jeshua, continued its leadership in a reduced Yehud, a small and rather isolated territory in the far-ranging and ever-expanding Persian Empire. In this context, the visions of Zechariah convey a sense of cosmic hope against a seemingly omnipotent earthly empire.

Though David and his royal line were fading in importance, memory of them continued to shape Judean hopes for things to come. During the Hellenistic period, hopes for the return of the Davidic house would continue to be expressed (Zechariah 12:7—13:1). As an alternative view, Israel's own God would be the King whose new return and new presence would be the basis for hope (Zechariah 14). A similar viewpoint would ultimately inform later apocalyptic visions of Daniel 7–12, that God would ultimately save Israel and defeat the evil empires of this world. The late prophet Malachi, placed in the Christian canon as the final prophetic book, ends with a prediction of God coming, to be preceded by a return of the fiery Elijah, who is to turn a sinning people back to the true Torah (for later Jewish tradition, a hope for the Davidic Messiah at Passover, and for Christians a harbinger of John the Baptist).

With Ecclesiastes (Qohelet), we hear a different postexilic voice. Like the Song of Songs, this work is attributed to King Solomon despite signs of Persian-period composition (e.g., *pardes* in 2:5, as in Song of Songs 4:13). Here we see a different side of, and response to, postexilic Yehudian life. This book may be read as a learned elite's response to life in the Persian period; one cannot escape the status quo. The calculations of life represented in this book display a reasoning presented by an older Solomon exploring what his lifelong pursuit of wisdom and experience has taught him. It is largely a lesson of time; the famous "vanity of vanities" framing his discourse (1:2; 12:8) is better understood as the fleeting moment of the constantly vanishing present, as "evanescence of evanescence." The now-famous exposition of chapter 3 recognizes the order of time, with different activities fitting the proper times of life. For Qohelet, insight into the Divine does not derive from divine revelation or visions, but from observation of how the world has been constructed. In seeing all things in their proper places and times, the book offers one insight into the Divine, and it does so through an observation about the divine construction of the human person.

According to 3:11, God has given into the human heart *olam*, literally "eternity" (NRSV "a sense of past and future"), "without the human person ever reaching the matter that God has done from beginning to end." From this verse, I take it that God has built into the human person an intuition about the nature of eternity, something of Divinity itself, but without human persons being able to grasp the other superhuman dimensions of that which God has done in the universe. The downside of this human construction is the profound human awareness of human limits, while the upside is a visceral human insight into the Divine and a sense of how the human person is linked to the Divine. As this specific feature involves time, eternity imprinted onto the human heart makes human beings profoundly aware of what transcends them. In a small sense, humans are therefore connected to what is beyond them, in particular the Divine. At the same time, this eternity in their heart makes them sharply aware of their mortality as well. The human person is a paradox of divine construction that ultimately points back to its Creator and in a fundamental way links and leads it back to its Creator.

The book ends (12:9-12, 12-14) in praise of Qohelet's wisdom, yet warns against making too many books (perhaps like this one!). For all, Solomon included, reverence for God and the Commandments remains necessary (12:13-14). This sense of the Commandments' importance was a view shared by all sides of the Yehudian community. It would also provide crucial direction for Judeans living abroad.

Life in Foreign Lands

With Esther, we turn to a new challenge for Judeans, namely, life in foreign lands or what Jewish tradition calls "Diaspora." Set in the court of the Persian king, the

story portrays Judean efforts to negotiate the challenges of court life. The tale re-
volves around five characters. The center or fulcrum point of the book is King
Ahasuerus. Arrayed on one side of the king are two Judeans, Esther and Mordecai, and on the other side two Persians, the vizier Haman and his wife. In many
ways, the characters are stock figures: the king is supposed to be fair, but being
entirely dim-witted he does not recognize the plots being hatched by his vizier.
The wicked vizier manipulates the king in order to destroy any rivals. Standing behind Haman is his scheming wife. Mordecai is a high official in the court and a
model of traditional piety in solidarity with the Judean people. Mordecai's niece,
Esther, is the story's main figure. She does not act according to identifiably
Judean ways, and her descent is said to be unknown to all except Mordecai.

After the demise of Queen Vashti, Esther is selected as the new queen. All is
well until the crisis of Judeans' persecution led by Haman. Up to this point,
Esther lives a privileged existence, and her heritage has not been an issue for her.
In the wake of the persecution, Mordecai coaxes Esther to accept her identity as a
Judean and to act on behalf of her people. Only her help saves the Judeans from
destruction. The evil characters emblematize the threats that Judeans faced in
foreign courts, while the good characters symbolize Judean prosperity as well as
difficulties of cohesion and identity within Judean communities outside the land
of Yehud. Judeans cannot achieve as individuals what they can achieve together:
Mordecai needs Esther's intervention, and Esther needs his guidance in learning
the importance of being a Judean and acting on behalf of the Judean people. Behind both stands a divine hand that guides events to a successful outcome. The
God of this work is not the fiery revelatory presence at Sinai; it is a silent force
that wends a way toward good for the people. The ways of this God who acts se-
cretly behind the scenes (4:14) can be understood by the one who identifies and
leads life as a Judean and encourages others to do likewise. This is not history in
any conventional sense.

In some respects, the book of Esther looks like a Judean farce, with its stock
characters (Berlin 2001). Note the idiocy of the king rejecting Queen Vashti; the
drunken feasts with stupid advice given by royal advisors who are supposed to be
wise; a Judean woman selected through a beauty contest to become queen in the
Persian Empire; the evil non-Judean falling into the trap he sets for the good
Judean; royal decrees favoring Judeans everywhere, with them able to take revenge
throughout the empire, and many non-Judeans out of fear pretending to be
Judeans. It is a Jewish fantasy remembered not as history, but celebrated as Purim,
a holiday in the ritual calendar (Esther 9). Humor in religious celebration is a response to minority status in foreign lands. Like the Torah itself, Esther recalls the
past through ritual to address the ingredients of Judean experience in foreign
lands. In celebrating the story ritually, Judeans together in community can imag-

ine and face threats to their existence, an achievement that in isolation they could not achieve as successfully.

Another theory of history that lurks in the background of the story is revealed through the story's allusions to the family lines of some of the main figures (Berlin 1995). Mordecai's line is traced back to the family of Saul (2:5). Haman is reckoned as an Agagite (3:1), evoking the figure of King Agag, an Amalekite enemy of Israel (Numbers 24:7, 1 Samuel 15; for the Amalekites as Israelite foes, see Exodus 17:8-16, Deuteronomy 25:17-19). As noted by Brettler (1995), the genealogies of Mordecai and Haman subtly recall King Saul killing King Agag in the aftermath of battle (1 Samuel 15). Implicitly, the story of Esther shows a Judean theory of Judean history: threats faced in early Israel are linked to mortal dangers faced by later generations of the Judean people. Through genealogical references, the story of Esther does what the books of Chronicles also achieve in the Persian period. Both narrative presentations link the situation and trials of Judean life in the Persian period back to the era of the monarchy. As a result, the narratives express a sense of continuity between these later Judeans and their preexilic forebears and therefore provides as well a sense of identity with them.

Like Esther and Mordecai, Daniel lives in a foreign court. Daniel is presented as a Judean who went into exile and succeeded as a court advisor for several empires, Babylonian, Median, and Persian. The first part of the book, chapters 1–6, is a series of court tales that illustrate Daniel's devotion and success. In this respect, Daniel recalls Judean figures prospering as counselors in foreign courts—not just Mordecai, but the biblical prototype of such figures, Joseph. All of them face hardship and even the threat of death, often concocted by competitors at court. Through these difficulties, the wise and pious Jew survives, due in part to his appreciation of his heritage and thanks in part to the hidden divine support operating behind the scenes. Daniel's very name elicits a model of piety, as his namesake was a righteous man of old (known from Ezekiel 14:14, 20).

The second part of Daniel, chapters 7–12, contains apocalyptic visions of historical events. They are presented as sixth-century visions of the future, but their interpretations indicate that the sequence of empires was known to a second-century audience, specifically during the crisis of 167–164 B.C.E. As 1 Maccabees 1–4 indicates, this period witnessed to a civil war largely pitting the rural Judean population eventually led by the Maccabees against some of the priestly elite and their supporters, in particular the foreign power of the Seleucid king, Antiochus IV Epiphanes. For example, Daniel 8:20-22 identifies the two-horned ram and the buck (or he-goat) as, respectively, the kings of the Medes and Persians and the king of Greece, whose kingdom splits into four. On view in this passage are Alexander the Great and the four kingdoms that emerged from his empire.

The last figure of this narrative is Antiochus IV: "He will destroy the mighty and the people of the holy ones" (Daniel 8:25). The historical narrative reflects matters down to the middle of the second century, even though the story is situated in the sixth century. The apocalypse of Daniel 10–12 also lays out a historical scenario in the future. Only when the visions get to the very end of this history is there a switch to real attempts at prediction. The king of the north is said in 11:45 to die between the Sea (the Mediterranean) and the beautiful holy mountain (Jerusalem), but Antiochus IV, whose Seleucid kingdom was based to the north of Yehud in Syria, did not die there. He died in Persia toward the end of 164 B.C.E. (1 Maccabees 6:16; 2 Maccabees 1:13-17; 9:1-29; and confirmed by other ancient sources). With the second part of the book of Daniel (chapters 7–12), we have left the Persian period and entered the Hellenistic period. At the same time, Daniel 7–12 illustrates ongoing concerns from the Persian period, in particular problems of foreign domination and internal strife within the community in Yehud, as well as hope of apocalyptic proportions.

In the biblical corpus we hear little of Judean communities in Egypt. Although these are known from Jeremiah and from the Elephantine papyri (as noted in chapter 1), they receive virtually no notice in the Bible. In part, this may be due to historical conditions, that they played little part in the community of Yehud relative to the Babylonian Yehudians. Yet, as the prophecy of Jeremiah 44 (especially vv. 26-28) suggests, they may have continued to be viewed as heterodox in their goddess worship (see vv. 15-19). The Elephantine papyri indicate that the Yehudian colonists struggled with their local Egyptian counterparts under Persian rule, but not a great deal is otherwise known of the challenges that they faced.

Textual Creations as Responses to Postexilic Life

David's Opera in the Psalms:
From Intertextual Singer to Scripturalizing Scribe

We do not think of the third part of the Jewish Scriptures, the Writings (Ketubim), as "historical works" in the same way as the Torah (Pentateuch) or the Former Prophets (the historical books from Joshua through 2 Kings). Even so, they offer views about Israel's past experience that helped it to address its present situation. Because of the nature of the Writings, their views of Israel's past at times require some effort to uncover. In the Psalms, historical views are found first of all in individual psalms that narrate the past in terms of either divine blessing (Psalm 105) or Israel's sins (Psalms 78 and 106). This is the past presented in service to religious praise and confession. Ritual reinterpretation of the past, found in these psalms, represents an ongoing response to loss.

Another view of Israel's history operates at a more general level of the Psalms, and this is one that is not easy to see. In the labels (or superscriptions) at the beginning of most Psalms, we are told who the putative authors were (mostly "of David"), biographical information about David, the type of psalm (a psalm or song or the like), the musical personnel, and other musical information. The labels with biographical information about David offer an interpretation of the psalms that they belong to; in other words, these psalms are interpreted as David's words from particular times in his life. These psalms were written after David's lifetime, as indicated, for example, by references to the Temple, which was built by his son Solomon. So it would appear that already as part of the biblical text itself, the psalm labels offer an interpretation of these psalms.

Many of the early laments in the book of Psalms are given superscriptions telling readers what situation in David's life the psalm addressed. So Psalm 3 is represented as David's words when he fled from his son Absalom, who, according to 2 Samuel 15–18, rebelled against his father and tried to have him killed. Schroeder (2001) has nicely shown how the transmitters who added the superscriptions to the Psalms connected Psalm 3 with this episode in 2 Samuel, because of the shared wording between Psalm 3:1 and 2 Samuel 18:31. Psalm 3:1 prays: "O LORD, how many are my foes,/Many rise against me." In 2 Samuel 18:31, it is recognized that David was delivered "from the hand of all who were rising against you." Because of the similar wordings, the transmitter of Psalm 3 who added the superscription saw Psalm 3:1 as alluding to 2 Samuel 18:31 and created the biographical information in the superscription based on this interpretation of the psalm.

According to this method of reading the Psalms, postexilic transmitters added biographical information about David to the superscriptions. The David of the stories in the books of Samuel became the reference point for the Psalms; readers are supposed to understand the psalms in terms of this David presented in Samuel. In turn, David is reconfigured as a model of deep religious piety for the late biblical audience. The Psalm superscriptions offered a way for readers to relate to the Psalms; they are to emulate David as model of piety and apply the Psalms to the circumstances of their own life. The picture of a model David is forged out of an intertextual relationship linking Psalms and Samuel. In this way, the authors of the Psalm superscriptions generated the first known interpretation of the Psalms.

The Psalms as a whole received a further interpretation, organized largely by the placement of the royal psalms, Psalms 2, 72, and 89, in conjunction with the superscriptions. Given their musical character, the five "books" of the Psalms may be heard as a religious opera in five movements devoted to the theme of Israel's relationship to God in the past, present, and future: (1) God's help of David (marked by the superscriptions about David's life and opened by the royal Psalm 2), in Book I, Psalms 2–41; (2) the monarchy and its glory under David and Solomon (also signaled by the superscriptions and the royal Psalm 72), in Book II, Psalms 42–72; (3) the demise of the monarchy (marked in particular by the royal lament in Psalm 89), in Book III, Psalms 73–89; (4) Yahweh's coming to Israel as the new King (sung in the hymns of Psalms 93–100), in Book IV, Psalms 90–106; and (5) the future divine restoration of Israel and universal praise of God in Book V, Psalms 107–50: "Let everything that breathes praise Yahweh. Hallelujah" (150:6). Sometime in the postexilic era, Psalm 1 was added as a new introduction to guide readers in the purposes of the Psalms; it is not simply ritual praise, but with its five books, it is torah, like the five books of the Torah. So the book of Psalms does not simply offer David's piety as a response to postexilic life. It additionally offers a vision of Israel's past and expresses corresponding hope for its future.

It is interesting to see that the inverse method of interpreting the book of Samuel by recourse to the Psalms is also at work during the later biblical period. In one conspicuous case, transmitters took a biblical psalm and added it to the narrative of 2 Samuel. Scholars have long noted that Psalm 18 and 2 Samuel 22 are the same royal psalm incorporated into these different books (with interesting textual variants). The most plausible explanation for the appearance of the same psalm in both biblical works is that a later transmitter of 2 Samuel knew the text of Psalm 18 from a liturgical collection of the Psalms and inserted it into the book of 2 Samuel. (The addition, "he said" in Psalm 18, preceding v. 1 in NRSV is a piece of prose narrative that no other Psalm superscription contains; it evidently was taken from the prose narrative of 2 Samuel 22:1-2.) Instead of the Psalm superscriptions reading the Psalm text in terms of the Samuel stories about David, with 2 Samuel 22 we see a reading of the David story in 2 Samuel interpreted in light of the Psalm. In summary, the placement of this Psalm 18 text in 2 Samuel 22 seems to mark at least a partial adoption of using Psalm texts with the narrative of Samuel to present David.

In the late postexilic period, perhaps also during the Hellenistic period, David became an emblematic figure linking the reading together of scriptural books. In other words, Israel's old religious works became sacred writings or scriptures in part through their being read in terms of one another, and the "intertextual David" of Psalms and Samuel is a reflection of this process. In later works such as the Psalms Scroll from Qumran Cave 11 (11 Q Ps^a), David would serve not only as a model of torah piety. He is also a scribe endowed with light like the light of the sun, an image that would have been particularly powerful for the Dead Sea Scrolls community, which lived largely by a calendar oriented to the sun. David's songs and psalms are said to have been spoken by him through prophecy: "all these he [David] uttered through prophecy that was given to him from before the Most

High." In this work, the psalms are torah, wisdom, and prophecy all at once, under the figure of David the scribe.

With this formulation, we are considerably removed from a sense of the ancient past of David the king. Instead, David the pious, inspired scribe seems to be a figure for the text's own enshrinement as sacred scripture. The identification of religious texts as sacred scriptures was not simply a process of collecting individual religious works, but of reading them together and in terms of one another. As a figure of torah, wisdom, and prophecy, David now emblematizes this scriptural understanding of Israel's religious works as an increasingly and deepening intertextual process. For the Psalms in particular, the prestigious and pious figure of the king stands for the increasingly prestigious status of these texts of piety, which console and lead Israelites to praise. David becomes both model and medium of revelation.

Solomon in the Song of Songs: A Love Story of Postexilic Hopes?

The Song of Songs is attributed to Solomon. In Jewish tradition the two lovers of the book have been understood as referring to God and Israel. Christian tradition has analogously applied the work to Christ and the church. With northern references to the bride (especially in chaps. 4 and 7), the book may symbolize the monarchy's courtship of the two kingdoms in the time of King Solomon, or perhaps his quest for an ideal united kingdom of north and south. The female is praised as more beautiful than Tirzah and Jerusalem (6:4), the ancient capitals of the two kingdoms. With this reference and other references to the geography of the north and the south, the body of the female may symbolically evoke the northern and southern kingdoms. Moreover, the female addresses "daughters of Jerusalem" (*benot yerushalayim*, 2:7; 3:5, 10; 5:8, 16; 8:4), an expression that suggests Jerusalem's surrounding villages, reflected also in the expression "daughters of Judah" *(benot yehudah)* around Jerusalem in Psalm 48:11. The female lover is herself called the Shulammite (6:13), with its consonants punning on both "Jerusalem" (in Hebrew, *yerushalayim*) and "Solomon" (Hebrew *shelomoh*). As noted in chapter 1, the work was produced in the Persian period. Perhaps the Song of Songs recalls the Solomonic past as two lovers courting as if for the first time. In so evoking the past, the book seems to express a postexilic yearning for a restored Solomonic "united kingdom."

The Priestly Production of the Torah

Incorporating a wide spectrum of materials, the three biblical works of Exodus, Leviticus, and Numbers were arranged in large measure according to symbolic space and time (Smith 1997). We may observe first the symbolic use of geography. In the most general terms, Exodus through Numbers exhibits a basic geographical symmetry: from Egypt to Sinai and from Sinai to Transjordan. The priestly arrangement of Exodus and Numbers presents the geographical progression in Numbers in part as an inversion of the progression in Exodus. At the heart of this geography is Mount Sinai, the Mount Everest in the priestly imagination, which understood the events there as the most important in world history. Sinai looms larger than later cultic sites in the land, including Jerusalem and Solomon's Temple. For the priestly tradition, Sinai would represent the site of the definitive foundation moment in Israel's relationship with God and model for cultic recollection in the land. Accordingly, this mountain defines life inside and outside the land. This site dominates the Torah in extending from Exodus 19–40, through all of Leviticus, then from Numbers 1 through chapter 10.

Chronology also serves to delimit Exodus through Numbers into two major stages. With the exodus from Egypt, Israel leaves chronology marked by years and enters into sacred time, signaled by connections made between their narrative and the feasts of the annual calendar. Exodus 12 marks the beginning of the sacred calendar, with its explicit connections with the Feast of Passover (Pesach). The Israelites' arrival at Sinai in Exodus 19 implicitly marks the Feast of Weeks (Shevuot). This is no coincidence, as the feast in postexilic times celebrated the giving of the Torah at Mount Sinai (2 Chronicles 15:10-14; Jubilees 6:17; reflected also in the Feast of Pentecost in Acts 2). The chronological markers in Exodus 40:2, 17 signal the turn of the year (Rosh Hashanah). The New Year in Exodus 40 evokes the new creation of Israel's relationship with Yahweh through the creation of the tabernacle and thereby harks back to the priestly creation of the world in Genesis 1.

Commentators have long observed that the end of the priestly tabernacle account in Exodus 39–40 consciously echoes the end of the priestly creation account in Genesis 1:1—2:3, as seen from parallel phrasings in Exodus 39:43a//Genesis 1:31a; Exodus 39:32a//Genesis 2:1-2a; Exodus 40:33b//Genesis 2:2a; and Exodus 39:43b//Genesis 2:3a. Exodus 39–40 is thereby connected to the creation story of Genesis: while the account of Genesis marks the creation of the world, the creation language of Exodus 39–40 heralds the new creation of Israel's religious life with its Deity. Leviticus contains a handful of chronological markers, and the overall impression is a lack of the passage of time.

Numbers returns to Passover in chapter 9. So a full sacred year passes at Sinai from the time of the exodus from Egypt to Sinai to the time of the departure from Sinai toward the land of Israel. Prior to and after Exodus 12 through Numbers 10, time is counted in years, but the special events within these chapters are marked according to the sacred calendar. These events therefore take place within the compass of sacred time, unlike the events preceding or following them. In short, the year from departure to departure marks one religious year, which celebrates Passover at either end.

At the heart of this sacred time and geography is Leviticus, which is surrounded by the tabernacle in the final block of Exodus and the camp arrangement in the initial block of Numbers. The center of the Pentateuch corresponds to the center of Israel's sacred life. The priestly edition incorporated the earlier priestly materials in Leviticus 1–16 and the Holiness Code in Leviticus 17–27. The first focuses on torah for the priesthood, the second for the people. Exodus 12–Numbers 10, but especially Leviticus, creates an increasing density of sacred events within an extremely short compass of time at Mount Sinai, unlike and beyond the normal passage of time. Time at Mount Sinai virtually stops, signaling that the events at the mountain of God are timeless; and the instructions given in that timeless moment were intended to serve for all time.

After Numbers 10, the narrative returns to time counted by years, yet even this shift does not mark the complete end of religiously marked time. The journey in the wilderness would happen over a period of forty years, marking the passing of the old generation and the birth of the new (Olson 1985). This period would be recalled at the Feast of Booths *(Sukkot)* as the period of the ancient Israelites living in booths during their journey toward the land.

The correlation between pilgrimage feasts and the Torah did not end with Numbers 10. The final shape of Exodus–Numbers resulted in a broader correlation between the three great pilgrimage feasts and the three great themes of Exodus–Numbers. The three feasts taken together correspond to the old, foundational events from Exodus to the edge of the land that would become Israel. In celebrating the exodus from Egypt, Passover *(Pesach)* begins the chain of events with the departure from Egypt. Weeks *(Shevuot)* continues by celebrating the divine gift of the Torah at Mount Sinai. Booths *(Sukkot)* ends the series by recalling the forty years in the wilderness following the departure from Sinai. Through the use of sacred time and space, the religious life of the pilgrimage festivals played a decisive role in the priestly formation of the Torah. This linkage between the festivals and Israel's foundational events between Egypt and the promised land was made gradually, with Passover already associated with Egypt during the preexilic period, but with Weeks and Booths with their Sinai and wilderness associations developing only later, in the postexilic period.

With this linkage of religious life and text, the Torah offers insight into Judean survival strategies in the postexilic community. One particularly important one is the Torah's revision of older traditions. Perhaps the most dramatic example is that Deuteronomy reinterprets material in Exodus–Numbers (as incisively shown in Levinson 1997). The complete devotion to God, as required by the Ten Commandments, specifically Exodus 20:3, "You shall have no other gods besides Me," is a cultic restriction is that is reexpressed in the Shema in its notion of "oneness" (Deuteronomy 6:4): "(As for) the LORD our God, the LORD is one" (see the discussion by MacDonald 2003). In all spheres Yahweh is the only one for Israel. In the postexilic context, the imperative to exclusive worship translated into the worldview that the universe has only one deity with any real power (see Deuteronomy 4:35, 39; compare 4:19). In short, Deuteronomy expresses a worldview of a single god over all, which extends the older command of single-minded devotion in Exodus.

The process of reinterpretation in Deuteronomy is operative also in its legal precepts. For examples, the cultic calendar of Deuteronomy 16 differs significantly from the priestly calendars of Leviticus 23 and Numbers 28–29. Deuteronomy 16 adds a restriction that sacrifice be made only at a single ritual site; the other calendars know nothing of this requirement. Deuteronomy shows a process of textual addition and interpretation within the Torah that comes to be understood as the contents of the eternal covenant. Yet even the priestly calendars themselves exhibit differences, and these are considerable compared especially to the non-priestly, non-Deuteronomic calendar of Exodus 23:14-17 and the later composite calendar of Exodus 34:18-26. As the multiple calendars in the Torah illustrate, the authors of Deuteronomy did not initiate the principles of addition and interpretation; instead, they made these principles central to their construction of Torah. The preservation of multiple calendars in the Torah is a witness to an ongoing dialogue within the community regarding its religious life. These calendars projected to the distant past at Sinai itself show the efforts of various leaderships at religious community building.

Reading, writing, and interpretation were all parts in the process of biblical composition, as demonstrated insightfully in the work of Fishbane (1985, 2003) and his students (such as Levinson and Schniedewind). In tradition, the Torah is regarded as eternal, as it derives ultimately from God; yet throughout it has been added to and interpreted. What was received as timeless has been handed down and supplemented; in other words, the Torah embodies the apparent paradox of being eternal yet additive. Rabbinic Judaism imagined the written Torah as a single divinely authored work linked to an accompanying Oral Torah. The principles and practices of interpretation associated with the Written and Oral Torah in rabbinic Judaism have an ancient basis in the very composition of the written Torah.

Monotheism and the "Historical Work" of Genesis–Kings, *Ezra–Nehemiah–Chronicles*

The construction of a narrative history is itself a response to identity issues. The linking of histories, especially of Genesis–Deuteronomy, Joshua–2 Kings, and Ezra–Nehemiah (reinforced by Chronicles), represented a major construction of continuity in identity at various levels. It makes a claim to social identity, that the

Israel of premonarchic times eventuated in the Israel of the Persian period. It offers the further claim that the land associated with Israel at the beginning and end of these works belongs to Israel through all these periods (and by implication, in any period). It also makes the assumption that the God of Israel is the same deity in all these periods. In other words, the construction of a single relatively continuous narrative for the past of a single people and land in turn conveys the claim for a single deity by rejecting other deities or at least pushing them into the backdrop of the national literature (see Damrosch 1987). A single narrative also diminishes issues about the historical background of other deities, their importance to Israel, and even any contributions that they may have made to the biblical picture of Israel's deity. With this narrative, the nature of deity is not limited to number, but it also involves its configuration: a single text of this sort tends to channel all major divine roles to this deity.

This deity also ends up championing the ideals of the social segments most responsible for its construction. For example, the priestly ideals of avoiding the impurity of death and sexual relations would tend to accent a holy god, disconnected from the realm of death and lacking in sexual relations. Holier than the holy of holies, this god would model the ideal for priests, and even the priestly people of Israel.

The Deuteronomic ideal of faithful observance of the Torah focuses on the deity as the divine voice that issues Torah. Otherwise, this invisible voice remains virtually unknown and largely unapproachable, except through religious observance and prayer. In short, the construction of a narrative time line itself became a means for asserting continuity across the massive ruptures in divine identity and Israelite experience. What was lost in past experience, traditional land, or family identity could be recaptured in sacred text and communal ritual.

Concluding Remarks and Reflections

The Bible offers a panorama on Israel's past as well as responses to the challenges that it faced. It also provides a partial glimpse into the cultural practices that Israel used to address these challenges. The destruction of Jerusalem was recalled as Israel's single greatest challenge, and the response to this loss of traditional marks of identity was to redefine identity with the additional claim that this new identity represents Israel's original one. The Torah, especially in the priestly traditions of Exodus–Numbers and in Deuteronomy, offers models for Israelite identity that focus on religious practice as the chief cultural markers of Judean identity. Rather than a life based on family land and practices, evidently the norms for most Israelites down at least to the eighth century, the Torah offers an alternative view of Israelite identity that subordinates family and land to priestly and Deuteronomic religious visions that would anticipate the emergence of Jewish identity in the Hellenistic period. Since the late 1990s scholars (such as Cohen 1999) who work on Judaism in the Hellenistic period have identified Jewishness as marked more by religious observance and belief and less by location in Yehud (later Judea) or even Judean descent, as conversion becomes more common in this period. Looking back over this discussion of the Bible, we may say that the roots of this shift from being Judean to being Jewish, from identity according to land to identity according to religious observance, are already developing in the Torah as a response to the crisis of the exile and postexilic life in foreign lands. The Torah, indeed the Bible as a whole, became part of Israel's portable shrine.

The exile generated Israel's most far-reaching changes in redefining its identity. Not only did all of its social, political, and religious institutions adapt to new circumstances. Israel's production of texts also served a revolutionary role in negotiating and expressing those changes. The texts became the landscape of the places lost in exile, and they captured in words what was lost in time. Like the priestly tabernacle, the texts enjoyed a portability and power of memory that served to link Israel's descendants. The Bible's own works witness to this transformation of strategy in re-creating Israel's identity. The many levels found in the longer works of the Bible show marks of rewriting Israel's past. From the monarchy, through the exile and the Persian period, the many authors of biblical works combined reading, writing, and interpretation as a means for coping with the challenges of their past as it was unfolding.

Celebrating these texts ritually in the context of worship was a complementary strategy for forging identity across generations. Biblical Israel's answer to the challenges that it faced over time was not simply a matter of getting the religious content right, but also of developing the scribal and ritual means to explore the meaning of that content as the challenges changed. The Bible preserved and provided for a dialogue over the meaning of Israel's past. Mount Sinai and Israel's other primordial moments were captured in the texts, and Israel's ritual would use its texts not just to ask what happened, but to ask what the past in the texts meant to their descendants in each period. In ritual, with its devotional use of texts, Israel's past was never completely gone. A centrally important dimension of the link across time was the Bible's assertion of one God; how this idea about divinity developed in ancient Israel is the subject of the next chapter.

Biblical Monotheism and the Structures of Divinity

*The detail of the pattern
is movement.*
—T. S. Eliot, *Four Quartets*

Introduction

As we saw the preceding chapter, Israel's survival strategies for dealing with the fall of the northern and southern kingdoms included making conceptual changes in understanding divinity, especially as it was considered to be operative in the human arena. How these conceptual changes came about may be understood better by looking broadly at the development of ideas about divinity in ancient Israel. As a beginning point, we should note that in Israel language about God (literally, "God-talk" or "theology") was intensively metaphorical. We can barely think of an image for God in the Bible that is not a metaphor based on human experience of nature or society. If we think of God in the Bible, what comes to mind are societal images of lord, redeemer, savior, help, shepherd, father. Or we think of images based on what humans do, for example, God as creator; or we may think of images based on what humans make: "A mighty fortress is our God." Or we may think of natural images: God as rock. With biblical God-talk, we are never too far from the language of society or nature. To enter into a discussion of biblical God-talk in ancient Israel requires being profoundly aware of its societal and environmental contexts. To sketch out what I would call structures of divinity in ancient Israel is to be cognizant of the deeply metaphorical nature of biblical language about divinity. As a human linguistic phenomenon, biblical discourse has a history; it changes over time. " *This Old House* "

To understand the story of God in the Bible, we need to back up to Israel's early expressions about divinity. The beginning of the time frame for investigating biblical God-talk has, by tradition, been marked by the biblical canon. This is a theological judgment, by virtue of Christian and Jewish traditions, which historically have chosen to understand the God of the Bible by locating revealed *what about extra-biblical texts as corroboration for metaphorical understanding?*

discourse about God in what the Bible presents. After all, for Christian and Jewish traditions, revelation about God begins with the Bible, not from extrabiblical texts. In contrast, ancient Near Eastern texts lie outside the Bible and therefore have no theological claim to inclusion in theological discussion. If ancient Near Eastern texts have no claim to inclusion, it is equally true that there is no theological basis for their use as a foil or contrast to the Bible, an approach long used (as discussed by Fishbane 2003). However, this approach has never properly been clarified from a theological perspective.

Let me give one common example of the kind of contrast or foil that scholars have applied to the ancient Near Eastern texts versus the Bible. Many past discussions contrasted Israel's monotheism against the polytheism of ancient Near Eastern texts. They also assumed that Israel was essentially monotheistic, and when it was not it was only because it had been tempted by the ways of its polytheistic neighbors. These discussions often began from a religious stance informed by a theological evaluation and then moved into a historical discussion that weighted the record in favor of biblical monotheism. Instead of asking how polytheism "worked," the assumption was that polytheism was a multiplicity of deities. In other words, the discussion never asked what the "oneness" or conceptual coherence of polytheism was for the ancient polytheists, or whether and how monotheism was a reformulation of polytheism. It was simply assumed that monotheism differs radically from polytheism, and that monotheism was radically superior. No one asked if in ancient Near Eastern religions, or even in early Israel, polytheism could have made more sense than monotheism, because it was always presupposed at the outset that polytheism was a lesser form of belief than monotheism. But what if in early Israel and its predecessor culture, polytheism made more sense than monotheism?

In the course of this chapter, I will suggest that in order to understand biblical monotheism better, we must understand the polytheism of early Israel as well as the polytheism of its cultural antecedents more broadly, as reflected through the Ugaritic texts of the Late Bronze Age and other sources. We may see Israel's articulations of monotheism as reformatted formulations of early Israelite polytheism, itself one version of polytheism among several polytheisms operative in the larger region of the Levant during the Late Bronze and Iron Ages. We may ask how these polytheisms had theoretical coherence, what was "mono-theistic" about them, and how they mapped out reality.

For the sake of clarity, it is important to make a number of general observations about the religious situation in Israel. First, monotheism developed in monarchic Israelite religion or at least in segments of its populace, and eventually it became normative for the authors of what became the biblical texts. Second, this monotheism did not originate historically at a pristine moment at Sinai with Moses and the covenant made there. In presenting this early time, the Bible even reminds us that "other gods" are a possibility, as the Ten Commandments warn the Israelites. Even Moses could ask, "Who is like You among the gods, O LORD?" (Exodus 15:11). So, as we will see in more detail later in this chapter, monotheism was a development in Israelite religion that was read back into its earlier religious tradition. Third, explicitly monotheistic expressions do emerge at a crucial midpoint in Israelite religion, but this is not to deny that there were ongoing forms of Judean polytheism, nor even to deny the pluralities within the godhead of biblical monotheism. Fourth, as far as we can tell, there was always something monistic about polytheism: it used different concepts to express "one-ness" in the universe. In turn, we may also say that after the emergence of monotheistic language in the Bible in the seventh and sixth centuries, there was often something quite "poly" about monotheism: it conveyed in one deity many different sorts of personalities associated with several deities in polytheism.

In this discussion I will focus on the early side of the Hebrew Bible, and not on later questions about Judean polytheism during the Persian period or in the Greco-Roman world. Instead, I will address early Israel and the background provided for early Israel by the Ugaritic texts, dating to the Late Bronze Age. In order to appreciate what we find in early Israel and then in the seventh to the sixth centuries, it is important from an intellectual perspective to have a sufficient backdrop to make sense out of the structures of divinity in early Israel. I begin the discussion with the structure of divinity at its broadest distinction between deities and divine monsters.

Structures of Divinity: Deities versus Divine Monsters

When I refer to structures of divinity, I am describing various categories of divinities and how these categories correspond to the way the universe was viewed. In other words, types of divinity and various deities corresponded in certain ways to the spatial realms of the universe as perceived by people living in and around the region of ancient Israel. In terms of divinity, the main structure of the cosmos is the division drawn between beneficial anthropomorphic deities on the one hand versus monstrous divine creatures on the other hand, as nicely sketched out for Mesopotamian mythology by the Dutch Assyriologist Franz Wiggermann. As Wiggermann (1992, 1996a, 1996b) shows, this line of distinction corresponds to an important and basic spatial distinction well known in anthropological research, namely, the "periphery" as opposed to the "center" (or "home"). This general division informs a series of conceptual divisions of time and space from the perspective of urban elites, between what is perceived by them as cultured and cultivated on the one hand, and uncultured and uncultivated on the other.

To illustrate this division, we turn first to the Ugaritic literature of the Late Bronze Age. The site of ancient Ugarit, modern Ras Shamra, lies on the Syrian coast about one hundred miles north of Beirut. The literature of this site, uncovered beginning in 1928, tells the stories of gods and goddesses, including the patriarch El, his wife Asherah, the storm-god Baal, and other divinities known in the Bible. A comparison of the Ugaritic texts with the Bible shows that, for all their differences, including the polytheism of the one and the monotheism of the other, the two belonged ultimately to the same larger cultural world. This is not to deny their significant differences: Ugarit, in the north, and Israel, in the south, stand at opposite ends of the eastern coast of the Mediterranean; Ugarit was intensely urban compared to the relative backwater of highland Israel; and the Ugaritic texts under discussion date to the Late Bronze Age, while the biblical texts span more than a thousand years, from the Iron Age though the Hellenistic period. Yet their many shared features indicate that they both belonged to a larger cultural world. So, as backdrop for understanding divinity in ancient Israel, we turn first to the Ugaritic texts.

The relationship between center and periphery in Ugaritic literature has been described well by Schloen. Quoting Edward Shils, Schloen (2001, 317n. 1) comments:

> For Shils, the social "center" is "the center of the order of symbols, of values and beliefs, which govern the society"; thus the terms "center" and "periphery" do not necessarily imply spatial separation. For Ugarit, however, it can be argued that the social center was focused in the physical center of the kingdom at Ras Shamra, which appears to have been the main locus of administration, of ritual, and of literary activity. In this case, then, the distinction "urban-rural" is more-or-less synonymous with "center-periphery."

At the heart of the "center" lies the household, which expresses domestic safety and protection, as well as familial patrimony and land. This center denotes family safety, but it is also the site of occasional domestic conflict. The periphery stands as a transitional zone between the center and the distant realms of the cosmos lying beyond human experience and control. Accordingly, one might prefer to speak of three zones: "center," "periphery," and "beyond the periphery." The distinction between the center and the periphery is expressed by a contrast in agrarian terms, the "sown" versus the "outback" or "steppe."

The mapping of divine space generally corresponds to the division of divinity made between deities and demons. On the earthly or horizontal level, deities inhabit places that are "near," while "monsters" or "demonic forces" do not. Within the "center" or area of human cultivation and civilization, deities have sacred mountains or cult sites, while cosmic enemies generally do not. These mountains literally point to the heavenly level where the deities live. The case of the mountain of the god Mot (Death) is the exception that proves the rule, since to get to Mot's home in the underworld, messengers do not travel to the top of the mountain, but lift up the mountain to descend to Mot. In terms of the cosmic or vertical level, deities inhabit heaven while monstrous forces inhabit either the underworld or the cosmic ocean that lies below the world, near the underworld. The divine topography is organized further according to realms ruled by the gods Baal, Yamm, and Mot. More specifically, realms are attributed to Baal (sky), Yamm (sea), and Mot (underworld). Space therefore is used in two different ways: mountains to mark proximity of deities enjoying cult and bestowing blessing of various sorts, and realms to mark cosmic competition.

Within this general home of human and divine order is a center point, Baal's mountain, Mount Sapan, the place where the gods feast. Baal's mountain is also called "pleasant place." This is garden language that in biblical texts is an expression for the center point of the cosmos. Later biblical texts represent this sown in particular as a garden, a reflection of the divine fructification of the center (as described by Stordalen 2000). The best-known case is the "garden of Eden" in Genesis 2–3. The mountain of the gods is also regarded as a garden, for example, in Ezekiel 28. In sum, the sown is the region of human habitation and cultivation, and accordingly within it lies the realm of cultic activity devoted to beneficial deities.

For ancient Ugarit, these distinctions for "center" may be subdivided according to the heart of the center and the further realm of earthly space viewed as beneficial. In Ugarit's world, the heart is the kingdom of Ugarit, and the wider band of positive space is marked by Egypt and the Aegean, reflecting Ugarit's historical experience as a major trading power around the eastern end of the Mediterranean Sea. This division may be schematized in the following manner for Ugaritic polytheism:

PLACE: VERTICAL SPACE
   Heaven

PLACE: HORIZONTAL SPACE

HOME	FOREIGN
Ugarit	Egypt/Crete
local cultivation (with its divine sponsor, the storm-god Baal)	foreign culture and crafts (with their divine sponsor, the craftsman-god Kothar)

SUPERNATURAL	
Home deities	Foreign deities
Cult and blessing	Blessing, but no cult

Just as the center bears a subdivision, the periphery likewise shows a distinction between what humans experience in the periphery and what lies beyond this periphery. This distinction is expressed spatially:

PERIPHERY	BEYOND THE PERIPHERY
Unpopulated zones: outback	Underworld (and the god of death, Mot)
Surface waters (springs, rivers)	Waters beyond ("the deep"; the god Yamm, whose name means "Sea")

In contrast to "home," the periphery or "outback" is characterized as a terrain of "rocks and brush." The outback marks a marginal or transitional zone and the site of human activities such as grazing and hunting; here begins the area of dangerous forces. Accordingly, in the cosmic geography of the Baal Cycle, the "outback" designates the place where Baal meets the god Mot (Death) at the edge of the underworld. The "outback" is also the site where Baal's foes are to be given birth and to confront him.

Divisions apply not only to cosmic space, but also to divine powers. Broadly speaking, the most fundamental division involves deities who meet human needs on the one hand, and on the other hand monstrous divinities who pose a threat to humans. Well-being, including fertility at various levels, was thought to derive from a number of deities. In contrast, monstrous divine powers were thought to provide no benefit, but only a threat to human well-being from the periphery. It is true that some deities violate this distinction. Let me give two examples. The monstrous enemy Sea (Yamm) is included in a list of otherwise beneficial deities (*CAT* 1.47.30 = 1.118.29). The inclusion of Yamm is understandable in view of Ugarit's special orientation to the sea. For the second example, we may turn to the goddess Anat, who shows an intensely violent side. Often her violence is directed against enemies to the benefit of the center (for example, *CAT* 1.3 II), but she occasionally exceeds such a positive purpose and strikes the hero of the story, as in the case of Aqhat (*CAT* 1.17 VI). Anat's character embodies a fundamental perception about the complex dimensions of divine violence, potentially dangerous not only to enemies but occasionally also to the community. Such cases as Yamm and Anat play off the general presumption about the destructive nature of cosmic monsters and the beneficent character of deities. These exceptions additionally show that deities are not simple constructs, but rather complex expressions of character. We could discuss some further examples of deities who show multiple sides, but they do not really undermine the general distinction between beneficial deities and monstrous enemies.

In terms of their representation, we see another basic difference. Benevolent deities are often rendered anthropomorphically, while destructive divinities appear as monstrous in form. In fact, theriomorphic (beast-form) representations reflect the dichotomy between deities and cosmic enemies. Cosmic enemies are monstrous or undomesticated in character, while the animals associated with benevolent deities (what have been called "attribute animals") generally reflect cultural domestication. This fundamental set of distinctions may be schematized in the following manner:

Benevolent Deities	Destructive Divinities
Human in form (anthropomorphic)	Monstrous animal form (theriomorphic)
Domesticated species as emblematic of deities: bull, cow, calf, bird	Undomesticated species as emblematic of monsters: snake, serpent

On the one hand, we see domesticated species reserved for beneficial deities. For example, the bull seems to be typical for El, as reflected in his Ugaritic title, "Bull El my Father." Bull icons, possibly representations of El, were also recovered from Ugarit (*ANEP*, no. 828). Again, there are occasional exceptions to the general rule. Although it is not always clear which goddesses are involved, lions and snakes are associated with some goddesses in various religious depictions (*ANEP*, nos. 470–74, 830). It is possible that lions denote the goddesses' warrior character while snakes signal some other positive aspect of goddesses (perhaps healing, an association of snakes that we see in Numbers 21:8-9 and 2 Kings 18:4). Perhaps it is the scale that is telling, for unlike the largely domesticated animals representing deities, the snakes or serpents representing destructive divinities are cosmic or at least superhuman in proportion. In fact, the cosmic enemies are represented as giant snake-dragons. The Bible contains literary references to this dragon often presented as multiheaded (Psalm 74:13, 14; Job 26:12-13; Revelation 12:3-4; 13:1). This tradition is quite old; it is known from a seal dating to the late third millennium (*ANEP*, no. 691). One Ugaritic text (*CAT* 1.3 III 40-42) describes Tunnanu (or less likely an unnamed cosmic enemy) as a snake-dragon, also with seven heads:

> Surely I bound Tunnanu and destroyed (?) him.
> I fought the Twisty Serpent,
> the Potentate with Seven Heads.

The god Mot reminds Baal of his defeat of Leviathan in similar terms (*CAT* 1.5 I 1-3):

> you killed Litan, the Fleeing Serpent,
> annihilated the Twisting Serpent,
> the Potentate with seven heads.

The biblical hymn of Psalm 148:7 calls on the cosmic sea creature Tannin (NRSV "sea monsters") to join in praising Yahweh. The kindly attitude toward cosmic monsters may not be an Israelite innovation. Indeed, this view of the monstrous enemies recalls El's special relationship with these foes, expressed through various "terms of endearment" and other nomenclature. The Ugaritic material is especially rich in terms of endearment between El and the cosmic enemies, expressed in a speech uttered by the goddess Anat (*CAT* 1.3 III):

Why have Gapn and Ugar come?
What enemy rises against Baal,
what foe against the Cloud-Rider?
Surely I fought Yamm, the Beloved of El,
surely I finished off River, the Great God,
surely I bound Tunnanu and destroyed (?) him,
I fought the Twisty Serpent, the Seven-headed Potentate.
I fought Desire (?), the Beloved of El,
I destroyed Rebel, the Calf of El.
I finished off Fire, the Dog of El,
I annihilated Flame, the Daughter of El,
that I might fight for silver and inherit gold.

Some of the Ugaritic cosmic enemies are associated with Yamm, others with the chief god El. Yamm and El share a common trait: both are opponents of the warrior storm-god, Baal. Perhaps this division of cosmic characters highlights El's relationship with Yamm, who is the premier figure of El's favor.

From the discussion of cosmic enemies so far, we may note three basic features shared by the Ugaritic traditions and the comparable material in the Bible. First, ancient Israel inherited the actual names of the cosmic enemies from the broader culture that Israel shared with Ugarit. There are four foes with basically the same names confronted by both Baal in the Ugaritic texts and Yahweh in the Bible: Sea (Hebrew *yam*, Ugaritic *ym*, with his additional name, River); biblical Leviathan *(liwyatan)* and Ugaritic *ltn;* Hebrew *tannin*, Ugaritic *tnn* (spelled out as *tunnanu* in one Ugaritic text, spelled Tunnanu in the English translation above); and Hebrew *mawet* and Ugaritic Mot, both literally meaning "death." For Baal, most are enemies of old, but Sea (Yamm) and Death (Mot) are ongoing threats.

Second, just as these cosmic enemies are mentioned as Baal's or Anat's old enemies, they are known in Israelite tradition as enemies of Yahweh, the warrior-god. Three of these enemies appear in Psalm 74:12-17:

Yet, O God, my king from of old,
    maker of deliverance throughout the world,
you are the one who smashed **Sea** *with your might,*
    cracked the heads of **Tannin** *in the waters;*
you are the one who crushed the heads of **Leviathan,**
    left him as food. . . .
You are the one who broke open springs and streams,
    You are the one who dried up the Mighty Rivers.
To You belongs the day, Yours too the night,
    You are the one who established the Light of the Sun.
You are the one who fixed all the boundaries of the world,
    summer and winter—it was You who fashioned them.

Here the cosmic enemies' defeat serves as prelude to the ancient event of creation. In contrast, Isaiah 27:1 presents Leviathan's defeat as a sign of the future end times. Isaiah 25:8 likewise proclaims a reversal of the power of the cosmic enemy, Death. The image of God there swallowing up Death reverses the comparable image of Death's demanding to swallow Baal known from Ugaritic literature. This notion of Death as a divine enemy is otherwise rare in biblical conflict stories. The older mythic tradition was hardly eradicated or fell out of use in ancient Israel, however. It survived strongly in biblical apocalyptic. We might say that pre-Israelite polytheistic narrative set in the past later appears in monotheistic form as Israelite apocalyptic set in the future. It would appear that Yahweh has assimilated the traditions associated with Baal. Both warrior storm-gods, these two gods prove later to be competitors (as we will see later in this chapter). Even in this competition, the traditions that still resonated with positive association were attributed to Yahweh. This incorporation by Yahweh of other deities' characteristics was a long-term trend in Israelite religion that shows what I have called (Smith 1990, 2002a) an increasing "convergence" of divine roles attributed to Yahweh.

Third, like the Ugaritic texts, biblical texts attest to the cosmic forces as the chief god's domesticated beasts. For the Ugaritic literature, the cosmic enemies are the enemies of Baal, but the beloved of El. The book of Job also knows these cosmic enemies as both human foes and divine playthings. So Job himself expresses the understanding of these figures as hostile powers, when he complains against God: "Am I Sea or Tannin [NRSV 'the Dragon'] that You set a watch over me?" (Job 7:12; see the reference to Sea and Leviathan in Job 3:8, and the mention of the Sea and the "fleeing serpent" in 26:12-13). Yet the book of Job later renders the cosmic enemies not as Yahweh's enemies but as objects of divine domestication. So God responds to Job that he treated Sea at creation not as an enemy but as a newborn babe (Job 38:8-11). Leviathan is the sea creature caught by God's "fish-hook" (41:1; 40:25 NJPS), drawn by a rope and nose-ring. God asks Job: "will you play with him like a bird?" (40:29 NRSV English; 41:5 in Hebrew and NJPS). Psalm 104:26 similarly identifies this figure as a creature made for play: "Leviathan whom you formed to sport with."

This view of Leviathan as a tamed pet may go against the expectation of an Israelite audience, which knows Leviathan primarily as a monstrous enemy, as in the Ugaritic texts that pit Baal or Anat against such figures. However, the biblical texts treating the monstrous figures instead as pets may echo their "beloved" relationship with El. In the Ugaritic passage, Sea is called "the beloved of El," and elsewhere Death receives a variant of this same title. So for Job, Yahweh is very much an El-figure, a creator-god who has cosmic monsters forces as beloved pets.

Because of the growing recognition of the many cultural features shared by Israel and its immediate environment, many scholars conclude that Israel inherited older traditions (as nicely put by Fishbane 2003). Several scholars have come to the further conclusion that Israel and Ugarit, as well as the other local polities located between them, belonged to the same larger cultural matrix. This claim does not mean that each of these societies did not take these cultural traditions in its own direction. Because we can see such specific cultural features of the older Ugaritic literature in the Hebrew Bible, we may suggest that the Bible drew directly on cultural traditions that predate Israel. The Ugaritic texts as well as other texts from outside the Bible found in this region form the backdrop to the Bible's use of these traditions. The Ugaritic texts (and other extrabiblical texts from the region) constitute what may be called "the Old Testament of the Old Testament" (to borrow a phrase coined by Moberly 1992). That is, these extrabiblical texts provide an essential understanding of the Hebrew Bible or Old Testament in a way analogous to the way that for Christian tradition the Old Testament has been understood as a necessary backdrop and preparation for the New Testament. This relationship of Israel and its environment may be best captured not by the expression, "Israel and the ancient Near East" (a customary label for this subfield of biblical studies), but "Israel in the ancient Near East." Israel is embedded in its environment, and the various terms specifically shared by both Yahweh and Baal are only one part in this common cultural relationship. Indeed, a look through the highly recommended volume *Dictionary of Deities and Demons in the Bible* (van der Toorn et al. 1999) shows the depth of continuity as well as interesting changes and differences between Israel and its surrounding cultures in the area of divinity and religion.

The Ugaritic material, in fact, differs from some biblical passages in a number of respects involving the cosmic enemies and the gods connected with them. First, there is the matter of whether these forces are considered divine. On the Ugaritic side, these figures are at a minimum treated as equal in power to the deities who fight them. There is a stalemate between Baal and Mot (*CAT* 1.6 VI), and once it seems that Baal is depicted as slumped beneath Yamm's throne (*CAT* 1.2 IV). Moreover, some of the texts mentioned above treat the cosmic enemies explicitly as divinities. For example, River, a title of Yamm, apparently bears the epithet "Great God" *(il rbm)*. Included in the same list (quoted above) as Yamm are El's beloved or pets, the other cosmic enemies; from this context it would appear that they are comparable in rank or status to Yamm. In another passage, Yamm's destruction is paralleled with the havoc caused by another god, Resheph. Mot receives the title *bn ilm,* meaning either "son of El" or "son of the gods." This is the same title used elsewhere for members of the pantheon. In sum, the Ugaritic texts present these figures at least as divine in rank and power, if not in formal designation.

In contrast, many biblical passages do not accord divine status to these figures. This statement should be qualified, since in early Israel such cosmic foes may have been regarded as divine, and it is only in the later attested corpus that they appear. We may get a glimpse of this possibility in the personal name Jemuel (Yemuel) known from Genesis 46:10 and Exodus 6:15, which has been interpreted as the Hebrew equivalent of Ugaritic *ymil,* "Yamm is god." Such evidence is rare, however, and the biblical corpus seems removed in time from the period when such cosmic foes would have been attributed divine status. Some examples will help to illustrate the contrast. Psalm 74 draws on the paradigm of the "center-periphery" found in the Ugaritic Baal story. Just as the beneficial god Baal defeats the cosmic monster Sea, the powerful God of Psalm 74 fights the monstrous enemy of the cosmic realm beyond the periphery. However, there is some reduction in the enemy in Psalm 74 compared to the story of Baal versus Yamm. In Psalm 74, when the enemies fight against Yahweh, they hardly compare in power with Yahweh. We may contrast Baal's initial setback in his conflict with Yamm, followed by victory but only thanks to magical weapons made by Kothar, the craftsman-god. In short, we see the old paradigm still in place, but with a reduction of the status of the enemy, who is hardly a peer of God.

Psalm 104 also alters the status of the cosmic enemy, but in an entirely different way. Psalm 104 mentions the cosmic waters, which briefly flee at the beginning of creation (v. 7). There is no real battle to speak of: God shows up for the conflict and utters a battle cry, the divine "rebuke" or "blast" in verse 7, reminiscent of divine thunder elsewhere in biblical tradition. However, there is no corresponding resistance on the part of the enemy. Moreover, the waters are not otherwise personified, and they are not described in monstrous form. We see here, then, the beginning of a transformation of the "center-periphery" paradigm. The enemy is no longer theriomorphic in form, and it is no threat compared to the Baal story or to Psalm 74.

A further transformation takes place in the character of the waters. They are changed from a negative, hostile force into a positive material of creation. No longer oppositional, the waters constitute an element that in its proper place plays its proper part in the order of creation. The waters now in their place play a beneficial role in the divine plan. They supply drink for the beasts in verses 10-13 and presumably for the world's crops in verses 14-18. According to verses 25-26, the waters, too, provide ships with a "sea-road" (to echo a phrase from Beowulf). The waters also serve as a home for all the creatures of the sea, including Leviathan, now a divine plaything (v. 26).

In terms of the "center-periphery" paradigm, the threatening waters in Psalm 104 are barely hostile, and they are transformed from their place beyond the periphery and incorporated inside the creation of God. As a result, they play multiple positive purposes within the wise creation. What has been traditional beyond the periphery is now integrated into the "center" of the beneficial God; and in turn, the wondrous "center" of the wise God extends out to the entire universe.

In doing so, this new order is suffused with the divine life force (Hebrew *ruach* twice in vv. 29-30, NRSV "breath" and "spirit"), which makes the symbolic center extend out to the reaches of the "periphery." Where Psalm 74 praises divine might, a feature that requires conflict and presupposes opposition, the creation of Psalm 104 presents a wise design. As verse 24 says, "You made them all with wisdom." The world is based on harnessing and arranging the components of creation for one another, and the traditionally hostile waters are transformed into a central element of the wise plan.

A third example of biblical creation, Genesis 1, reduces the cosmic waters as a divine enemy even more than Psalm 104. The audience of the creation story of Genesis 1 is prepared for a cosmic conflict, set up by the opening references to the waters of the abyss (*tehom;* NRSV "the deep") in verse 2. With the references to the chaos waters, readers are all prepared for a description of God smashing these watery enemies. In Psalm 74 this battle is explicit; in Psalm 104 it is muted, with only the divine "rebuke" (or "blast" of v. 7). This "rebuke," by comparison in Genesis 1, is transformed into a divine word: "Then God said" (v. 3). Elsewhere in the Bible and the ancient Near East, there is creation simply by the divine word, and one could argue that Genesis 1 involves creation by word rather than creation by battle or conflict (as proposed by Fishbane 2003). However, the references in Genesis 1 to the *tehom* (v. 2) and later to the *tanninim* (v. 21, NRSV "sea monsters") clearly echo the older tradition of divine conflict. These *tanninim* are related to the Ugaritic cosmic enemy called Tunnanu, described earlier in this chapter. In view of these connections with the background of the cosmic enemies, Genesis 1 evidently transforms creation by conflict into creation by the word as a statement about divine power lying beyond the traditional norms of divine power. Accordingly, Genesis 1 omits not only the conflict but also any personification of the cosmic waters. With no hint of conflict or even hostility, God speaks (not even rebukes), and the divine will is achieved. This substitution of divine speech for conflict is designed to heighten the picture of a powerful God above human expectations, beyond the traditions of cosmic conflict. The watery creatures are now not monstrous, and they are contained in the created order in Genesis 1:21, characterized repeatedly in Genesis 1 as good: "And God saw that it was good/very good" (vv. 4, 10, 12, 18, 21, 25, 31). Where Psalm 74:12-17 presents creation in terms of power and Psalm 104 stresses the divine wisdom of creation, Genesis 1 emphasizes its goodness.

The cosmic opposition, *tanninim,* lying beyond the periphery, is transformed in Genesis 1 from cosmic enemy (like Ugaritic Tunnanu) into part of creation. Genesis 1 goes a step further beyond the creation tradition of battle conflict, in partially removing these sea creatures from the beginning of the narrative as expected. While Psalm 104 presents the fleeing waters at the outset of its description of creation, Genesis 1 envelops these *tanninim* into the fabric of creation, without any recognition that they ever were anywhere near the periphery. In this way, Genesis 1 even more than Psalm 104 stresses the inclusion of the old watery beings into the good creation. The periphery remains somewhat in the form of the cosmic oceans at the beginning of Genesis 1. They remain to a great degree beyond the firmament. So boundaries between inside and outside are drawn, perhaps corresponding to the Israelite, priestly sense of boundaries securing the ideal purity of the community boundaries. However, the waters within the firmament provide a proper place for the fishes of the sea, including the *tanninim*. Indeed, in drawing a vision of the entire world in terms of priestly categories of time and space, Genesis 1 rearranges the world with a plan partially blurring center and periphery in a single system. For Genesis 1, the center versus the periphery does not map the world, perhaps signaling the demise of the Temple and land as center in priestly imagination in favor of the Israelite god's holy lordship over all the universe.

The presentation in Genesis 1 carries an especially powerful force for an audience that knows and presumes the traditional stories of its warrior-god's victories over the ancient cosmic enemies. Such a presentation assumes that the audience knows how such stories convey God's mastery over the universe. Genesis 1 plays on this knowledge and thereby extends the picture of divine mastery. Yet there is more to this passage. This transformation in the character of the divine foe involves an alteration not only of theme but also of literary order. In placing the *tanninim* within the narration of the created order in verse 21 instead of the beginning of the account, the literary order of Genesis 1 contributes to a monotheistic vision. In this regard the text manifests a monotheistic perspective, which alters the perception of reality with its created order.

This monotheistic reading applies not only to the sea creatures. It also works for the sun and the moon, called only "the greater light" and "the lesser light" (Genesis 1:16), titles that were not necessarily polemical as such but quite traditional, as shown by the titles "great light" for the Ugaritic sun-goddess, and "light of the heavens" for the Ugaritic moon-god (compare also the sun-goddess's titles "Great Sun," and "Light of the Gods, the Sun"). In Genesis 1 these figures are no longer presented as divinities. Instead, like the sea creatures, the celestial bodies are placed within the created order. In their context in Genesis 1, the heavenly bodies now reflect the original light presented in verse 3, arguably God's own light (like the divine light of Psalm 104:2) rather than a created light, one that shines divine well-being into the world like the shining of divine Torah to Israel (cf. Psalm 19). In other words, the power of the old sun-deity is transformed in Genesis 1 into the divinely created sun that reflects the primordial Light of God.

We will note below in the Ugaritic texts and early Israel that the sun was part of the pantheon and therefore an object of ritual devotion. This ritual devotion may have been transmuted into the primordial Light of God that may have informed a new ritual context in ancient Israel, namely, priestly mystical experience interpreted as the light of Torah. (For two other models of biblical visionary or mystical experience, we might compare the priestly mystical chariot in the prophetic book of the priest Ezekiel, mentioned in chapter 2, and the earlier mystical vision of Exodus 24:9-11 discussed in chapter 4.) Accordingly, in Genesis 1, the old light of the sun-deity continued to shine through its massive priestly transformation as God's own. Indeed, in Genesis 1 all old divine entities apart from God are transformed, and any ambiguity between Creator and creatures is resolved, with no middle ground left in its monotheistic vision.

As this discussion indicates, Genesis 1 shows displacement from the traditional picture of both the chief god and the monstrous forces. The book of Job, too, shows some important displacement. The book does not simply echo the earlier roles attested in the Ugaritic texts, at least when it comes to the chief god. For Job modifies the portrait of God compared to either of the Ugaritic gods, El and Baal. In Job 38:1 God appears not in a westerly storm cloud, a traditional way of presenting Baal's theophany, or in human dreams, El's usual medium of communication with humans. Instead, God appears in the storm of the dust cloud, the "whirlwind" (*hassearah*, Job 38:1), the dessicating wind blowing off the eastern desert, a natural force that would have been associated mythologically, if anything, with Mot, the god of death (see Fitzgerald 2002, 136–39). This motif in Job signals that God is the God not only of the domesticated human sphere, but also of realms undomesticated, even unknown by humans; therefore, the divine cannot be controlled or tamed by human assumptions. For humans the divine is accessible and therefore to that extent domesticated, yet this is also the God who moves about in the unknown reaches of the universe. This God is the known and unknown. This God belongs not only to the center, but also to the periphery and well beyond. (Whether this reflection—or that of Genesis 1—might be related to Israel's own sense of being peripheral in the world is difficult to know.) So, despite long familiarity with the traditional view of God, Job recognizes that this God is one whom he now meets for the first time (Job 42:5). "Home is where one starts from," we are told by T. S. Eliot (*Four Quartets, East Coker*), and the point applies to human perception of the divine in Job. To know the God of Job, one only starts at home and visits realms beyond the home, as Job shows in his discovery of the Divine in the whirlwind.

I would like to end this section with a further consideration about these conflict narratives. These conflicts may involve either power or lack of power.

Enuma Elish

For example, in the Babylonian myth of *Enuma Elish* (sometimes called "The Creation Epic" or "When on High," based on the first line of the work), the warrior-god Marduk defeats the cosmic sea, Tiamat, a foe at the outset presented in majestic terms. Marduk's victory is definitive, and his mastery over the universe is complete. In the Assyrian versions of this myth, the name of the god Ashur is substituted, making this Assyrian chief god into the hero of the story. We might say in the case of *Enuma Elish* that the god's mastery over the cosmic enemies expresses the well-being of those who transmitted and used the text in the Assyrian and Babylonian contexts of the mid-first millennium. For the Mesopotamian users of this text at this point, *Enuma Elish,* then, is largely about the rise of the Assyrians and Babylonians as world empires. In the case of *Enuma Elish*'s earlier composition, however, its conflict narrative is not expressive of political power. It is thought that *Enuma Elish* may have been composed originally in the Early Iron Age when Assyria and Babylonia were not yet world powers; the text seems to express political aspirations that would be realized only later. A lack of divine mastery is also apparent in Baal's need for help from other deities and his lack of definitive victory over Sea and Death. Baal's situation perhaps echoes Ugarit's circumstances living in the shadow of the Egyptians and the Hittites, the great powers linked to Ugarit by sea and by land. Clearly, the conflict story has the flexibility to express political strength or aspirations to political power.

In the case of Psalm 74, the lament presents a recollection of divine victory of the past at a time of human powerlessness, even desperation. Psalm 74:12-17 appeals to divine strength at a moment of perceived divine weakness or indifference, as shown by the lament over Jerusalem's destruction in verses 1-11. In this case, Yahweh's mastery is not fully realized; for ancient Israelites this divine dominion is a debatable matter. Similarly, in passages such as Isaiah 27:1, prospects of divine victory are held out for a future time. Yahweh here has not yet exercised complete mastery over the cosmos. Isaiah 51:9-11 likewise can proclaim the power of Yahweh over the cosmic enemy as an expression of hope in the face of human weakness at the time of exile. If Genesis 1 is to be situated against the backdrop of foreign empires' imposing their power on Judah, as many scholars argue, then again divine mastery stands in inverse relation to the political status of the text's author. From all of these various biblical and extrabiblical texts, it is clear that divine power can encode not only human power but also human powerlessness. The conflict between the divine hero and the divine enemy may reflect the condition of a community against an earthly threat that may be overwhelming.

In short, narratives of divine conflict composed at moments of political power or powerlessness are expressions of vision and hope. Some conflict narratives may be used to present an existing political order, an emerging order, or even a nonexistent order that is hoped for. This order, real or unrealized, is seen as a source of blessing, or at least it expresses hope for blessing as of yet unknown, of things unseen. It is hope and not simply power that seems to be the key to these texts of conflict.

The Divine Council and the Divine Family: From Polytheistic Ugaritic through Polytheistic Israel to Monotheistic Israel

The Levels of the Divine Assembly and Family at Ugarit

After the fundamental division between cosmic enemies and beneficial deities, the next major division in the structure of divinity involves the beneficial deities themselves. It is not uncommon for ancient texts to refer to the general collectivity of deities as a "council" or "assembly." Indeed, this divine social structure seems to be the dominant way to refer to the gods and goddesses as a group. Mesopotamian literature attests to "the assembly of the gods" in a number of different contexts. The Ugaritic texts also use this language to refer to the deities. The expression "meeting of the gods" is found in a section of a text called the Kirta (or Keret) Epic, but more commonly the terminology for the general assembly involves the word "assembly" or "council" (as laid out in Mullen 1980). The usages with this term might be divided into three basic expressions: "the assembly of the gods," "the assembly of the divine sons," and "the assembly of the council." The word "assembly" may also refer to more restricted groupings of deities centered on particular gods such as El or Baal.

Used with the language of divine council is the notion of the divine household. The divine council is coterminous in the Ugaritic texts with the divine family household. In general, the notion of the family, together with the language of divine council, provided a cohesive vision of religious reality. The immense importance that the patrimonial household holds for understanding both human and divine society in the Ugaritic texts has been underscored in recent years, especially by Schloen (2001). The pantheon is a large multifamily or joint household headed by a patriarch with several competing sons. As a whole, the pantheon has four levels (as I discussed in Smith 2001). From various scenes in the Ugaritic texts, we see the four levels in the divine household:

Level 1: The elderly god El and his wife Athirat

Level 2: The divine children: Athtart and Athtar (the evening and morning star), Shapshu (sun) and Yarih (moon), Shahar (dawn) and Shalim (dusk), Resheph (Mars?); also Baal, the warrior/storm-god.

Level 3: Kothar (the craftsman-god)

Level 4: The divine workers: messengers (angels), gatekeepers, servants

The four levels of the pantheon correspond to different tiers of the divine household. The top two levels of the pantheon are occupied by the divine parents and their children, while the bottom two tiers of the pantheon consist of deities working in the divine household. The divine family of El and Athirat is called in generic terms "the seventy sons of Athirat," a conventional number for a large group (see Judges 9:5; 2 Kings 10:1; see also Exodus 1:5). Broadly speaking, the "seventy children" designates the divine council as a whole.

The highest rank is held by El, the father of deities and humanity. El presides over the pantheon and issues decrees. El's capacity as ruler of the pantheon is expressive of his function as patriarch of the divine family. With El is his consort, Athirat (later biblical Asherah), mother of deities and humanity. The goddess may influence El's decisions, for example, when she asks him to allow the building of Baal's palace (*CAT* 1.4 IV). She may even participate in the decision-making process, for example, in the selection of a royal successor to Baal (*CAT* 1.6 I). Scholars have often suggested that Athirat in these instances reflects the role of the royal wife who intercedes with her husband in political matters that affect the well-being of her sons. This idea would be consistent with the fact that the royal title "lady" is also a title for Athirat.

The second level of the pantheon consists of the main children of El and Athirat. The deities belonging to the second level include major figures of the pantheon: Shapshu (Sun), Yarih (Moon), Shahar (Dawn) and Shalim (Dusk), Athtar (Morning Star), and Athtart (Evening Star). As can be seen from the meanings of their names, many of these deities are celestial or astral in character. Indeed, three pairs of astral deities in the second level mark the times of day. The sun and moon deities balance daytime and nighttime. The sun-deity travels from west to east through the underworld during the night; at sunrise she crosses the sky from east to west over the course of the day. The deities Dawn and Dusk mark the transitions from night to day, and from day to night. In this they are joined by Athtar and Athtart, the morning and evening star (sometimes called "the Venus star"). With these three pairs, we see a certain symmetry expressed about the cosmos and its daily cycle, ruled by the figure of El. This astral grouping is apparently characterized as "the children of El" and "the assembly of the stars" (*CAT* 1.10 I 3-4). Even El occasionally reflects a celestial background. In a later record of this mythology by Philo of Byblos, El himself is identified as a star (*Praep. ev.* 1.10.44).

In addition to this basic celestial group are other deities, including Anat. This goddess is an unusual member of the second level of the divine household. She seems to be El's daughter, but she also appears to be Baal's sister. Another unusual member of this tier is Baal himself, the warrior/storm-god. Because his father is explicitly named as the god Dagan, Baal is evidently an outsider; Dagan would seem to be a level-one god in an alternative system. Despite Baal's status as an outsider, he claims some sort of generic familial relation to El. Like the other deities, Baal refers to "Bull El" as his father.

It is to be noted that combat and conflict generally involve this level of the divine family. References to conflict against cosmic enemies are confined largely to Baal and Anat. Similar rank along lines of military prowess is implied for other figures of this rank. Athtar's nomination to Baal's throne (*CAT* 1.6 I) would suggest a martial view of him, though he hardly measures up to Baal (or at least his throne). Given her military character elsewhere as well as her hunting, Athtart would appear also to reflect this martial dimension of the second tier of the pantheon. A further distinctive point about the second level involves nature. Many deities of the second rank are associated with nature or natural phenomena in the Ugaritic texts. This point extends to Baal, Yamm, Mot, and Athtar, but also to Shapshu, Yarih, Shahar, and Shalim. Natural fertility is also a matter of the second tier. Deities have sometimes been thought to have been or be forces of nature, but such an association appears in the Ugaritic texts to be confined to the second tier.

An important caveat: the language of identification of natural "forces" with deities is reductionist and potentially misleading. Perhaps it would be better to say that the earthly manifestation of deities in this tier takes place in specific natural realms and through natural phenomena. It is important to be careful about how to put this point, because nature, though emphasized in a text like the Baal Cycle, is rarely stressed in proper names, prayers, or incantations. In iconography, too, Baal's weaponry comes to the fore, although it is to be noted that the so-called Louvre stela (*ANEP*, no. 490) depicts the storm-god's spear with features of a plant. The god is typically depicted as a standing warrior (*ANEP*, nos. 481, 484, 827). With his thunder and lightning understood as his powerful voice and his weapons, Baal's warrior role coheres with his role as storm-god. Before moving to the third level, we should note that in the Baal Cycle, Baal's power is balanced with the executive power of El. In other words, family hierarchy balances power between the elderly patriarch and the strong son. So family structure does not express simply levels of power, but also a number of shifting fulcrum points of social power.

The third level of the pantheon is poorly represented in the Ugaritic texts, as in the biblical texts. In view of this situation, it seems better not to regard it as an entirely separate level. When the literary context calls for the services of an important worker, one emerges from the ranks of the workers who belong to the

fourth level. For Ugarit's cosmopolitan urban culture, the worker who emerges
from the ranks is the craftsman-god named Kothar wa-Hasis. As we will see, in biblical texts the worker who emerges from such ranks functions in other capacities.
In Kothar's case, he serves the upper two tiers of the royal family, and he is
needed by them to provide his services. He is ordered by El to build a palace for
Yamm (*CAT* 1.1 III). Kothar also makes a weapon for Baal (1.2 IV), and later he
builds a palace for him (1.4 VI-VII). Kothar occupies a position below the great
deities El, Baal, Athirat, and Anat, and he performs numerous services for them.
As divine servant and general factotum of the great deities, Kothar services the
great deities with not only his craftsmanship but also his spells, advice, and wisdom. Indeed, in one passage (*CAT* 1.4 VII), Kothar's wisdom clearly exceeds that
of his divine superior, Baal. His homes in Egypt and Crete signal his place outside
the immediate orbit of the upper two divine levels and their homes. It may be
that this tier represents a particular development at Ugarit reflecting not only
foreign trade, as indicated by Kothar's homes, but also the important place of
craftsmen in Ugaritic society. Moreover, as a foreigner, Kothar would be marked
as outside the indigenous pantheon. Kothar is the only example of the third level,
and later this tier is poorly represented in all periods (for some periods, we will
see no figures at this level). The texts occasionally introduce and highlight third-
tier figures in ways never done for members of the fourth level. Unlike fourth-
level figures, they receive names, and they often perform important, specialized
duties. That some distinction should be maintained between the third and fourth
levels may be supported by administrative lists from Ugarit, as they sometimes
lists workers without names while at other times they do provide names.

The fourth and bottom level of divinities is exemplified by household workers of the following sorts. Best known are "servants." Some are specified as domestic female servants. In contrast, "messengers" and "gatekeepers," who guard
the household or go out into the world, are male roles in the divine household.
Other minor gods are to be placed at this level, for example, divine military
troops serving a major warrior-god (e.g., *CAT* 1.5 V). In sum, the divine household exhibits numerous structural and linguistics hallmarks of the patriarchal
household.

One should note that presentation of the divine household is based on the
literary texts. The lists of deities do not conform entirely to this idea of the
household. However, some elements of the hierarchy seen in the literary texts are
expressed by such lists (*CAT* 1.47 = 1.118). For example, the lists generally begin
with the older generations of deities including Ilib, El, and Dagan, and then pro-
ceed to Baal, followed by other high members of the second level. These figures
are in turn followed by many lesser divinities, including figures of particular rele-

vance to liturgy. For example, the bottom parts of these lists include the divinized lyre, likely a reflection of the use of this instrument in cultic liturgy. This progression and hierarchy is hardly uniform, and we do see some exceptions in the listing (for example, Shalim, a second-level deity, who is named last). Despite differences in methods of organization and the ranking of some deities, however, the literary texts and the lists do share some of the same hierarchical principles.

The Levels of Divinity in Israel

It is possible to provide ancient Israelite texts with the same sort of analysis of four divine tiers that we applied to the Ugaritic texts. For, like Ugaritic literature, the Bible manifests the language of the divine assembly and family, as well as specific deities. Before we enter into this analysis, it is important to take into account some of the complexities involved with Israelite evidence. We may note five in particular. First, the Ugaritic literary texts may offer a more systematic picture than the biblical texts, which show only vestiges of this systematization by comparison. We need to recognize that the entire divine family idea may have varied between Ugarit and other Late Bronze Age cultures in the Levant and the later Iron Age states of Israel and its neighbors. In other words, given the lack of evidence, it is difficult to be sure that the entire paradigm as I have laid it out in the preceding section remained intact in the societies of Israel and its neighbors. Second, with the passing of time, the names of the deities in Israel, as also among Israel's neighbors, also seem less and less proximate to the picture at Ugarit, as emphasized by Lemaire (1994). Third, I offer these schematas of levels to allow us a better sense of shifts in divinity within ancient Israel, but I would not pretend that these account for all of the available evidence, much less the considerable information that we do not know. Fourth, I believe that in fact the schematas overlapped historically and were not really stages as such. Fifth, I also imagine that multiple pantheons were always in dialogue and conflict throughout Israel's religious history. Egypt and Mesopotamia show multiple pantheons of deities in competition at various points over history. So, even if Israel and its neighbors had fewer deities in their pantheons compared to Egypt and Mesopotamia, we might still suppose that these varied in structure from shrine to shrine or from region to region.

Despite these limitations, I have represented the pantheons over the course of Israel's history in a rather linear manner, in order to help us see some of the complexity of Israel's configurations of divinity. For all its problems, this approach is intellectually superior to working with the old assumption of Israelite monotheism versus the polytheism of other ancient Near Eastern cultures. In view of these considerations, the best we can do is to identify the family language for Israel's divinities and to work with what that evidence provides.

The Pantheon of Premonarchic Israel

The four levels of the premonarchic pantheon in Israel may have looked like this:

Level 1: El and Asherah

Level 2: Baal, Astarte, Shahar, Shalim, Resheph, and Deber
Yahweh, the outsider from Edom/Midian/Paran/Seir/Sinai

Level 3: ?

Level 4: Messengers (angels) and servants

The name El in the word "Israel" suggests that it was this god and not Yahweh who was the original head of the divine household in Israel's earliest pantheon. Moreover, the pairing of El with "Breasts and Womb" in Genesis 49:25 sounds like El's consort, Asherah. The second level of divine children would seem from various later references to include Baal and Astarte, as well as Shahar (Isaiah 14:12, NRSV "Dawn"), and Shalim (in names, such as Abishalom/Absalom; see the discussion of Huffmon in Van der Toorn, Becking, and Van der Horst 1999, 755–57), as well as the goddess Astarte. We may suppose that given their place in Ugaritic religion and their later appearance in monarchic Israel (discussed shortly below), Resheph and Deber are probably level-two deities in this period. Baal is the god of Gideon's family (in Judges 6), and his name appears in proper names from inscriptions of this period (as observed by Hess 2003). Although later tradition would see Baal and other deities apart from Yahweh in early Israel as foreign gods, this interpretation of their background does not seem to be true. Despite this distortion in religious memory, it preserves at the same time a recollection of Baal as a god in the highlands of premonarchic Israel.

By contrast, Yahweh seems to derive from the southeast of the Israelite highlands in a region variously called Edom, Midian, Paran, Seir, and Sinai (Sinai//Seir//Paran, Deuteronomy 33:2; Seir//Edom and Sinai, Judges 5:4-5; Teman//Paran, Habakkuk 3:3; Sinai, Psalm 68:8, 17). Like Baal in the Ugaritic pantheon, Yahweh seems to be an outsider warrior-god who makes his way to the top of the pantheon. It is true that some early Israelite texts such as Judges 5 elevate Yahweh in a way that recalls the exaltation of Baal or Marduk, but such expressions do not alter at least the ceremonial status of the older level-one gods like El and Enki-Ea within the pantheon; they remain important figures. What is reflected by such praise of the level-two warrior-gods is their increasing importance, to the point of their somewhat overshadowing the older, level-one gods, at least in some texts. As a result, we hear nothing of El in many Ugaritic or biblical texts, as they exalt Baal or Yahweh, respectively.

We might go further and think that Yahweh's dominance in some early Israelite contexts was so great that placing him at the second level does not really do justice to his character or importance in early tribal Israel. This is, of course, the dominant view of the texts that represent Israel's past (for example, Judges 5). As we shall see shortly, however, El remains very much an identifiable figure in early Israel. So, despite the dominant representation of Yahweh in early Israel, this does not mean that the structure of the four levels was dramatically modified, only that the fulcrum point of power between the two levels hardly subordinated the second level to the first; instead, we see in the main gods of the first two levels a coordination of powers or expressions of authority in the world. This is true of El and Baal in the Ugaritic texts, and this seems to be the case for El Elyon and Yahweh in a number of biblical texts. This would nicely explain both the dominance of Yahweh in early Israel and the survival of the picture of El Elyon at the top of the pantheon, precisely the picture for Baal and El that we saw in the Ugaritic pantheon.

Moving to the third level, we have no such figures attested in this period. This may be because of the lack of evidence; after all, it is very fragmentary for early Israel. Or it may be that level 3 is not a full-scale level. Despite this problem, it may be preferable to retain level 3, since such specialized worker roles do emerge as needed in narratives. For example, there is "the senior servant" of Abraham's household in Genesis 24:2. Like Kothar in the Ugaritic texts, we have specialized craftsmen in building stories, for example, Bezalel and Oholiab in Exodus 35–36, and Hiram of Tyre in 1 Kings 7. Later, the figure of the *satan* emerges from the level-four divinities in a specialized, named role. So such special workers do emerge in various areas of specialization. Craftsmen, to be sure, are not the same as household workers, but it seems that they often work like household servants at the behest of the royal household. Level 4 figures are common in early Israel, primarily in the form of angelic figures. In this period, "angels" is simply a term for divine messengers, and as such they are divine.

To illustrate the situation in the top two levels in early Israel, we turn to two later biblical texts that enshrined this old idea. The first is one that presents Yahweh in an explicit divine council scene, but not as its head. This text is Psalm 82, which begins:

> God (elohim) *stands in the divine assembly/assembly of El* (el),
> *Among the divinities* (elohim) *He pronounces judgment.*

Here the figure of God, understood as Yahweh, takes his stand in the assembly. The name El was understood in the tradition—and perhaps at the time of the text's original composition as well—to be none other than Yahweh and not a separate god called El. As Parker (1995) has observed, however, the god who presides in the council customarily differs from the god who stands to speak. In other words, the poem implicitly distinguishes the presiding god who sits enthroned from the one who stands in the assembly. In fact, the position of sitting enthroned is the characteristic presentation of El in the Ugaritic texts, and it is considered typical of depictions of this god (for example, in *ANEP*, nos. 493, 826). The assembly in Psalm 82 consists of all the gods of the world, for all these other gods are condemned to death in verses 6-7:

> *I myself presumed that you are gods,*
> > *Sons of the Most High (Elyon),*
> *Yet like humans you will die,*
> > *And fall like any prince.*

A prophetic voice emerges in verse 8, calling on God to assume the role of judge of all the earth:

> *Arise, O God, judge the world;*
> > *For You inherit all the nations.*

Here Yahweh in effect is asked to assume the job of all gods to rule their nations in addition to Israel. Verse 6 addresses the gods as "the sons of Elyon" (NRSV "The Most High"), probably a title of El at an early point in biblical tradition as reflected by the threefold mention of El Elyon in Genesis 14:18-20. If this supposition is correct, Psalm 82 preserves a tradition that casts the god of Israel not in the role of the presiding god of the pantheon, but implicitly as one of the sons. Each of these sons has a different nation as his family inheritance and therefore serves as its ruler. Yet verse 8 calls on Yahweh to take over the traditional inheritance of all the other gods, thereby making not only Israel but all the world into the inheritance of Israel's God. Psalm 82 is a polemic directed against the old worldview, which would suggest that the older worldview retains some force for the author of Psalm 82.

    This family view of the divine arrangement of the world appears in a rather different setting in the versions of Deuteronomy 32:8, as preserved in the Greek translation called the Septuagint and in the Dead Sea Scrolls. As reviewed by Himbaza (2002), the reading "sons of Israel" in verse 8 is found in the traditional Hebrew text of Jewish tradition called the Masoretic text (MT for short), but the reading "sons of God," *bny 'lwhym*[, appears in one Dead Sea Scrolls manuscript of Deuteronomy from Cave Four (called 4QDeuteronomy^j). We have a similar reading "sons of Go[d]," *bny 'l*[, attested in another Cave Four manuscript of Deuteronomy (called 4QDeuteronomy^q). In addition, "sons of God" appears in the Septuagint as *huion theou* (with variants with "angels," *angelon*, sometimes added), which reflects the same reading in the two Dead Sea Scrolls manuscripts of Deuteronomy 32:8. The original text of verses 8-9 would then be translated:

When the Most High (Elyon) allotted peoples for inheritance,
when He divided up humanity,
He fixed the boundaries for peoples,
according to the number of the divine sons:
For Yahweh's portion is his people,
Jacob His own inheritance.

The author of this poem, with the reading "number of divine sons," probably understood Most High (Elyon) and Yahweh to be one and the same god, the god of Israel. For the poem goes on to refer to the other gods as "no-gods" (v. 17, NRSV "not God") and to describe Yahweh as the only god (v. 39). It is clear that for this author there really are no other gods. It would seem that for the author of Deuteronomy 32, the old worldview in verses 8-9 serves as a relatively neutral backdrop to tell the story of how Yahweh came to be the god of Israel (critically discussed by Sanders 1996). In using the idea of divine governance in verses 8-9 as backdrop, however, the author also preserves the older, traditional idea of divine family and council. As Parker notes (1995), the older tradition underlying verses 8-9 involves not one but two divine levels of divine figures, one El Elyon, as he is called in Genesis 14:19, 20 (NRSV "God Most High"), and the other his divine children who reign over the nations of the world, and within the structure Yahweh is the patron god of Israel.

Scholars have generally argued that the transmitters of the traditional Hebrew text (MT) recognized this polytheistic worldview in Deuteronomy 32:8-9 and changed the older reading. For the MT shows not "divine sons" *(bene elohim)* as reflected in the Greek and the Dead Sea Scrolls, but "sons of Israel" *(bene yisrael).* Scholars have understood the MT here as an "anti-polytheistic" alteration (Tov 2001, 269). A less deliberate theological intention has also been entertained by Himbaza (2002), who sees a different tradition of interpretation rather than censorship at work in the MT of Deuteronomy 32:8. Yet a similar change can be detected in Deuteronomy 32:43, with MT reading "nations" versus Septuagint "gods" and Dead Sea Scrolls "sons of the gods" (as discussed in Fishbane 2003), and this contrast too suggests a deliberate shift from the polytheistic setting of the poem to a more generic presentation. In any case, the older tradition of Israelite polytheism has been submerged, compared to the more palatable view expressed in the MT. The texts of Deuteronomy 32:8 in the Septuagint and the Dead Sea Scrolls show an old form of Israelite polytheism: although it clearly focuses on the central importance of Yahweh for Israel within the larger scheme of the world, this scheme provides a place for the other gods of the nations of the world.

Moreover, even if this text is mute about the god who presides over the divine assembly, it maintains a place for a god who was originally not Yahweh. Of course, the author of the poem as well as later tradition could identify the figure of Elyon ("Most High" in many translations) with Yahweh, just as many scholars have done. However, Elyon seems to denote originally the figure of El Elyon (Genesis 14:19, 20), presider par excellence not only at Ugarit but also in Psalm 82. To be clear, I am not suggesting that the two poems themselves date to the premonarchic period, but that they display traditional ideas that seem to have been operative in early Israel. In rejecting the old worldview, it is evident that the two poems belong to a later time, perhaps the eighth or seventh century, and possibly later.

One could speculate further and suggest that given the prominence of the title El Elyon in a passage associated later with Jerusalem, namely, Genesis 14, one might infer that this worldview was at home in particular in the Jerusalemite tradition. Given the northern background or tradition often attributed to Deuteronomy, however, one might argue that despite the reformatting of this world theology in Deuteronomy 32, it was operative prior to the book of Deuteronomy also in the northern kingdom. Although the idea of the four levels of the divine household predated the monarchy, the application of the four levels to the nations of the world in this world theology would have made particularly good sense in the monarchic period, as the divine family is nicely grafted to the world political situation. So perhaps this world theology should be seen in both the northern and southern kingdoms of Israel in the period from the tenth century through the eighth century. In any case, the important point to underscore here is that despite their rather different purposes and forms, both Deuteronomy 32 and Psalm 82 show an older world theology that looks quite different from Israel's later monotheism of the seventh and sixth centuries.

The Pantheon of Early Monarchic Israel

The first half of the monarchy shows a shift toward Yahweh-El as the head god:

Level 1: Yahweh-El, the king of the Gods, and his consort, Asherah

Level 2: Sun, moon, and the host of heaven

Level 3: ?

Level 4: Messengers (angels), Resheph, and Deber

Yahweh and El were likely identified at an early point in the monarchy, if not earlier in many parts of ancient Israel. The poetic parallelism of Yahweh and El in the early poems of the Balaam oracles (Numbers 23–24) suggests a strong Transjordanian tradition that identified the originally separate gods, El and Yahweh (as shown most penetratingly by Levine 2000). Similarly, the description of Yahweh in 1 Samuel 1–3, which tells the story of Elkanah and his wife, Hannah, at the shrine of Shiloh, is shot through with El names (like El-kanah and Samu-el) as well as the tradition of El's tent-shrine, his mode of revelation in dreams, and his role as helper in cases of infertility (as insightfully studied by Seow 1989). In the divine council scene in 1 Kings 22:19, Yahweh is surrounded by the heavenly host, just like El in the Ugaritic texts. It is evident in 1 Kings 22:19 that Yahweh has the place of presider formerly held by El. It is also evident from texts such as Isaiah's vision of Yahweh surrounded by the seraphim (Isaiah 6) that Yahweh assumed the position of presider by this time (the early date of the traditions of this chapter have been defended by Hartenstein 1997).

What is at work at this stage is not a loss of the second level of a pantheon headed by Yahweh. Instead, it is more likely that the collapse of the first and second levels in the early Israelite pantheon was caused by an identification of El, the head of this pantheon, with Yahweh, formerly a member of its second tier. Now Yahweh-El was the head of the top level, which included the military roles and power that he held as a leading member of the second tier in the premonarchic Israelite pantheon. At first glance, this identification of Yahweh-El as a single figure seems to run counter to our discussion of Deuteronomy 32 and Psalm 82, which distinguish, or assume the distinction between, El and Yahweh. What seems to have been the case is that the older idea of El Elyon and the other gods of the world theology discussed in the preceding section was modified during the early monarchy in contexts where El and Yahweh were seen as Yahweh-El, yet rejected in other contexts (Psalm 82), and probably used for purposes of rhetorical presentation in still other contexts (such as Deuteronomy 32). It is unlikely that El Elyon was important in the state religion in this period. In contrast, it is possible, perhaps even likely in view of the presentation in the family stories in Genesis, that either El or Yahweh in his El characteristics enjoyed a greater devotion in family religion during the early monarchy.

As a result of this identification, it would seem that Yahweh-El gained Asherah as his spouse, as Olyan (1988) has argued convincingly. Earlier El had Asherah as a consort in the Ugaritic texts. So it would make sense that as a result of the identification of Yahweh and El, the divine couple, Yahweh and Asherah, stood at the top of the Judean pantheon. The historical reconstruction tracing Asherah the goddess in the Ugaritic texts down to asherah the symbol in ancient Israel has been discussed and debated since the mid-1980s, as reflected by the range of views in Becking et al. (2001), Dietrich and Klopfenstein (1994), Olyan (1988), Hadley (2000), and Zevit (2001). Many scholars believe that the asherah in the Jerusalem Temple was none other than the symbol of the goddess (2 Kings 17:16), either a tree or wooden pole (NRSV "sacred pole"), and that the image was hers ("the image of the asherah/Asherah," 2 Kings 21:7). According to this scholarly view,

Asherah was a goddess venerated in the Jerusalem Temple of Yahweh and therefore she was regarded as his consort.

To this evidence scholars would add the eighth-century inscriptions from
Kuntillet Ajrud and Khirbet el-Qom that mention *lyhwh wl'shrth*. Some commentators regard the words here as "to Yahweh and to his Asherah," with the name of
the goddess. Others see the second word as "and to his asherah," since divine
names generally do not take a pronominal suffix. With this reading, the symbol
could represent the goddess. As an alternative, the symbol is said to be "his," in
other words, Yahweh's (cf. Zevit [2001, 403]), and so perhaps the symbol no
longer referred to the goddess as such and by this time belonged to the repertoire
of symbols of Yahweh. How this process would have worked is not entirely clear.
Perhaps Yahweh and Asherah were once considered consorts, but this association
had somehow diminished by the time of the Kuntillet Ajrud inscription. (This is
the view I take of the inscription, since it provides the closest reading of the grammar.) Still other scholars believe that the inscription reflects Phoenician
influence. They take the word to mean "and to his shrine," in accordance with
Phoenician; the same interpretation may apply to the newer appearances of this
word in inscriptions from the site of Tel Miqne, ancient Ekron.

I mention this diversity of views to indicate that despite the dominance of the
first view in the American scene, scholarly consensus on this question has not
been met. In any case, the bulk of scholars who comment on these inscriptions'
references to asherah use them to support the idea that Yahweh and Asherah were
a divine couple in ancient Israel and Judah. Indeed, prophetic condemnations are
often taken as evidence for such worship; after all, so goes the reasoning, why
condemn something unless it is a problem? Yet it is possible that while the two
were a couple in early Israel, perhaps by this time the goddess was no longer associated with the symbol. If so, Israelite ditheism at the top tier of the pantheon
under the name of Asherah may not have lasted this long. Even if this were the
case, however, references to the Queen of Heaven in Jeremiah 7 and 44 would
suggest the reassertion of a major goddess in late-monarchic Israel.

As a result of the identification of Yahweh and El, the astral family of El was
associated with Yahweh-El. This astral group appears with Yahweh in 1 Kings 22:19.
The prophet Micaiah ben Imlah says of his vision: "I saw Yahweh sitting on His
throne, and all the host of heaven was standing in attendance before Him at His
right and at His left." The later text of Job 38:6-7 may reflect a witness to this old
notion of the heavenly hosts with God:

> *Who set its cornerstone*
> *when the morning stars* (kokebe boqer) *sang together,*
> *and all the divine beings* (kol bene elohim) *shouted for joy?*

In this verse, Yahweh the creator-god (like old El) asks Job if he was present when Yahweh set the cornerstone of the world's foundations, an ancient event celebrated by the divine beings, here specified as stars. In this passage, the morning stars clearly correspond by poetic parallelism to the "divine beings," *bene elohim.* This is similar to the poetic parallelism between "stars" and "children of El" that we noted earlier in the Ugaritic texts (*CAT* 1.10 I 3-4).

The old astral association apparently lies also behind the polemic against the king of Babylon in Isaiah 14:12-13. The king is accused of attempting to ascend into heaven and to exalt his throne "above the stars of El" (NRSV "above the stars of God"). The king is called by the name Shahar (Dawn), one of the astral gods of the Ugaritic and early Israelite pantheon. The passage seems to allude to an old but otherwise unknown story of Shahar's unsuccessful bid for power in the heavenly pantheon. This story would become the basis for the later story of the battle in heaven between the angelic forces of God and the fallen angels, but its polytheistic background would be forgotten. Dawn (Shahar) also appears as an element in Hebrew proper names. Dusk (Shalem) is attested sporadically in biblical literature, for example, in the form of proper names such as Abishalom/Absalom. Given their earlier and later references to them as deities, the sun and moon likely continued as deities at this stage of Israelite religion as well. In sum, the old idea of the astral family, formerly connected with El, continued into Israelite religion under Yahweh-El.

One god traditionally belonging to this second level may have been rejected in Israel because of the threat that he may have posed to Yahweh-El. The conflict with Baal drives the cycle of stories in 1 Kings 17–19. With these stories, we may see what seems to be the first instance of the Israelite rejection of another deity, which may be viewed also as a rejection of what the eminent Egyptologist Jan Assmann (1997, 3, 28, 44–54; see 1990) calls the "translatibility" of divinity. In the ancient world, deities of various nations were identified with one another. Sometimes, this worldview was captured in scribal lists. For example, one tablet from Ugarit has four columns of deities (from four different cultures) equated with one another. In other instances, we see treaties listing deities of the treaty partners who would recognize the validity of one another's gods. In the international world, various empires and states understood that different deities could be identified with one another. Within Israel, we see at least toleration for Baal, as shown by the element "Baal" in personal names alongside names with Yahweh in inscriptions known as the Samaria Ostraca (ca. 770s). It is even possible that King Ahab and other Israelites accepted the translatability of Israelite Yahweh-El and Phoenician Baal, as they were both storm-gods. It would seem, however, that the tradition enshrined in the Elijah stories rejected this translatability of Yahweh-El with Baal. This is not to be confused with a general rejection of foreign deities, a feature that will emerge in the late monarchy. The rejection of Baal was seen as a precedent for this later shift.

In the third level of the pantheon, no particular figure comes to the fore in the texts that we have. The fourth level continues the usual figures of messenger-deities (angels). Yet, in addition, we have an important and interesting presentation of Resheph and Deber in Habakkuk 3:5. These two figures are known as gods in Ugaritic literature. In Habakkuk 3, which may be dated to the monarchy (see "your anointed" mentioned in v. 13), we see the two old gods as two members of the divine military troops accompanying God:

> God comes from Teman,
>> the Holy One from Mount Paran.
> His majesty covers the heavens,
>> his splendor fills the earth.
> For it is a brilliant light,
>> with his rays (emanating) from his hand,
>> and there his strength . . .
> Before him goes Deber [NRSV "pestilence"],
>> and Resheph [NRSV "plague"] follows at his feet. (3:3-5)

In this passage, God proceeds in battle, with Deber and Resheph marching along. In Ugaritic literature, these gods belong clearly to the second level, but here in Habakkuk 3 they have been subordinated to the Israelite head god. In this context, they function in a fourth-level capacity held by the military troops who belong to second-level deities. With Yahweh-El as the only main god, other specifically named gods (perhaps apart from the celestial deities) seem to make their way down the divine hierarchy to level four. If this is correct, it is important because it shows the process leading to the later demotion of Israelite level-two deities to the fourth level, which we will discuss shortly.

Israelite Pantheons in Conflict in the Late Monarchy

Toward the end of the monarchy, we see at least two models of the pantheon in conflict. The first resembles the preceding model of the early monarchy:

Level 1: Yahweh-El and Asherah and/or the Queen of Heaven

Level 2: Sun, moon, and stars

Level 3: ?

Level 4: Messengers (angels) and servants

According to this model, Asherah was represented by her symbol (NRSV "sacred pole") in 2 Kings 21:3 and her "carved image" (NRSV) in 2 Kings 21:7 (see also "the sacred pole" in 18:4). The references to the Queen of Heaven in Jeremiah 7 and 44 (possibly under Mesopotamian influence) further suggest that Yahweh-El retained his consort in some circles. As shown by Halpern (1987), Zephaniah 1:5 also provides evidence for the association of the host of heaven with the cult of Yahweh. Second Kings 21:5 mentions Manasseh's construction of "altars for all the host of heaven in the two courts in the house of Yahweh." The tour of Temple idolatry in Ezekiel 8–10 might include a reference to an image of the goddess in the house of the god (8:5), as well as solar worship of some sort (8:14).

In contrast, the Israelite pantheon imagined by Deuteronomy and perhaps championed during the late monarchy of Josiah looks considerably different:

Level 1: Yahweh-El

Level 2: Zero

Level 3: "The *satan*" (Job 1–2; Zechariah 3)

Level 4: Messengers (angels) and servants

At the highest level of the pantheon, the only deity remaining is Yahweh. As a result, the head of the gods becomes tantamount to the godhead. Asherah has been demoted; her symbol perhaps by this time had become part of the repertoire of the Yahwistic cult, and even then it is rejected (so 2 Kings 18:4; 21:3, 7). The ditheism of Yahweh and Asherah at the top of the household was opposed by some prophetic and Deuteronomistic critics from the eighth century onward and perhaps transmuted into more acceptable forms, such as personified Wisdom. Like the asherah, Wisdom is rendered as a tree in Proverbs 3:18: "She is a tree of life to those who grasp her." The verse goes on with its description of female Wisdom, perhaps with a wordplay on the word *asherah,* "and the one who holds her is happy." The word for "happy" *(meushar)* shares most of the same basic consonants with the word *asherah* (as pointed out to me by Anthony Ceresko in a personal communication).

At the second tier, the old astral divinities in Israelite religion, the "sun, moon, and stars," are criticized within the cult of Yahweh (2 Kings 23). As noted, this celestial devotion was traditional in ancient Israel, but within this new pantheon it is rejected. It is possible that the criticism of the astral deities was generated by a perceived threat of the Neo-Assyrian astral cult during the Iron II period, as suggested by the increase in astral symbolism at this time (noted by Keel and Uehlinger 1998). A perception of a new threat may have inspired some in Israel to turn against older deities who would have been traditional and indigenous to Israel. We can see this change not only with astral deities, but also from references to divinities such as "the Tammuz" (Ezekiel 8:14). This figure was Mesopotamian in origin, and so a perceived threat from Assyrian influences was not without foundation. We can see a similar importation of Assyrian influence in this period in the form of the Queen of Heaven. As we observed in chapter 2, this otherwise unnamed goddess was venerated by Judeans, according to Jeremiah 7 and 44. The Assyrian influence is evident in the "cakes for the Queen of Heaven" (Jeremiah 7: 18; see also 44:19). These cakes are called *kawwanim*, which has been long recognized as an Akkadian loanword into Hebrew. In Akkadian the word is used of the cakes for the goddess Ishtar. It is evident that this goddess influenced the figure of the Queen of Heaven in Judah. Indeed, there may have been even an identification of this Mesopotamian goddess with an indigenous goddess such as Astarte. If so, many Judeans may have accepted the translatability of their local goddess with an Assyrian goddess.

In these cases we can detect Assyrian influence, and it may have been this very influence that inspired a reaction in late-monarchic Judah against other deities more broadly, even those with a long history in Israel. At this crucial juncture in Israel's religious history, some in Israel rejected translatability with such clear foreign influence. So they rejected foreign deities. In addition, they turned against older traditional deities, apart from Yahweh. Interestingly, deities of the old second level with specific names would also be rejected, while some of the features associated with them, such as the idea of the divine council, would continue.

Signs of this broad shift against other deities are evident in the new divine hierarchy, especially at the lowest level of the Israelite pantheon. As the Ugaritic texts show, the lowest tier involved a number of deities who served in a variety of menial capacities. A common task for such gods was the job of messenger, the literal meaning of the Greek *angelos,* from which the English word "angel" derives. As with the middle levels, this tier went through a change in perspective in Israel. The old "divine sons" (*bene elim,* Psalm 29:1), formerly understood as level-two deities, survived in the form of "divine sons" (*bene haelohim,* Job 1:6; NRSV "heavenly beings") and "holy ones" (*qedoshim,* Zechariah 14:5), but it would appear that they are understood as angels, no longer "sons" in any real sense. With the exception of Yahweh, who occupies the top level, the old second tier is apparently identified with the fourth. This shift from the second level to the fourth is reflected in how the old number of seventy gods found in the Ugaritic texts survived in the later Jewish notion of the seventy angels, one for each of the world's putative seventy peoples (*1 Enoch* 89:59; 90:22-25; the Jewish Aramaic translation of the Torah known as *Targum Pseudo-Jonathan* to Deuteronomy 32:8; Babylonian Talmud *Shabbat* 88b; Babylonian Talmud *Sukkah* 55). These are powers that act in the name of their patron god and give thanks to the power of that deity.

It is important to observe that angels are not regarded in later tradition as independent gods. The Dead Sea Scrolls frequently refer to angelic powers as *elim,* literally, "gods," but in the wake of the earlier telescoping of the pantheon and the collapse of its middle tiers, this word probably conveyed a notion of heavenly powers (under the One Power) rather than full-fledged deities. So when one of the hymns from the Dead Sea Scrolls (the *Hodayot,* 1QH 7:28) asks in the same words as Exodus 15:11, "who is like You among the gods?" the question does not carry the same freight; it has lost its earlier polytheistic context.

The old second level went through a further development. As just noted, the conflation of the second and fourth levels led to an identification of second-level divinities as fourth-level angels. Additionally, in later apocalyptic literature these angels exercise the kind of great power and reflect the sort of high status formerly associated with the old second level. Some angels display such great power that they seem to be just below the level of the one God of the top level; they hardly seem to be menial fourth-level divinities. Instead, they sometimes manifest power that places them close to the heavenly throne, and they receive personal names to a degree not seen in earlier presentations of angels, perhaps also a sign of their exaltation.

An extraordinary elevation of some angelic figures can be seen in the discussion in Segal (1997) and in Hurtado (2003). Particularly striking in Segal's account is the angelic figure Metatron, called "the Lesser YHWH," in *3 (Hebrew) Enoch,* which also describes his position on a throne alongside God (one might also compare the figure in the Babylonian Talmud *Hagigah* 15a and *Sanhedrin* 38b). To my mind, this figure appears to reflect the special status held earlier by the angel Michael, himself a possible echo in role and status to the old god Baal in relation to El in the Ugaritic texts. That angels in later periods were exalted along the lines of the old second-level gods can be seen also in the application of the old myth of the fall of Shahar in Isaiah 14 that we saw above. This passage alludes to the attempt of a second-level deity to gain divine kingship; with this attempt unsuccessful, the god is expelled from heaven. We seem to see the vestiges of a parallel myth in Genesis 6:1-4. This mythic pattern, especially in Isaiah 14, later became the model for the story of the battle in heaven between God's angelic forces and the rebellious fallen angels cast into the underworld. This story is known from New Testament references to the fall of Lucifer in Luke 10:18 and 2 Peter 2:4, and the heavenly battle in Revelation 12:7-9.

It is within this context that we can better understand the transformation of the *satan* from a divine adversarial angel belonging to the divine children (*bene haelohim* in Job 1–2) into a figure of evil, as he is known from later Jewish literature (*Jubilees* 23:29; *Assumption of Moses* 10:1), including the New Testament (for example, Luke 11:15-19 paralleled in Matthew 12:24-27 and Mark 3:22-23, 26). In the Hebrew Bible, the term is not a name but a title that apparently means "adversary" in a political and military sense or "accuser" in a legal sense. As shown by Day (1988), the *satan* seems to begin as a characterization of hostile humans (1 Samuel 29:4; 1 Kings 5:4 [v. 19 in Hebrew]), an adversarial role later attributed to level-four divinities. In Numbers 22:22-35 we see an angel function-ing as *satan* doing God's bidding in blocking the path of Balaam riding on his ass; the animal can see the *satan,* but Balaam cannot, evidently making a mockery of the prophet. By the time we get to Zechariah 3:2, the *satan* has a heavenly role: in the divine council, he stands beside God to accuse the high priest Joshua, but the *satan* is rebuked, as God champions Joshua. In the book of Job, the *satan* is the prosecuting attorney of the divine council, who has the job of testing Job's piety. A fourth biblical reference to *satan,* in 1 Chronicles 21:1, attributes divine anger to *satan* instead of God, as found in the earlier source text, 2 Samuel 24. This substi-tution is often said to be motivated by a desire to displace the responsibility for divine anger from God to *satan.* In this case, the *satan* here seems more like the angelic *satan* figure of Numbers 22.

From Zechariah and Job 1–2, we might say that the *satan* serves as a special worker within the divine household and therefore he may be assigned to level three (as suggested by Lowell Handy [1994]). Broadly speaking, it would seem that *satan*/the *satan* figures function to express divine judgment while the God who commissions them provides mercy and kindness, for example, to Job and to the priest Joshua. In these texts, the figure of (the) *satan* may be seen as express-ing the negative divine disposition toward humans within the godhead, while the figure of God expresses within the godhead the positive divine disposition of mercy and generosity toward humans. It is also evident that the *satan* figure is subordinate to God and ultimately derives his reality from God. In later Jewish literature, this figure is externalized from the godhead, becoming a figure dwelling not in heaven with the divine council but in the underworld. Moreover, this figure now threatens humans independent of the divine will. A prayer in the Dead Sea Scrolls (the Cave 11 Psalms scroll, col. 19, line 15) asks God: "do not let Satan have power over me." This request compares to the last line of the Lord's Prayer, also called "the Our Father": "and deliver us not into the power of the evil one."

The question is why this transformation of the *satan* from heavenly to hellish figure took place. I would like to offer a simple guess (compare the detailed sur-vey by Koch 1994). Before the postexilic period, the universe was already under-stood as a three-level construction consisting of heaven, earth, and underworld. Different divinities live in heaven and the underworld, reflected in the categories of "center" and "beyond the periphery" introduced at the outset of this chapter. As we saw, the level-two figures compete with one another in the zone of earth. In the postexilic period, this construction of the world included human afterlife, perhaps due to influence from other cultures (probed in an interesting book by Wright [2000]). Earlier all humans with the possible exception of royalty went to the underworld (biblical Sheol), a shadowy realm for the deceased. In the Hel-lenistic and Roman periods, we see the idea of people going to either heaven, a place of eternal blessing, or hell, now viewed as a place of terrible punishment. Resurrection to heaven or condemnation to the underworld became a new paradigm for postmortal existence, instead of the shadowy existence in Sheol. With this shift came divine personnel to rule this nether realm. The old god of Death, denied or muted in the new monotheistic conceptualization of Israel, did not continue in his capacity as ruler of the underworld. It is possible that the *satan* assumes the old power of the god of Death, but not so much with the power to kill (Death's old special function), but with the role of punishing the wicked after death. The *satan*, already regarded as a legal or political adversary, became a cosmic adversary, perhaps due to influence from or identification with comparable figures from the Persian or Greco-Roman context. For example, *satan* is identified or synonymous with the "devil" (as in the Targum to Job 3). In other words, *satan* became the personified cosmic principle of opposition to the divine will and human life. Even so, for all his cosmic malevolence, this *satan* depends ultimately on the good reality sustained by God. Take God out of the system, and the figure of *satan*, however powerful he may seem, has no meaning or reality. Evil is ultimately dependent on good.

All in all, the four levels of the new Judean pantheon show significant lines of continuity with earlier and contemporary pantheons of Israel. With its middle tiers removed, the new Judean pantheon consisted of the one omnipotent God and the lower divinities. In the newly configured heaven, there were lesser powers subordinate to this one supreme Deity, and their power ultimately derived from this "One Power." This new reduced Judean pantheon of the late monarchy was essentially monotheistic in its view of reality. With changes in the four levels of the Judean pantheon as backdrop, we may now turn our attention to the conditions that shaped Judean monotheism in the seventh and sixth centuries.

Monotheism: From Crises to New Religious Vision

Israel's monotheism, considered one of the major hallmarks of biblical religion, represents a profound response to the external threat of Mesopotamian empires and the internal challenge of social deterioration. The looming threat of Assyria undermined the world theology traditional to monarchic Israel. The world theology was premised on the correlation of divine and human kings: as long as human kings were in power, it was a sign of divine power and protection. By ancient Near Eastern standards, however, the demise of a nation could also signal the impotency of its patron god. When the northern kingdom of Israel fell, it could seem that the patron god of the north might be correspondingly powerless. An alternative Near Eastern response, namely, that the patron god was punishing his kingdom, was advanced in the wake of the north's fall. However, the southern kingdom of Judah would have a more difficult time when it came to their own captivity in 587–586; many Judeans would question whether God was powerless.

To meet the challenge of Assyria as an empire, there was a reconceptualization of Israel's worldview. In Assyria's religious self-understanding, its own god, Ashur, was viewed as a divine emperor over all the gods of the other nations. As the god Ashur was the same name as Assyria, Ashur even embodies the imperial ideology of the Assyrianization of the world (see Holloway 2002). Israel would mimic this view for its own god, but with a most crucial difference: the power of its supergod would not be viewed as corresponding to the power of its king. Contrary to the standard way of looking at reality at this time, the massive power of Yahweh was seen in opposite terms, compared to the powerlessness of Judah. This revised worldview drew the opposite conclusion for Judah's world enemy. In the emerging view of Judah's monotheistic proponents, Mesopotamia's massive power was viewed as standing in inverse proportion to the power of its gods. As Mesopotamia's earthly power was massively increasing, the power of its gods was viewed as decreasing, to the point of becoming nothing. The new picture can be compared to the stock market: as Judah's stock tumbled to virtually nothing, dropping through the floor, Yahweh's climbed to the very top; and correspondingly, Assyria's stock shot through the ceiling, but its deities' stock fell precipitously and crashed. In short, the other gods were now viewed as nothing. The inversion of earthly and heavenly powers led to a new vision of a single divine reality who directed the destinies of both powerless Judah and powerful Mesopotamia.

In addition to this external shift of conditions, internal changes within Judean society also contributed to the emergence of a monotheistic worldview. Through the eighth century, Israel's world theology was based on the notion of the divine family. Up to this point, the primary basis for social identity in Israel was the family. Indeed, in a society where the highest form of social identification was the family, the notion of the divine family made considerable sense as a metaphor for divinity. However, the eighth century began to see a significant change in the status of the family as the primary basis for social identity. With the demise of the north, the families there lost their ties to their family lands, due to either flight to the south or captivity to Assyria. The Assyrian invasion of 701 marked a further erosion of the family, as several thousand inhabitants went into captivity (Sennnacherib boasts 200,150!), what we characterized in chapter 2 as Judah's first captivity or exile. It would seem that family identity was deteriorating as the primary expression of social identity (a development probed in important works by Halpern 1991, 1996 and Schloen 2001).

We may see a manifestation of this development in the notion that children are no longer responsible for the sins of their parents (Jeremiah 31:29-30; Ezekiel 18; 33:12-20; Deuteronomy 24:16). A culture with diminished lineages, one less embedded in traditional family patrimonies due to societal changes in the eighth to sixth centuries, might be more predisposed both to hold to individual human accountability for human behavior and to see an individual deity accountable for the cosmos. In other words, an individual God made more sense in Israel after the eighth century, while in earlier times a divine family would have more sense.

Between foreign and domestic challenges, we see the backdrop for the development of Judean monotheism. Monotheism was an interpretation of Israel's reality in light of developments in the eighth through the sixth centuries. It took Israel's traditions and monolatrous practice and offered a new vision of the God informed by the challenges of these times. This was a response at once revolutionary in its interpretation of the world yet evolutionary in forging this new view out of older, traditional components. This approach differs strongly from the one taken by Assmann (1997), who views biblical monotheism as revolutionary. Moreover, Assmann does not situate biblical monotheism within its historical and cultural context in Israel. As I hope this chapter demonstrates, such contextualization is absolutely necessary for understanding monotheism in Israel. Such contextualization allows us to see the lines of continuity and change that issue in biblical monotheism, as it was remembered in the Bible.

Given these cultural and historical conditions that I have laid out for Israel's monotheism, we might have expected monotheism to be a response during the seventh and sixth centuries not only in Israel, but also among some of its neighbors, such as Ammon, Moab, and Edom. At this point, we cannot fully answer the question why monotheism did not develop in these areas, since too little is known about the situation within these cultures in this period or during subsequent periods. We have no Ammonite, Moabite, or Edomite Bible. However, this very lack may point to a crucial factor for Israel's singular monotheism: the ongoing production of major religious texts in Israel following the loss of kingship and other institutions in the wake of the Babylonian conquest. The articulation of Israelite identity in connection with its one deity represented a major cultural project of exilic and postexilic Israel.

Indeed, the story of Israel's monotheism does not end simply with the sixth century. Israel's deity ends up championing the ideals of the social segments most responsible for its construction in the sixth century and later. For example, the priestly ideals of avoiding the impurity of death and sexual relations would tend to accent a holy god, disconnected from the realm of death and lacking in sexual relations. Holier than the holy of holies, this god would model the ideal for priests, and even the priestly people of Israel. The Deuteronomistic ideal of faithful observance of the Torah focuses on the deity as the divine voice that issues Torah. Otherwise, this invisible voice remains virtually unknown and unapproachable, except through observance and prayer. The postexilic elaboration of monotheism extends further, to the ongoing production of large religious texts about the past that seem to help generate and modify the idea of a single deity in the universe. As noted at the end of chapter 2, the construction of deity at this point was not limited to number, but it also involves its configuration: a single text of this sort tends to channel all major divine roles to this deity. Israel's master narrative about the past, namely, Genesis through Kings, helps to produce a master god.

I do not mean to suggest that the genre of biblical narrative itself represents a claim of monotheism. This idea has been argued in various forms for decades. It is an argument that asserts that the biblical narrative is the genre of monotheism, while ancient Near Eastern myths constitute the genre for polytheism. Many critics, such as Fishbane (2003), do not find this correlation between genre and divinity compelling. I am trying to suggest a rather different point. I would see the construction of a long time line from Genesis through Kings with one main divine protagonist as a postexilic claim about the continuity of monotheism throughout Israel's past. In the postexilic context, one of the most important assertions of monotheism lies in the construction of the first half of the canonical Hebrew Bible, the Torah and the Historical Books.

I want to explain this point, but before I do, let me say a word about the date of the Pentateuch and the Historical Books (or, as they are known in Jewish tradition, the Torah and the Former Prophets). I do not think it anachronistic to suppose that some form of these works had been achieved at least by around 198 B.C.E., the time of Ben Sira, and I would be inclined to believe that this was already a project in some form by the end of the Persian period (ca. 333 B.C.E.). Recent text-critical studies have questioned such assumptions, especially given the complexity of the situation in the Dead Sea Scrolls and recent reassessments of the dates of the Septuagint, in particular the prophetic books and the writings. Still, based on the internal evidence of the Torah and the Historical Books, I see little reason to doubt that some form of their construction as a connected narrative work had been achieved by the end of the Persian period; certainly it was achieved by the time of Ben Sira. Through many social segments and political forces at work in the production of biblical works, their editorial alterations, and their transmission, the text as a whole ended up presenting a linear time line from the first humans to the last king of Judah. If one were to add Ezra–Nehemiah–1 and 2 Chronicles as a further segment in this narrative chain, we would have to say that the overall time line presents some jumps in time. However, it still seems intended to provide a picture down through the time of Ezra and Nehemiah, with 1 and 2 Chronicles doubling back and recapitulating the narrative of Genesis–Kings. With or without the postexilic works of Ezra and Nehemiah, we have a long narrative line. This narrative line presents a continuity of Israel's past experience; or we might say that in this presentation, it also makes a claim about continuity of experience and identity from the beginning of Israel down to these postexilic writings.

This claim extends to the nature of Israel's deity as presented in the biblical time line. Although this narrative line was constructed out of widely varying understandings of the divine, the single line offers the idea of a single main deity for Israel over the course of its historical experience. Polytheism was pushed to the shadows (Genesis 49:25) or denied (MT Deuteronomy 32:8-9) or reinterpreted (Psalm 82), but such individual verses seemed hardly significant in the face of the dominant presentations of Torah and Temple, with their monotheistic divinity. The singular godhead, as refined in the dominant priestly and Deuteronomistic traditions, was derived from the earlier head god, and then it was read back and superimposed onto older presentations of the head god preserved in the Bible. Those involved in reading, reinterpreting, and rewriting older scriptural texts within the postexilic period came to see the older expressions of the head god in these texts as little different from their own ideas of the godhead. The great narrative line of the Law and the Prophets offers in itself a statement of monotheism. It is clear at various points that this is a constructed continuity, not simply a presentation of continuity. For example, Exodus 6:2-3 seems very aware that the patriarchs did not know the deity by the name that the priestly tradition associated with the call of Moses. Attributing or modifying the titles of other deities for the Israelite deity likewise issued in a deity who represented what all of these other deities were and did without being like them or without them having any genuine reality. The construction of the great text in turn offered the specifically Israelite vision of the monotheistic godhead.

From this discussion, it seems that monotheism in its various understandings over the course of the Bible is an interpretive lens through which older religious notions are refracted and reinterpreted. Accordingly, monotheism is part of the larger interpretive enterprise evident in the religious texts of the Bible. It is shaped to different settings and messages found across a variety of biblical books. As a result, monotheism is not in itself a system or an idea divorced from larger religious beliefs or understandings; it is an interpretation of reality that in turn further shaped other aspects of Israel's worldview. In the next chapter, we briefly revisit the development of the Judean pantheon's four levels and monotheism. We will see how Israel's collective memory and amnesia helped to generate the monotheistic vision of the Bible out of the older Israelite polytheistic worldview and then to interpret vestiges of the older Israelite polytheistic worldview in light of the new monotheistic vision.

The Formation of Israel's Concepts of God:

Collective Memory and Amnesia in the Bible

Time past and time future
What might have been and what has been
Point to one end, which is always present.
—T. S. Eliot, *Four Quartets*

Introduction

At the outset of chapter 1, I raised the question about whether biblical narratives about the past should be regarded as "history." Until relatively recently, biblical books about Israel's past such as Joshua, Judges, 1–2 Samuel, and 1–2 Kings have been regarded as history. Lately, it has become clear that history constitutes a limited and sometimes problematic category when it is applied to these biblical works that narrate the past, and other proposals have been made. Since around 1990, innumerable publications have been authored by scholars advocating what has been characterized as a so-called minimalist view of the Bible's history, questioning the historical value of the Bible or the dating of its "historical-looking" materials. In their hands, the Bible and its "historical-looking" claims are treated as myths. The united monarchy and the exile are taken as figments of biblical imagination, and their perpetuation in the scholarly literature is regarded as an uncritical parroting on the part of biblical scholars. In the wake of this attack on the Bible's historicity, others scholars have turned to defend it. For example, Dever (2001) has reviewed the "minimalist" literature in quite some detail and with no little invective of his own. Dever is particular defends the Bible's historicity at nearly every turn.

The presentations by the "minimalists" and their opponents tend to crash on one side or the other on the question of historicity. In general, the "minimalists" tend to dismiss or reduce the Bible's historicity (or most of it), whenever its parts show a later redaction, or when the material in the biblical book is arguably mythic or legendary in content, or when the books do not show features that can anchor a dating. These writers sometimes claim to allow the possibility of earlier tradition being embedded in texts of the Bible, and, on the face of it, this is a reasonable-sounding position. However, the problem is that such claims about earlier tradition are rarely taken seriously in minimalist presentations of Israel's history, and one also encounters from time to time dubious historical reasoning that minimizes the historical value of the Bible's narratives. At the same time, many of the "minimalist" opponents tend to ignore the complex questions surrounding the dates and composition of biblical witnesses to historical events.

Where does the field of biblical studies stand on the question of the Bible's historical value? As this picture of the field of biblical studies would suggest, it often veers from one side of the theoretical problem to the other. Scholars rush to defend the Bible's historicity or to attack it. There are also efforts at compromise, by indulging in some combination of the two. To assume one side or the other is, however, to agree to the terms of the engagement, namely, that biblical narratives about the past are historical or they are not historical. "Biblical historians" cannot even agree on what constitutes history, as shown by the differences between Halpern's *First Historians* (1988) and Brettler's *Creation of History* (1995). Biblical historians agree that the biblical narratives of the past constitute history, but their arguments over the definition of history raise serious questions about the adequacy of the label for biblical works.

Given the massive differences among historically oriented biblical scholars over what constitutes history, one may ask if a basic problem afflicts the operating assumption that biblical narratives about the past are to be regarded primarily as history, either in the classical sense (for example, in Herodotus or Thucydides) or in the modern sense (as used by academic historians). Both classical and modern historians are concerned with critical examination with multiple sources—in short, verification, or at least some conscious assessment of sources. This discussion indicates that the theoretical questions impinging on the Bible and its representations of the past necessarily involve a number of critical issues. In general, our consideration of biblical texts requires returning to fundamental questions: What are we biblical scholars dealing with in the Bible, what or who are we as we deal with it, and what means can we deploy to plumb the difficulties in these questions and to assess these issues? In this chapter, I focus on the last of these questions. In particular, I wish to advance the claim that the academic study of collective memory offers important intellectual help for understanding the biblical representations of Israel's past.

— cf Lewis & Clark guy

Collective Memory and Amnesia

To begin, there are two fundamental points to be made about the nature of the Bible's treatment of the past. First, the Bible is not a record of "events," as Childs commented over forty years ago: "We do not have in the Old Testament 'an original event'. What we have are various witnesses to an event" (Childs 1962, 85). Second, the Bible is teaching (*torah* in Hebrew), much of it bearing a religious character. Ancient Israelites and the biblical traditions that they spawned, as well as modern Bible scholars, largely recognize the Bible's pedagogical purpose, and this teaching function extends to the Bible's narratives of the past. The biblical texts present a series of "teaching moments," recollections of past events that provide religious lessons. Given the Bible's representations of the past as teaching, what is needed are some intellectual means for negotiating back and forth between Israel's collective memories of its past on the one hand, and, on the other, the historical contexts that gave rise to those memories.

One means at hand is the sociological and historical research concerning collective memory and the impact of that memory on the historians who both belong to, and have written about, those cultures. This is not to say or claim that biblical scholars have not explored the topic of memory. On the contrary, it has long been a subject of biblical and ancient Near Eastern scholarship (for example, Childs 1962). In more recent years, there have been significant discussions by scholars on the role of memory in several ancient Near Eastern cultures; for example, by Assmann (1990, 1997) for Egypt; by Jonker (1995) for Mesopotamia; by Schottroff (1967) and later by Brettler (2001), Fleming (1998), and Hendel (2001a, 2002a) for ancient Israel; by Brandfon (1987) and Bloch-Smith (2003) for the study of the Bible and archaeology. We may also note the discussions of Yerushalmi (1989), Funkenstein (1993), and many other scholars concerning memory and Jewish tradition; and by Gerhardsson (1961), Riesner (1988), and others for the New Testament. These discussions would suggest a need for a discussion of memory and history as contained in the narrative presentations of the past in the Bible. For example, Yerushalmi (1989) and Brettler (1995, 2001) have fathomed the critical distinction between memory of the past and history, and especially how memory affects the issue of history in the Bible (in other words, how memory served to generate the presentations of the past in the Bible). To their credit, Brettler and other scholars have initiated a critical investigation of the multiple relations between Israel's cultural memory and the Bible's presentations of Israel's past. Brettler, for example, has nicely shown how the biblical authors rendered the past through various typologies, interpretation of earlier texts, and literary shaping.

Despite these important advances, Bible scholars have not generally engaged the available critical discussions of memory and history in the field of history and sociology. Since the early 1970s, cultural memory on the one hand and history writing on the other (with their intertwined relations) have informed a great number of treatments in the fields of medieval and modern history. A huge amount of scholarly literature has appeared on the topic, including the journal *History and Memory*. In many works on history and cultural memory, the names regularly identified with the academic lineage of this topic are the sociologist Maurice Halbwachs (1877–1945) and a team of historians, including Jacques Le Goff (1924–) and Pierre Nora (1931–). I also note the contributions of Philippe Ariès (1914–84) and those made by a more recent figure, Danièle Hervieu-Léger.

Maurice Halbwachs

Halbwachs, a disciple of Émile Durkheim, was professor at Strasbourg between World War I and World War II. Halbwachs numbered among the early founders of what would later become known as the *Annales* school, associated today with the name of Fernand Braudel. Halbwachs is credited with making three foundational contributions to the modern study of collective memory: the opposition between memory and history; the role of physical location in collective memory; and the importance of social power in cultural memory.

First, throughout his work Halbwachs underscored the opposition between memory and history. Collective memory represents the collective pool of memory shared by individuals, and it consists further of memory passed down to subsequent generations. For Halbwachs, memory is what a culture collectively carries forward about its past, while history involves a critical assessment of the past. Operating on an affective level, cultural memory confirms similarities between past and present. In contrast, history for Halbwachs reconstructs the past from a critical distance and strives to convey the sense that its connections with the present are devoid of emotional commitment. Collective memory, as Halbwachs explored in his early work *Les cadres sociaux* (1975; originally published in 1925), is expressed through shared images that embody an elaborate network of social mores, values, and ideals esteemed by social groups. The interconnections among the shared images in turn form and shape the social frameworks *(cadres sociaux)* of collective memory. Memory, Halbwachs argued, was an unreliable guide to history since it conveys distortions of the past. For Halbwachs, history and memory differed in another respect: history begins where memory ends. Stated differently, the historian's critical assessment of cultural memory marks a break point in the way that memory normally functions.

Second, for Halbwachs collective memory turns on location. In remembering, cultures locate or localize images of the past in specific places. In and of themselves, images of memory remain fragmentary until they are projected into concrete settings. Remembering therefore might be characterized as involving the integration of specific images formulated in the present into particular contexts associated with the past. The images of the past in these locations give expression to the present understanding of what the past was like. Memorialists in a culture may transpose a mental map about the past onto an external topographical plane.

During the 1930s, Halbwachs traveled twice to the Holy Land. In his major study during this phase of his work, *La topographie légendaire des évangiles en terre sainte* (1971; originally published in 1941), Halbwachs pursued his examination of the biblical Holy Land as a mental landscape, imagined by Christian pilgrims during the Middle Ages in Europe and superimposed onto the terrain of the Middle East in gradually increasing levels of commemoration. Drawing on the researches in historical geography by the École Biblique's Pères Vincent and Abel, Halbwachs noted discrepancies between the actual history of the terrain and the terrain as imagined by Christian pilgrims. Holy sites, often with little or no historical basis, became the created locales embodying the foundational events in the collective memory of Christian culture. Examining the place of memory, then, focuses not so much on "real events" or "data" as the image of them transmitted via, and interpreted through, recollection.

Third, memory was largely for Halbwachs a question of social power. The various places where past images are celebrated reveal the essentially social character of the processes by which groups fashion and conduct such celebrations. In the words of Patrick Hutton (1993, 79): "What we remember depends on the contexts in which we find ourselves and the groups to which we happen to relate. The depth and shape of our collective memory reflects this configuration of social forces that vie for our attention." The process of commemoration is a collective, deliberate effort on the part of a culture's memorialists both to preserve and to adapt slowly over time. It is a process that transpires so slowly that its incremental changes are imperceptible to those who participate in them. For Halbwachs, a historian is in a position to observe such change, while those immersed in such a process of memory and tradition resist change and the idea of change in a tradition, and in fact they deploy acts of commemoration in order to effect such resistance. Or, as Halbwachs comments, "each group immobilizes time in its own way."

Halbwachs's research on cultural memory enjoyed considerable recognition among later scholars, especially in the fields of history, anthropology, and Jewish studies. Halbwachs perhaps made his initial, though indirect, impact on biblical studies via Yosef Yerushalmi, who acknowledges Halbwach's influence on his

Hayden White ?

book *Zakhor* (1989). Halbwachs's work would also inform the explosion of interest in cultural memory among French historians in the mid-1970s.

Philippe Ariès

A second figure who would fuel the discussion of history and memory in the mid-1970s was Philippe Ariès. Under the influence of the *Annales* school, Ariès's book *Centuries of Childhood* (1962) drew on his own family experience to understand the role of memory in history. Like Halbwachs, Ariès noted the importance of family memory, but in his own case he saw how the cultural memory influenced historians of culture. Ariès's personal memory of his family's past helped him appreciate the public role of family in the historiography of the French Revolution. Accordingly, he understood that historical writing was often an extension of particular traditions of collective memory. For Ariès, historians must self-critically negotiate between the operations of memory and history, because historians operate as recipients of cultural memory even as they seek to pursue critical history. ✳

Jacques Le Goff and Pierre Nora

Cultural memory became a very prominent topic in the *Annales* school's agenda of historical anthropology in the mid-1970s. Among the major figures influenced by the *Annales* school and in particular by Halbwachs's ideas were Pierre Nora and Jacques Le Goff. In 1977 Jacques Le Goff, Braudel's successor as president (and also director) at the École des hautes études en sciences sociales (formerly École practique des hautes études), produced a seminal volume on the subject. In this work, Le Goff discussed the various human realities impinging on history writing. For Le Goff, collective memory, assimilated by members of the culture who later become historians, influences them as they produce histories involving their culture. Le Goff speaks of examining the presentations of the past not only as a question of understanding historical realities. Le Goff makes the important point that historians may examine past historical works to construct a history of the representations of the past. By the same token, Le Goff insists that such an undertaking is not to replace efforts to recover the past; instead, the two tasks stand together and may illuminate one another.

Professor and colleague of Le Goff at the École des hautes études en sciences sociales, Pierre Nora continued Halbwachs's particular interest in places of commemoration. Produced for the bicentennial of the French Revolution, the three volumes of *Realms of Memory* (1996–98; originally published in 1984–92) edited by Nora survey different elements of French national memory: commemorative monuments and shrines, national histories, civics manuals and history textbooks, public archives and museums produced in the name of a French identity since the

Middle Ages. In examining sites of recollection that were part of his own cultural experience, Nora recognized the impossibility of maintaining a clean separation between memory and history. Nora the French historian studied the commemoration of France in France from the eighteenth century into the twentieth. As a result, Nora could recognize the impact of cultural memory on his own understanding of history and on that of his predecessors. The recognition that cultural memory deeply informs historians' work demarcates Nora from Halbwachs, whose choice to study commemorative sites in the Christian Holy Land maintained a distance between himself as historical investigator and the commemorative discourses he chose to investigate. In the intellectual tension resulting from a historian's involvement in the collective memory of the culture whose history one studies, Nora saw that the horizons of historians are shaped by the collective memory of the societies to which they belong, and in turn historians give shape to collective memory. For Nora, "history was verified memory."

Nora's further contribution involved recognizing the shifts in technologies and their impact on a culture's receptivity to its own collective memory. New technologies shift cultural receptivity away from older forms of cultural memory. For Nora, the nineteenth-century historian's document supplanted oral tradition as the repository of cultural memory, albeit in a new, professionalized garb. At the same time, the rise of such a form marked a rupture between past collective memory and its ongoing transmission in the twentieth century. In short, writing does not effect a rupture in collective memory; rather, it signals it. Nora (1984–92, 1.xxv [in the French original, cited and discussed in Hutton 1993, 148]) puts the point this way: "One looks for places of memory because they are no longer milieux of memory." For Nora, this situation for historians is intellectually challenging and threatening. The contemporary awareness among historians questions the viability of any history, or at least of any national history. While the inclusion of diverse particular histories into the narrative of collective history has marked a giant step forward, at the same time it has been suggested that the writing of any larger history is little more than performing the politics of the present. For Nora, this is what historians have been doing all the time. The difference involves the recognition that this is the case and the sense that this situation poses serious intellectual challenges.

Danièle Hervieu-Léger

This brief survey of French historians concludes with the figure of Danièle Hervieu-Léger, who like Le Goff before her served as director of studies at the École des hautes études en sciences sociales. Her seminal contribution appeared in 1993, *La religion pour mémoire,* translated as *Religion as a Chain of Memory* (2000). This book applies the insights of Halbwachs and Nora to questions of religion. Hervieu-Léger begins with a critique of what she sees as the overstated case for secularism inevitably triumphing over traditional religion in the modern world. She sees traditional religion as a phenomenon not stamped out by secularism but displaced by it, with religiosity manifest in a wide variety of settings and modes. Hervieu-Léger (2000, 24) comments on religion: "the subject, even in the act of disintegrating, shows astounding resistance; it re-emerges, revives, shifts ground, becomes diffuse." The single greatest challenge to traditional religious life therefore is not secularism as such, but the destabilization of traditional authority that secularism has helped to undermine. Hervieu-Léger notes how collective memory, operative at different levels in Christian churches, is in a process of disintegration and how various church personnel seek to retain and to reappropriate collective memory to speak to new contexts.

Overall, Hervieu-Léger's account of social memory echoes treatments by her predecessors. Memory and tradition involve a body of religious perceptions constituting a shared understanding, mediated by individuals and/or groups and potentially shifting in response to continuingly emerging needs and questions. Correspondingly, religious tradition necessarily permits aspects of shared memory to recede. Religious memory for Hervieu-Léger is a socially located phenomenon, not a transcendent good bestowed upon those who invoke and transmit it. Shifts of location, geographical as well as cultural, yield corresponding shifts in religious memory. Hervieu-Léger identifies several features of what she calls "the chain of tradition reinvented": the destruction and restructuring of memory provided with formal explanatory links; the conflictual nature of collective memory; conflicting efforts on the part of shifting hierarchies to homogenize collective memory; and the role of what she calls "elective fraternity" in the reappropriation of reinvented memory. Almost all of these features follow from the insights of Hervieu-Léger's predecessors, yet it is her particular interest in religion and its displacement that offers additional promise for the study of Israelite religion.

Implications for Collective Memory in the Bible

To turn the discussion of collective memory to the Bible, we can glean a number of lessons from historians of memory. We may note seven points in the order of the presentation of figures discussed in the preceding section. First and foremost, the Bible does not simply record fact or fiction, history or literature (largely modern distinctions of considerable value and difficulty). Instead, many biblical texts might be better characterized as constituting the record of Israel's cultural memory. "Remembering" is sometimes the Bible's own term for recalling the past (Deuteronomy 32:7: "Remember the days of old . . ."). Although there have been significant discussions by Bible scholars on the role of memory in Israel's past, it represents a significant paradigm shift to regard the Bible in general not as the locus of Israel's historical record (or not), but as the partial record of Israel's cultural memories of its past that contain some amount of historically accurate information.

Halbwachs's paradigm of memory/history would allow for a sifting of historical reality from later accretions, which is how critical biblical scholars continue to think about the historical study of the Bible. However, the work of Nora and later writers acknowledges the complications involved in such a model, when memory constitutes one of the basic ingredients in the historical record. Collective memories entail constantly shifting historical perceptions, and the record of any historical reality is deeply marked by the forms that it assumes in collective perceptions and memories, even at the time of an event's occurrence. To return to a basic point concerning the Bible and Halbwachs's foundational comments on memory, one basic purpose of memory is to use the past to teach in the present. The representations of the past are shaped to the contours of this teaching function not only in texts like Psalms (such as 78, 105, 106), but also in long narrative works. The Passover of Exodus 12–13 has been a long-noted marker of teaching, and as we saw in chapter 2, an educational purpose informs the presentation in the Pentateuch from Exodus 12 through Numbers 10 as a single sacred year, from Passover to Passover with the Feasts of Weeks and the New Year appearing in between. We also saw a highly didactic function operative in the so-called Deuteronomistic History (Joshua–2 Kings).

 Second, Halbwachs's work teaches us to recognize the role of memory of our own religious traditions, which have influenced not only Bible scholars' initial interest in entering the field of biblical studies but also our interests and our horizons, our questions and our answers. Thanks to Nora, we sense how two levels of commemoration, the ancient and the modern, flow into one another, and cannot remain separate, as Halbwachs believed. The ruptures in traditional religion in the modern world are profound, and they deeply affect both religious and non-religious biblical scholars. This subject lies beyond the scope of this presentation, since by itself it would require a lengthy book on the history of modern study of the Bible.

At this point, it would perhaps be appropriate to acknowledge my own background in setting the horizons for this study. It is evident to me in retrospect that my background as a Roman Catholic has sometimes influenced my choice of subjects to study. For example, I wrote a book on pilgrimage in the Bible and its use as a literary pattern in the book of Exodus (Smith 1997). Pilgrimage is not a subject exclusively of interest to Catholics, but it is a traditionally important topic for us. With this work on collective memory, I believe that I have also been influenced by the Catholic emphasis on tradition; social memory is a function of tradition, and the ultimate project of the Bible as a revelation is a product of Israel's traditions. I would also say that my accompanying interest in how Jewish tradition developed such themes and expressed them in what became traditional Jewish texts emanates from my personal and professional ties to Jewish scholars and Jews more broadly. As a result of my scholarly engagement, I also understand that the eventual differentiation of Judaism and Christianity was a complex succession of overlapping identities and communities that would not be fully differentiated for centuries after the New Testament, and not simply some sort of split or "parting of the ways" forced by the Jewish apostle Paul and his initiative to advance the Christian gospel among non-Jews (see especially Hurtado 2003, and Becker and Reed 2003). Finally, my scholarly interest in understanding God (whether in my earlier books on God or in this one) stems from deep-seated religious sensibilities. This conglomeration of personal horizons may be, from an intellectual perspective, both liberating and restricting; in my experience, they enhance empathy for such themes, even as the same horizons may delimit understanding of the subject under investigation. In particular, my sense of the complexity of biblical viewpoints and traditions that later seem to stand at odds seems to me influenced by what I sense are the complex relations between Judaism and Christianity both in the early centuries C.E. and today. According to what Halbwachs and Nora have shown in the field of history, readers should be suspicious about how an author's horizons have shaped her or his analysis. This point applies to my examination here of biblical memory: does the shape of the presentation below about memory of God in the Bible correspond well to the shape of the actual biblical evidence, or have some of my own horizons subtly, or not so subtly, affected the analysis in a negative way?

Third, from Halbwachs and Nora as well as others, we may appreciate the role of social context and power of groups in shaping their collective memories, as Hutton (1993, 113) remarks: "The influence of an idea is relative to the cultural power of the tradition within which it is located." Viewing the task from the perspective of social groups and strata and their influence on the shaping of cultural memory, the task of the biblical historian may be to undertake what Le Goff understands as a history of the Bible's representations of the past as well as a recovery of that past. Bible scholars have long emphasized social power in the production of texts, but we have attended less meticulously to the role of social groups and their power in generating cultural memories of Israel's past in the Bible. This topic entails noting the shifts in the impact of various social strata and segments in generating collective memories. From Halbwachs and especially from Ariès, we learn the importance of the family in shaping memory and the significance of the emerging monarchy for submerging and remerging collective memories. Where the field has long focused on the power of priestly lines and the importance of annual feasts and sanctuaries, more recent work has called attention to the role of the family (for example, in the important but rather different books by Bloch-Smith 1992, van der Toorn 1996, and Schloen 2001). In general, what I am highlighting here are the shifts in the social locations of recollection among families with their family shrines and the "high places" of clans, the priesthood of various sanctuaries, and the appointed priesthoods at royal shrines. All of these social settings and the shifts that they experienced affected the biblical records of Israel's collective memories. Brettler's characterization of the Bible's presentations of the past here is salutary: the Bible "is national history, precisely the type of history which even in modern times has been most open to being rewritten or created and is most easily influenced by memory in all its permutations, with all of its problems and benefits" (Brettler 2001, 11).

I would push Brettler's point about collective memory: the Bible is largely a collection of the partial records of family, priestly, and royal commemorations. I would further stress the impact of the pre- and postexilic Jerusalem priesthood and royalty in generating broad societal narratives that submerge and co-opt the collective memories of family and non-Jerusalemite priestly lines. Below we will see the impact of different groups on the memory of God in Israel's past.

Fourth (and related), Halbwachs and Nora focused on the role that actual physical sites play in shaping cultural memory. In his preface to the second volume of *Les lieux de mémoire*, Nora makes a number of observations about land, cathedral, and court as sites of memory. Here we might read for Israel: family patrimonies, the so-called high places and local shrines, and royal shrines and capitals. Nora (1996–98, ix–x) comments: "Quite apart from the social structures, types of organization and regimes, and historical eras that they evoke, each of these three words has accumulated, whether at a specific moment in time or as a gradually thickening patina, a certain weight of historical images and representations—images and representations which have been revised throughout the ages and which still influence us as archetypes of social memory."

If we apply these principles to the memory of major biblical personages, they are enshrined in official histories not simply according to the "historical facts," but according to the settings where their reputations were enshrined. We saw in chapter 2 that the history about David and Saul depended on their later supporters. Represented as a rather ideal figure in the official history contained in the book of 2 Samuel, the memory of David became more glorious as time passed. By the time of the Dead Sea Scrolls, he was recalled as a model of piety (as at the end of the text called "Some Precepts of the Torah," 4QMMT), speaking under prophetic inspiration (in the Cave 11 Psalms Scroll, 11QPs[a]). One obvious exception to David's exaltation was the story of his adultery with Bathsheba, which many scholars believe was written later by critics who disapproved of the official ideal memory of David. Similarly, how Moses was remembered likely varied, depending on the local traditions associated with him at various sites. For those sites that did not survive, the memory of Moses at such places would not have remained in competition. One dominant view of Moses in the Bible seems to be his status as super-prophet and conveyor of Torah, which apparently shows the stamp of northern Israelite prophetic circles and the circles that produced Deuteronomy. Other traditions about Moses known, for example, from Transjordanian Israel may have been lost, suppressed, or rewritten (as Baruch Levine in a personal communication recently reminded me.) Below, I will make a similar case for how God was remembered, especially at Mount Sinai.

As a related point for Nora, locations of memory also offer clues as to rupture in living memory. This point applies to the northern kingdom from 722 and to Jerusalem from 586, at least for those who lived outside the land, especially in Babylon (Psalm 137). As we saw in chapter 2, the efforts to reconfigure community in the face of the exile generated a reconfiguration in Israel's identity; the identity question, who is an Israelite, changed grounds as a result. Similarly, the living traditions of polytheism represented by a figure such as the Queen of Heaven (discussed in chapters 2 and 3) evidently survived in Egypt following the catastrophe of Jerusalem in 586, but it is not clear that her cult survived equally well elsewhere. We do get some inkling of a few other deities in the Jewish texts from Elephantine, discussed in chapter 1. Anat-Yahu, as well as Anat-Bethel, Eshem-Bethel, and Herem-Bethel, were recognized as divinities of some sort by Judean colonists at Elephantine. (What sort is debated.) Other polytheistic traditions and perhaps some traditions regarding Yahweh may also have been submerged or forgotten due to the changes in community life for those who were deported to Babylon. Although we know little of such developments, the fact that nothing is heard in the Bible of older Israelite divinities in exile (except Yahweh) may be a witness to their reduction or even their demise because of the rupture of exile. This could have been by polemical design on the part of Judean exilic leadership. Yet if other divinities were known, one might have expected polemic directed against them, something the biblical authors do not otherwise shy away from. Instead, the lack of other deities in exile perhaps happened by default; their cult as configured in the land perhaps failed to serve the needs of the community in exile and therefore was forgotten. Particularly at risk would have been the religious traditions at local shrines. By contrast, familial and priestly religious practices would have been able to continue in some form in the exile.

Fifth, we might also reflect on Nora's point that the rise of writing and written sources of history marks a transition away from oral memory as the culturally prestigious form of recollection. I would put the point a little differently for ancient Israel, as the oral and written forms of memory should perhaps not be separated too neatly (rather, various forms of oral and written memory should be seen as

constituting a spectrum). Oral transmission likely remained a significant component in Israel's social memory despite social and political ruptures that it suffered.
However, something important happened in the eighth century in the area of writing at elite levels of Israelite society. As the eighth century appears to be an important watershed for writing in ancient Israel (as discussed in Schniedewind
2004), this time perhaps begins the displacement of oral culture as the prestigious
medium and means for maintaining and transmitting Israel's collective memory.
The rising prestige of writing among ancient Israel's religious elites may signal, in
Nora's terms, the rupture between a traditional past and an awareness of its demise. While significantly fewer earlier Israelite texts are known from outside the
Bible or alluded to within it prior to the eighth century, the massive appearance of
extrabiblical written material beginning in the eighth century may mark a major
shift in the roles of oral culture and writing in preserving Israel's collective memories. Various works across the surviving biblical corpus would point to the rise
of writing as an additional culturally prestigious form of cultural memory at this
time. These may include the so-called Yahwist and Elohist sources (discussed
near the beginning of chapter 1) as written sources or in redaction together in the
eighth century; the Neo-Assyrian context claimed for Deuteronomy 12–26; the
redactions claimed for the Deuteronomistic History (Joshua–2 Kings) during the
reigns of Hezekiah and Josiah; the first separate prophetic works in the eighth
century; a seventh-century redaction claimed for Isaiah; and the redaction of
Proverbs 25–29 by the "men of Hezekiah" (Proverbs 25:1). In Nora's terms, the rise
of writing from the eighth century onward in ancient Israel would signal a rupture between a traditional past and an awareness of its demise. It would seem that
some traditional contexts of (and societal anchoring for) oral memory do not retain their cultural prestige in the face of monarchic and priestly support for written forms of cultural memory. With the massive appearance of writing in eighth-
century sources, we might see signs of a shift in the relative power of the contexts
that support and generate oral and written forms of cultural memory.

Sixth, from Yerushalmi we learn the importance of societal tragedy on the production of writing about the past. In Jewish history, particularly during the biblical and medieval periods, narrative recollections of the past were inspired in large
measure by intensely traumatic events. Yerushalmi does not probe his insight in
the periods related by narrative works of the Bible, but it is clear that the two great
biblical periods of historical writing responded to massive social and political loss.
The looming threat of the Neo-Assyrian Empire beginning in the 730s and its incorporation of the northern kingdom in 722 marks the period of the initial compilation of the Deuteronomistic History and probably some amount of the narrative of the Pentateuch as well. The fall of Jerusalem and the destruction of the
Temple in 586 witnessed the further compilation of the Deuteronomistic History

and the composition of the books of Ezra–Nehemiah and Chronicles as well as other works that draw on the stuff of history, such as Esther. It is arguable that to tell the story of the past is to explore the reasons for the present state of matters; figuratively speaking, to "get past" it. Historical writing seems, then, to capture in memory what has been otherwise lost in life. In short, to write back through the past is to enable moving through present loss and toward the future.

Seventh, Hervieu-Léger discusses the destruction and restructuring of traditional memory provided with formal explanatory links, the conflictual nature of collective memory, the conflicting efforts on the part of shifting hierarchies to homogenize collective memory, and the role of what she calls "elective fraternity" in the reappropriation of reinvented memory. These are all features that biblical scholars would recognize in the accounts of Israel's past in priestly traditions in the Torah (Pentateuch) and in Deuteronomy as well as the historical books influenced by it, Joshua through 2 Kings (accordingly called the "Deuteronomistic History"). The past is provided with new connections to the present, and there are differences over such presentations of the past and evidently conflicts over such competing accounts. Hervieu-Léger is interested in how traditional religion oriented around the French parish of the countryside recedes first in the face of the emerging nation-state, then is challenged by an increasing loss of traditional locus and practice of religion due to the modern forces of society, only to reappear in various forms of elective fraternity.

Hervieu-Léger's general scenario may be applied by analogy to Israelite religion. Traditional religion (and here for ancient Israel read traditional religion of clans, with local "high places" and shrines) is submerged first in the face of the rising nation-state, with its royal sanctuaries (here read the rise of the Judean and Israelite monarchies). This traditional religion then recedes further due to an increasing loss of traditional locus and practice of religion (here read the loss of local patrimonies and lineages and nonroyal sanctuaries especially from the eighth through the sixth centuries). This loss corresponds to the appearance of new forms of elective fraternity (here read prophetic and perhaps priestly and Deuteronomic movements gathering social force in reaction to the limitations of family and monarchic religion in the eighth through the sixth centuries). At work is a rule of memory surviving in inverse proportion to historical order and power of social location: the family, with its memories generated largely through oral means, is socially weaker relative to the priestly forces behind the textual formation and transmission of texts in regional shrines, and family memory is submerged further beneath the weight of priestly lines working in sanctuaries and then filtered through royal shrines, and ultimately through the royal shrine with a single priestly hierarchy in Jerusalem. Yet homogenization of societal narratives went only so far. Just as collective memory in France could maintain a variety of versions of national history, so within the Jerusalemite context several narratives, specifically priestly and Deuteronomic ones, could be maintained and modified, at once rejecting and responding to one another.

The change of systems producing collective memories in turn produces changes in the information stored. From our distant vantage point, this change can look like censorship: an active, deliberate process of altering elements of past narrative no longer perceived as appropriate or orthodox. As we will see later in this chapter, some signs of censorship are arguably apparent. Loss of collective information can also function in a less deliberate mode, whereby tradition remembers what is useful and tends to forget what is no longer of use. This model works reasonably well for oral transmission of memory, but once written memory passes into a body of traditional texts, the tradition does not seem to throw out what it forgets; instead, it tends to rewrite what it does not remember. This form of written transmission is evident from both the Bible and other ancient Near Eastern texts. Additionally, later tradition may retain older material that can be conformed to later understandings or often does not conspicuously contradict them. The sort of cultural amnesia entailed by rewriting need not be regarded as dysfunctional. Instead, there is, according to Harvard psychologist Daniel Schacter, an adaptive advantage to forgetting; it is how systems of memory naturally function. Schacter comments (2001, 188): "A system that renders information less accessible over time is therefore highly functional, because when information has not been used for longer and longer periods of time, it becomes less and less likely that it will be needed in the future."

I would like to conclude this discussion of general literature on collective memory with a fundamental point about memory in the Bible. For ancient Israel, to recall the past was an act designed to affect the present. As we saw earlier in this chapter, Yerushalmi named his book concerning the collective memory of the Jewish people *Zakhor*. This title, literally the command to "remember," derives from the Ten Commandments, where Israel is instructed: "Remember [*zakor*] the Sabbath day to sanctify it" (Exodus 20:8). As Yerushalmi reminds his readers, this commandment does not only involve a mental act of memory; biblical memory is not the opposite simply of forgetting. Instead, "to remember" combines a mental process with religious performance. Memory in this case is designed to induce Judeans to sanctify the day. That this act of memory is not simply a mental one may be illustrated by the parallel version of this same commandment in Deuteronomy 5:12: "Observe [*shamor*] the Sabbath day to sanctify it." To remember involves both mental act and performance. It is also essentially a religious action, or more specifically a ritual act. The Sabbath is the premier weekday of religious observance.

In ancient Israel, memory commonly served in ritual settings, with communal prayers addressed to Yahweh to remember Israel in days of distress (Lamentations 5:1; see v. 20; compare Esther 9:28). In Psalm 137 the request to God to remember Israel's enemies follows a personal vow to keep Jerusalem in memory, even at the psalmist's happiest experience. Stories in the Torah (Pentateuch) present Moses pleading with God to remember (Exodus 32:13) or Yahweh remembering (in particular, remembering the covenant). In these passages and many others like them, an appeal to divine memory is part of the effort to induce the Deity to act on Israel's behalf, or at least to demonstrate intention to act of Israel's behalf (see Exodus 6:5; compare Leviticus 26:42).

Other religious acts also invoke ritual memory. Sacrifices are sometimes called an *azkarah*, a "memorial offering" (NRSV "taken portion," Leviticus 2:2; 24:7; see also Isaiah 66:3, NRSV "memorial offering"). Later Judaism enshrined memory as a central ritual act. For example, the *Yizkor* (literally, "may he remember") prayer is to be recited four times per year, on Yom Kippur, the Day of Atonement, and on the three pilgrimage holidays of Passover, Weeks, and Booths, on the eighth day of the holiday. This Jewish service recalls deceased relatives and friends (somewhat comparable in this respect to the Christian feast of All Soul's Day on November 2), as well as Jewish martyrs. The *Zikronot* service during Rosh Hashanah (the New Year) consists of biblical "remembrance verses." Perhaps best known among the Jewish holidays for remembrance is the recalling of the exodus during the Passover Seder. The Passover explicitly characterizes its ritual as designed to ritually translate the past into the present, to be as true of present participants as it was thought to be for the original generation of the exodus:

> In each generation, every individual should see himself as if he departed from Egypt, as it is said (citing Exodus 13:8): "And you shall tell your children on that day, 'On account of this the Lord acted for me when I departed from Egypt.'" Not our ancestors alone did the Holy One—blessed be He—redeem but also us with them, as it is said (citing Deuteronomy 6:23): "And us He brought out from there in order to bring us, to give to us the land that He swore to our fathers."

For Christians, an analogous act of memory is bound up in the performance of the Eucharist, the reenactment of the Last Supper; in the words of Jesus as recorded in Luke's Gospel, "Do this in remembrance of me" (Luke 22:19). This addition in Luke, which correlates the Last Supper with the Passover meal, strikes me as a quintessentially Christian realization of a quintessentially Jewish act of commemoration. As in this case, Jewish liturgies echo ritual memories in ancient Israel. As a hallmark of Israelite religious practice, ritual memory extended from family religion with its invocation of deceased ancestors all the way to national prayer. For this reason, stressing the religious dimension of memory and not simply memory in general seems particularly suitable to the study of Israel's past as represented in the Bible. Moreover, religious memory in its various aspects was central to the Bible's presentation of divinity and divinities in Israel's past.

Re-membering Divinity at Mount Sinai

In light of this discussion, we may probe the significant recasting of memory about Israel and its deity in the story of Mount Sinai. As the alleged foundational moment of Israel's experience of God, the story of Mount Sinai expresses Israel's primordial identity. The biblical representation of the events on Mount Sinai charts Israel's religious constitution and understanding of reality. We may note four foundational reinterpretations of Israel's religious identity generated through its memory of Mount Sinai.

From Single Service to God to Monotheism at Sinai

The most conspicuous recasting of Israel's recollection of Sinai, especially in light of the discussion of Israel's deities and the four levels of divinity in chapter 3, is the idea of Israel's monotheism. The Ten Commandments recognized that there are other gods ("You shall have no other gods besides Me," Exodus 20:3). In the book of Deuteronomy, Israel's later memory of the Sinai event remembers this sense of God and gods a bit differently. The book contains one introduction, in 1:1—4:43, that is thought to have been added secondarily, probably sometime after the exile, to the book's original introduction, beginning in 4:44 ("This is the teaching that Moses set before the Israelites . . ."). In the NRSV, this beginning is marked by a break between verse 43 and verse 44. A postexilic date for this added introduction is proposed because this section refers to Israel in exile "among the peoples" (4:27), namely, in several nations more broadly, a circumstance that fits the postexilic period. In discussing the Sinai experience of God, 4:35 associates Israel's monotheism with Sinai: "You were shown in order to know that the LORD is God; there is none apart from Him." Israel's later memory of God retrojects to its earliest time a monotheistic view of its Deity.

It is because the Bible enshrines this refashioning of Israel's earliest memory of God in this way that people usually think of monotheism as the basic religious view of Israel in the biblical period. It is not only Exodus 20:3-5 that shows a more complex situation when it came to deities in ancient Israel. As we saw in chapter 3, the reality was far more complex. In early Israelite religion, *elohim* could denote "God" or "gods" or "divinities." In early Israel it could be a clan deity (often a chief god such as El), called "the god of the father." Or *elohim* might denote upper-level gods or lower-level gods serving in the divine council; or ancestral spirits, or even a demonic god, or other divinities of destruction. In short, early Israel was populated with *elohim* of various sorts. In chapter 3 we saw how divinities could be basically categorized in four tiers or levels. By the time of the exile, however, a new pantheon with only two levels of deities was being proposed against this worldview. The head god now became the godhead, with the fourth and lowest tier occupied by angels, whose power was thought to derive ultimately from the one deity. In heaven there was only one power, and this power on earth could be manifest through messengers and others on earth. In Deuteronomy 4:35 this later monotheism is presented as part of the original revelation at Sinai. In the new introduction to Deuteronomy, the monotheistic vision was recalled as one of Israel's earliest memories.

God at Sinai: From Divine Body to the Voice of Holiness

The books of Exodus and Leviticus present various collections of teaching as parts of the Sinai revelation. As scholars have long noted, these collections include the Ten Commandments (Exodus 20), a set of legal rulings generally called the "Covenant Code" (Exodus 21–23), priestly instructions for building the Tabernacle (Exodus 25–31, which are then executed in Exodus 35–40); two major sections of priestly instructional literature in Leviticus, the first being instructions of sacrifices and other matters for priests in chapters 1–16, and priestly instructions for nonpriests in chapters 17–26 (the latter section scholars call the "Holiness Code"). In addition, Deuteronomy 12–26 is presented as a retelling of the Sinai teaching, yet it displays many differences from the same events presented in Exodus and Leviticus. For instance, there are some variations in the version of the Ten Commandments found in Deuteronomy 5 compared to the version in Exodus 20. (The variation concerning remembering the Sabbath day versus observing it was discussed in the preceding section.) Similarly, the introductions in Deuteronomy 1:1—4:43 and 4:44—11:31 retell the story of Sinai in ways that depart from the narratives in Exodus.

This variety in witnesses about Sinai and the revelation that took place there shows an ongoing discussion in ancient Israel about how this event was to be remembered. In other words, there was a continuing discussion and debate about how events on Mount Sinai were to be recalled. It was not a debate over history as such, but a discussion over which and whose collective memory and religious norms were to be championed. In the end, the text functions as a sort of compromise document that preserves both the older traditions of Exodus and later interpretations emerging from priestly and Deuteronomic circles ranging in date from the late preexilic period through postexilic times. The collections of teaching date to different periods, yet these are all enshrined in Israel's collective memory of the foundational events at Mount Sinai.

This process of enshrining later text as original Torah text did not end with the Bible. With the Temple Scroll from Qumran (11QT), we not only see the harmonization of legal material in Deuteronomy with its counterparts in Exodus, Leviticus, and Numbers, we also witness the Temple construction as included in Torah, even though in the Bible the Temple does not appear until 1 Kings 6–8. By interpreting the Temple as the tabernacle of Exodus 25–40, the Qumranites could regard the Temple as part of the original Sinai revelation to Moses. In sum, what emerged from later time periods was enshrined as the primordial divine word; what came out of particular times was presented as being timeless in its importance.

Let me illustrate this diversity of memory in the Bible's picture of Sinai with an example. As our discussion has generally focused on divinity in Israel, I would like to use an example of how God was recalled at Mount Sinai. One of the oldest pictures of God at Mount Sinai that we can now see is in Exodus 24:9-11. This passage relates the following event (rendered a bit literally, with some explanatory material added in brackets):

> Moses and Aaron, Nadab and Abihu, and seventy of the elders of Israel ascended [Mount Sinai]. And they saw the God of Israel. And under His [God's] feet was like brickwork of sapphire, and like the very heavens for [in terms of] purity [clarity or brilliance]. Against the leaders (?) of the Israelites, He [God] did not raise his hand; and they beheld God, and they ate and drank.

The combination of four features in this passage is unparalleled in the Bible. First, the passage shows Israel's leaders seeing God, a point that goes against the understanding elsewhere that people did not or could not see God (Exodus 33:20; Judges 13:22). Select individuals do see God occasionally in the Bible, such as the prophet in Isaiah 6:1. Or people say that they saw God (or at least an *elohim*), such as Hagar in Genesis 16:13 and Jacob in 32:30. Or they express the hope that they will see God (an expression of entering into the presence of God), as in Psalms 17:15; 27:4 (?); 42:2; and 63:2. Or, finally, they convey the belief that such an experience belongs to the upright, for example, in Psalm 11:7. Even so, seeing God was recognized as potentially dangerous. The author of Exodus 24:9-11 seems to be aware of this belief, for the passage adds in verse 11 that God did not raise the divine hand against these Israelite leaders, an action that could be expected since they saw God. (It is possible that v. 11, at least this first clause, may have been added when the section was first written down or later when it was transmitted, in order to explain why the leaders could have this experience.) As a mark of his special relationship with God, Moses is singled out elsewhere for being able to see God ("and the form of Yahweh he beholds," Numbers 12:8). In contrast, Exodus 24:9 strikingly mentions other people seeing God.

A second possibly old feature is an unusual detail in this passage: its allusion to the architecture of God's heavenly palace. The passage likens the material of the heavenly temple to sapphire brickwork. This sort of brickwork for heavenly palaces belonging to gods is known from other ancient Near Eastern texts, such as the Ugaritic Baal Cycle (*CAT* 1.4 V 19, 34-35). The idea of the heavenly brickwork survives down through ancient Israel even though it is not mentioned elsewhere in the Bible. The brickwork of the divine palace is mentioned in the Dead Sea Scrolls, in a text called the Songs of the Sabbath Sacrifice (4Q405, fragment 19, line 6). Of course, it is possible that the allusion to the brickwork in Exodus 24:9-11 is not so old, since it appears in a Dead Sea Scroll text. In view of the other features, as well as the antiquity of the brickwork in the Baal Cycle, however, I am inclined to see this detail as early as well.

A third old feature is the reference to God's body, in this instance the divine feet. This sort of anthropomorphism is exceptional, and if other anthropomorphisms of God are any indication, they seem more at home in the milieu of Israelite religion in the period up to the eighth century, for example, in the so-called Yahwist source (mentioned at the beginning of chapter 1). Afterward, such presentations of the divine body seem to fall out of usage or are purposefully submerged by Israel's priestly and Deuteronomic leadership.

A fourth feature in Exodus 24:9-11 used in conjunction with seeing God is eating and drinking on the mountain of God. This motif also seems to be quite old (see also Exodus 18:12). If we were to compare this detail to the meal on the mountain mentioned in 1 Kings 18:42, it would provide the Sinai meal with a setting in the northern kingdom in the ninth century. As a further connection of Exodus 24:9-11 to the north, we may note Elijah's journey to Horeb in 1 Kings 19, especially verse 8. The prophet's journey evidently reflects a northern literary tradition of pilgrimage to this mountain. (Pilgrimage may be also one of the purposes of a stopover desert site such as Kuntillet Ajrud, which shows signs of northerners. If there is a historical tradition of such pilgrimage, then it may have served as the channel of commemoration for this northern tradition.) If we compare Exodus 24:9-11 to the presentation of Samuel presiding over a meal at a shrine on a local high place in 1 Samuel 9:12, 19, we could push back the date of the presentation in Exodus 24:9-11 to the premonarchic period, perhaps as a northern recollection of Moses. In short, Exodus 24:9-11 looks like a northern memory of Sinai to be placed in the time of the early monarchy. The problem is that we do not have access to any Early Iron I or II confirmation (much less any Late Bronze Age evidence) of the Mount Sinai experience, and the biblical parallels mentioned here hardly confirm the antiquity of the actual text of Exodus 24. Indeed, it seems that the complex of some components in 24:9-11, with their quite

unparalleled expressions, may be quite old. (This conclusion stands in contrast to
the view expressed in a very learned discussion by Hartenstein [2003b], who one
must admit has some late extrabiblical parallels in his favor.)

Despite these limitations, it does seem that the religious meal on the mountain
of God along with the visual experience of God belong to the oldest traditions
now available, and these at least predate the priestly and Deuteronomic representations of God at Mount Sinai. That the later tradition was generally uncomfort-
able with this straightforward presentation of Moses' experience on the mountain
can be seen in Exodus 33–34, where Moses' visual experience of God was not denied but highly qualified. Mentioning the traditional belief that no one can see
God and live, God tells Moses that he can see God, but it is the divine back and not
the divine face (33:20-23). It would appear that the complex presentation of the visual experience of God here served as a sort of narrative commentary designed to
qualify the more anthropomorphic description of 24:9-11. The implication is that
24:9-11 belongs to an older level of Israelite tradition than chapters 33–34, and the
two texts present the memory of Moses' seeing God at Sinai in two very different
ways.

The later Deuteronomic and priestly recollections of the Sinai experience of
God move off from Exodus 24 in their own directions. Deuteronomy 4 offers a
further "new recollection" of God at Mount Sinai. First, only Moses ascends the
mountain. Second, there is no meal. Third, there is no body part of God mentioned in the presentations, nor is there any particular visionary experience (a
point emphasized by Hartenstein 2003b). Unlike Exodus 33, Deuteronomy 4
makes no effort to include the visual experience of God, even in a highly qualified
manner. As Yadin has noted (2003), the book of Deuteronomy stresses that God
was not seen, but appeared only as a disembodied voice emerging from the divine
fire: "And Yahweh spoke to you from the midst of the fire; you heard the sound of
words, but perceived no shape, only a voice" (Deuteronomy 4:12). The point is reinforced later in the same speech: "From heaven He made you hear His voice, to
discipline you; and on earth He showed you His great fire, and you heard His
words from the midst of the fire" (4:36). The voice from the fire is strongly, even
pointedly, nonanthropomorphic. I say pointedly in part because these verses in
Deuteronomy 4 may be designed to clarify the ambiguity in the older introduc-
tory material in 5:22-27 (Hebrew 5:19-24, also NJPS), which does not say whether
the Israelites saw anything.

The priestly representation of God at Sinai is quite minimal. If the scholarly
attribution of Exodus 20:18-21 (15-18 in Hebrew and NJPS) to the priestly tradition
is correct, the experience is limited to thunder, lightning, and smoke. In priestly
passages, this sort of divine appearance is characterized as "glory" (kabod), which
conceals as much as it reveals of God (Exodus 24:15-18). Elsewhere in the Sinai de-

scription, the priestly tradition offers more—but barely. The priestly presentation of Moses at the tent of meeting says only that "he would hear the voice addressing him" (Numbers 7:89). Both Numbers and Deuteronomy agree on the memory of God at Sinai as being distinctly different from what is preserved in Exodus 24:9-11. The cumulative picture offered in the present arrangement of the Sinai revelation largely overwhelms the few vestiges of the older tradition; the God that was seen in human form is now remembered as the divine voice that utters words from the formless fire or glory. The new picture of God in what became the dominant version of Sinai events is a barely visual one. In the accumulation of narratives at Sinai that open "And God said to Moses, . . ." we hear the divine voice time and again communicating the divine teaching. If there is any presentation of God apart from the divine voice in these works, it is a formless, non-anthropomorphic notion that stresses the divine holiness. The priestly presentation of God throughout Leviticus hammers home the theme that God is holy, and accordingly Israel is to be holy (Leviticus 20:26). In the Deuteronomistic retelling of the Sinai revelation, we see a comparable shift toward the divine voice as the medium of revelation. The priestly memory of God at Sinai, like the Deuteronomic one, functions not as a history of events at Sinai, but as Israel's reformed collective memory designed to inculcate a religious vision for Israel to follow: Israel should be holy as God is holy. The biblical narration of the past at Sinai renders in the form of a description of the past a prescription for the present. This is not history that analyzes the past with as little regard for the present as possible; it is tradition linking past and present.

These presentations of God in part refashion earlier traditional collective memory in the image and likeness of its later authors and transmitters. The priestly ideals of avoiding the impurity, especially with respect to death and sexual relations, would tend to accent a holy God, disconnected from the realm of death and lacking in sexual relations. Holier than the holy of holies, this God would model the ideal for priests, and even the priestly people of Israel. This God would also lack for family relations, as marked in the life-cycle events of marriage and death (the latter studied by Bloch-Smith 1992 and van der Toorn 1996). The priestly version of the holy God who has no relations sounds like a monotheistic vision directed not simply against other gods, but against family religion that would center on life-cycle events and family relations. The ideal of faithful observance of the Torah in Deuteronomy focuses on the Deity as the divine voice that issues Torah. Otherwise, this invisible voice remains virtually unknown and largely unapproachable, except through religious observance and prayer. In short, the representation of the Sinai revelation in the priestly sections of the Torah as well as the book of Deuteronomy recalls as Israel's earliest memories certain pictures of God. To some degree, these are traditional, yet with their representation as part of the Sinai revelation these ideas about God supersede other traditional notions, one particularly at home in family religion, namely, God as father, or, as he is called in Genesis, "the god of the father(s)."

The Shifting Nature of Revelation at Sinai

From Israel's recollection of Sinai, Mount Sinai and the revelation there appear central to the travel itinerary from Egypt to the land. However, this connection between the Sinai revelation on the one hand, and the exodus and the entry into the land on the other hand, is not nearly as evident elsewhere in the Bible. As scholars have long noted, Sinai is omitted from accounts of exodus and entry in Exodus 15, Deuteronomy 26:5-10, and 1 Samuel 12:8. According to scholars, Exodus 15 relates the exodus in verses 1-12 and the journey to the land in verses 13-18 (discussed in the next section below). In Deuteronomy 26:5-10 Israelites are instructed to bring the firstfruits of their harvest to the priest and to recite: "my father was a wandering [or better, 'refugee'] Aramean. He went down to Egypt.... The LORD freed us from Egypt...He brought us to this place." 1 Samuel 12:8 relates: "When Jacob came to Egypt, your fathers cried out to the LORD, and the LORD sent Moses and Aaron, who brought your fathers out of Egypt and settled them in this place." In all three of these recollections, Sinai is entirely omitted from the narrative. Similarly, Psalms 89 and 105 include long descriptions of the exodus, the wilderness experience, and the Israelites' entry into the land, but there is no word about Sinai. Also, Psalm 114 beautifully balances exodus and land, sea and Jordan River, but it makes no mention of Sinai. In other passages, the mountain is included in the itinerary, but again without any reference to the Sinai revelation (for example, Psalm 106).

In the postexilic work of Nehemiah, we finally get a clear linkage of the Sinai revelation with the exodus and conquest traditions. Nehemiah 9 presents the picture that we are familiar with from the Torah (Pentateuch), and it begins in verse 6 with the sort of monotheistic claim that the book of Deuteronomy retrojects to Sinai. From the overall evidence of other biblical passages, we might conclude that the Sinai revelation associated with Moses was not integrated with the exodus and land traditions until the postexilic period. In the context of postexilic Yehud, departure from the land of slavery, the teaching of Torah, and the entry into the land would serve as a charter for the postexilic community's own story of their predecessors' departure from Babylon, their establishment of a community led by the priesthood, and their resettlement in the land (as discussed in chapters 1 and 2).

However, these texts constitute only the external evidence. Against using this approach for a postexilic date for the linkage of the exodus, Sinai, and land, we might argue that the external evidence only helps us to track the timing of when the Sinai revelation as we have it found its way into other traditions outside the Torah (Pentateuch). Understood in this way, the other biblical passages tell us only when the picture of the Sinai revelation with the exodus and the conquest traditions was finding acceptance more broadly within the Israelite community, or at least among community authorities. The other biblical witnesses to Sinai would not actually indicate when the idea of the Sinai linkage to the exodus and the conquest first developed.

The internal evidence of the book of Exodus itself, though more complicated, suggests an earlier date. Before addressing this evidence, let me clarify that I am not suggesting that the exodus, Sinai, and the land may not be old traditions in ancient Israel. On the contrary: in chapter 3 we saw the old tradition of Yahweh as an outsider from Edom/Midian/Paran/Seir/Sinai (Sinai//Seir//Paran, Deuteronomy 33:2, with a linkage—perhaps secondary—to Moses in 33:4; Seir//Edom, Judges 5:4; Teman//Paran, Habakkuk 3:3; Sinai, Psalm 68:8, 17). Similarly, the exodus is mentioned already in Exodus 15. These traditions, especially of Sinai, are quite old (possibly premonarchic), but whether revelation largely in the form that it presently takes in the Pentateuch (Torah) with all the major sections of priestly instructions had anything to do with this older Sinai tradition seems unlikely. Nor does the presumed antiquity of some sections of teaching (such as the Ten Commandments or the Covenant Code in Exodus 21–23) confirm the antiquity of their association with one another within the larger narrative. Moreover, it would appear that most, if not all, of the various collections of teachings have been secondarily recontextualized in a dramatically refashioned presentation of Sinai, with revelation mediated by Moses to the people.

Unlike the date of the external evidence, the internal evidence for the time of this refashioning suggests a preexilic date, as it is operative already in the nonpriestly material about Moses at Sinai. The nonpriestly tradition brings Moses and the people to the mountain of Horeb (the alternative name for Sinai, mentioned in Exodus 17:6 and alluded to in 18:5). That the priestly tradition arranges its own description of the Israelite arrival to Sinai in Exodus 19:1-2 suggests the original independence of the nonpriestly material, mostly in what source critics have called the Elohist source (as noted in chapter 1). This nonpriestly material lacked the collections of priestly instructions, such as the tabernacle instructions in Exodus 25–31 with their execution in Exodus 35–40, and the book of Leviticus. Whether the nonpriestly material included either the Ten Commandments or the Covenant Code is debated. That the Covenant Code had been connected to the "E" source in the prepriestly tradition (a view that used to be common in biblical studies) would make sense in view of Exodus 18:16, 20 with their reference to "the law and teachings of God," unless this passage was constructed later in order to justify the addition of a collection such as the Covenant Code. In either case, it would seem that the linkage of the Sinai tradition to the exodus and the conquest is first found within the nonpriestly material of Exodus itself, which most scholars now date to around the eighth century. Even if one moves the date by a century or more, it would still mean that the picture we have of the Sinai revelation is largely a creation of monarchic-period memory, far later than the time when Moses is said to have lived. The biblical description of Sinai may preserve some old sherds of memory (perhaps the figure of Jethro the Midianite, for example), but these are vestigial in their present form in the Torah (Pentateuch). It would seem that we cannot get back much further in Israel's traditions to the historical setting of Moses. Just as important, the various traditions remember Sinai itself very differently: some pass over it in silence, while others—in particular the priestly and Deuteronomistic traditions—make it the most important event in world history.

Sinai: Mountain above All Others

Another major shift involves the prominence of Mount Sinai itself. Apart from the so-called Elohist traditions in Exodus and the poetic piece in Deuteronomy 33:2-4, we know of no monarchic-period material that views Mount Sinai (or Horeb) as the site of divine revelation mediated by Moses. It is possible that the so-called Elohist represented a major development in the generation of a northern tradition of foundational religious origins. With the addition of priestly sections such as the building of the tabernacle, the instructions in the book of Leviticus, and the priestly sections of Numbers, Sinai grows in sheer mass in the Torah (Pentateuch). In the priestly tradition, the Sinai revelation moves from being one major event in the narrative to becoming the most important event ever. It is the single greatest moment of revelation and it overshadows all other religious traditions.

One of the results of this shift is that Sinai looms over all other religious sites in the land of Israel. In early Israel many sites maintained religious sanctuaries, and the priesthoods of these various sites evidently competed for prominence. Sanctuaries located at Shechem and Shiloh made efforts to maintain their importance in the face of royal patronage for religious sanctuaries in Jerusalem, Dan, and Bethel. All of these sites would have enjoyed their own foundational stories; indeed, the Bible preserves a number of these, for example, Genesis 14 for Jerusalem and Genesis 28 and 35 for Bethel. For the priestly tradition as represented in the Torah as we have it, Mount Sinai becomes the Mount Everest of the Bible; it overshadows and displaces all of these sites.

This shift in priestly religious memory affected the way older traditions were preserved. The poem of Exodus 15 describes the victory over Egypt in verses 1-12 and the divine accompaniment of the people to God's mountain in verses 13-18.

For decades, scholars have debated the identity of the mountain in the poem, which goes unnamed (vv. 17-18):

> *You brought them and planted them on your mountain,*
> *the place You made for your dwelling, O LORD,*
> *the sanctuary, O LORD, your hands established:*
> *May the LORD reign forever and ever!*

It has been thought that because of the reference in verses 14-15 to the Philistines, the Edomites, and the Moabites, the poem referred originally to a sanctuary in the land. The poem would have first been used in a founding tradition or religious celebration of some religious site in Israel. For comparison, we can see the traditions of Shiloh celebrated in Psalm 89, which then discusses the divine preference for Jerusalem. Scholarly proposals for the identity of the mountain in Exodus 15 have ranged widely; my own favorite is Shiloh because of the close wording shared by Exodus 15:17 and Psalm 78:54: "He brought them to His holy realm [or hill], the mountain His right hand acquired." Despite the proximity of wording, this is a pretty thin thread of evidence, and the jury is still out on the issue.

What is interesting for the issue of collective memory is the present setting of the poem in Exodus 15. In the context provided by the priestly arrangement of Exodus, the poem has been inserted between the departure from Egypt and the journey to Sinai. In the new context provided by the priestly tradition, the poem serves as a narrative punctuation mark to the prose material surrounding it (Smith 1997). In turn, the prose traditions on either side of the poem serve to provide it with a new interpretive context. The mountain for the priestly creation of the Torah is no longer a mountain in the land; verses 13-18 now serve to point to Mount Sinai. The new priestly context for the poem of Exodus 15 created a shift in its enshrinement within Israel's cultural memory. The mountain as represented by Exodus 15 moved from the land to Mount Sinai, and as a result Mount Sinai stands out among all the sanctuary sites that would have been considered God's holy mountain. In the context of late-monarchic and the later religion of Israel, this was actually quite a major claim, since implicitly the priestly presentation of Sinai with its use of Exodus 15 suggests the demotion of Jerusalem and its royal patronage. The use of the past in effect reaches back before the monarchy and creates a more significant sanctuary tradition; such a tradition would help the priestly leadership of the community in postexilic Yehud to endure the monarchy's fall.

Looking over these shifts in the collective memory of God at Sinai, we see a new understanding of divinity. As noted earlier, the Torah's priestly ideals would tend to accent a holy God, while the Deuteronomic ideals of faithful observance of the Torah focus on the Deity as the divine voice that issues Torah. The monotheistic visions of the priestly and Deuteronomy traditions rewrote the Sinai revelation to such a degree that it succeeded in reformulating Israel's identity, which it claimed as its oldest religious identity. Perhaps the most revolutionary effect of the Torah's presentation of the Sinai revelation was to transform later memories of Israel's religious past into its primary record of its origins. This new picture of origins likely displaced old mythological frameworks used to describe social or political origins, which survive only vestigially in the Bible in pieces like Psalm 74:12-17. The Sinai revelation was a new foundational story that would overshadow and perhaps submerge other foundational stories claimed by particular shrines in the land. Other older memories, which perhaps lay closer in time to Israel's origins, such as the exodus story or some of the land traditions, were either linked to the Sinai event or overwhelmed by it (or both). For example, it would appear that the exodus story itself had become the dominant national story in the northern kingdom, if the golden calf polemic against Jeroboam I's bull-calf shrines at Dan and Bethel is any indication (as suggested by the parallel wordings in 1 Kings 12:28 and Exodus 32:4 and 8; see the discussion of Jeroboam in chapter 2). The priestly redaction of Sinai and the rest of the Torah retained the memory of the exodus, but it linked it to the covenant at Mount Sinai, regarded as the even more important event by the priesthood. As a result of these displacements, Israel's own polytheism was likely one of its original features submerged beneath the sheer mass of the Sinai description.

With these massive alterations in the memory of Sinai, we see a deliberate process of modifying the past. The changes in cultural memory here function in a rather deliberate, programmatic manner. Perhaps some changes may have been less deliberate, but on the whole these literary alterations bear the marks of conscious reformulation of cultural memory. In this way, collective memory re-created Israel's origins in the image and likeness of its later commemorialists. The Sinai complex of texts is a stunning example of programmatic change in cultural memory. For in adding collections to the Sinai event, Israel's later priestly and Deuteronomic writers would attribute to ancient revelation what had developed later during the monarchic, exilic, and postexilic periods. In other words, the Sinai complex enshrines as the eternal teaching of God what had developed in later times. The Sinai material thus harbors a central paradox of collective memory that in turn becomes a religious or theological paradox: revelation is at once eternal and historical, a single divine reality consisting of multiple parts from different periods; in short, a divine and eternal unity, yet a human, time-bound amalgamation.

Sinai was hardly the only example of massive shifts in collective memory. Israel's commemorialists used additional interpretive means for channeling Israel's traditions toward the notion of a single deity. Probing what may be called "methods of monotheism" will help in identifying several cases of undeliberate changes in religious conceptualization that involve both cultural memory and amnesia.

"Methods of Monotheism" and Collective Memory

The development of a monotheistic perspective went hand in hand with what I would like to call "methods of monotheism," namely, the various ways by which ancient Israel reconstituted the diversity of its deities into a single God. Here we may note three in particular. The first may be called "convergence," the assimilation of other deities' traditions/traits to Yahweh. I am not referring simply to what we have already seen in chapter 3 with the identification of El and Yahweh, and the resulting association of El's consort, Asherah, and his astral family. As I argued in *The Early History of God* (1990, 2002a), convergence also involves the attribution of other deities' characteristics or mythology following the denial of other deities. These other deities originally had little, if anything, to do with Yahweh (or El). Already in chapter 3 we noted how the names of Baal's cosmic enemies were the same names as Yahweh's cosmic foes. As further examples, we may note the assimilation of Baal traditions to Yahweh: Mount Saphon, Baal's mountain, identified with Yahweh's Mount Zion in Psalm 48:2; and Baal's title, "Rider of Clouds," modified and applied to Yahweh in Psalm 68:4 as "Rider in the Steppeland" (in NJPS 68:5 this is translated closer to the Ugaritic as "Him who rides the clouds"). We also noted in chapter 3 how the associations of the old sun-deity were applied and transformed into God's own light in Genesis 1. This application of solar language to Yahweh was likewise part and parcel of the monotheistic method of convergence.

A second method of monotheism involved differentiation (also proposed in Smith 1990, 2002a). A denial of "other gods" was accompanied by the claim that older traditions formerly associated with Yahweh did not belong to Yahweh. For example, we noted in chapter 3 denunciations of asherah and of the "sun, moon, and the stars." With this second method of monotheism, we see Yahweh differentiated from the earlier Israelite past. These features were quite traditional in ancient Israel. However, they were reinterpreted as features not of Israel but of foreign peoples. In the case of the asherah in particular, it was recognized as an old feature, but in Judges 6 it is recalled not as the traditional practice of Israel that it once was, but as an old foreign practice that sometimes Israel idolatrously adopted for itself.

A third method involved reinterpretation of older polytheistic vestiges. Powerful examples of this process of reinterpretation include two texts that we examined in chapter 3. The first was Deuteronomy 32:8-9:

When the Most High (Elyon) allotted peoples for inheritance,
   when He divided up humanity,
He fixed the boundaries for peoples,
   according to the number of the divine sons [MT: sons of Israel]:
for Yahweh's portion is His people,
   Jacob His own inheritance.

In chapter 3 we looked primarily at how this text preserves the old notions of the divine family and its world theology. By the same token, it is evident that the author of this poem, even with the reading "number of the divine sons," evidently understood Elyon and Yahweh to be one and the same god, the god of Israel, for the poem goes on to refer to the other gods as "no-gods" (v. 17, NRSV "not God"), and to describe Yahweh as the only god (v. 39). It is clear that for this author there really are no other gods.

Like Deuteronomy 32, Psalm 82 opposes the older theology, as Israel's deity is called to assume a new role as judge of all the world. Yet at the same time, Psalm 82, like Deuteronomy 32:8-9, also preserves the outlines of the older theology that it is rejecting. From the perspective of this older theology, Yahweh did not belong to the top level of the pantheon. Instead, it would appear that in early Israel the god of Israel belonged to the second tier of the pantheon; he was not the presiding god, but one of his sons. However, Psalm 82 did not seem to receive any kind of later Masoretic rewriting or reinterpretation, because Psalm 82 was more susceptible to a monotheistic rereading. It was apparently easier to interpret Psalm 82 in monotheistic terms, by assuming that El Elyon was simply a title for Yahweh. As long as biblical texts could be reread in terms of this new monistic vision, what we call monotheism, they could remain in the biblical record. Rereading of this text would permit a collective amnesia about the separate origins and history of Yahweh and El.

Even in cases where conscious censorship has been claimed, as in Deuteronomy 32:8-9, collective amnesia is also at work. For in treating these other gods as the gods of other peoples, Israelite society was also in the process of forgetting that what they condemned in some of these gods had once been their own. Both foreign and indigenous deities were subsumed under the rubric of the "other gods" belonging to the other nations and not to Israel. Other developments may also have worked with monotheistic language, for example, the linguistic phenomenon whereby the names of other deities became generic nouns. Thus Astarte became a term for fertility, Resheph for flame, and Deber for pestilence. As a result, variations in the presentation of divinity became more uniform in accordance with Israel's later collective memory. As a further result, a number of old religious features were altered.

Cultural Memory and Amnesia of Divinity through the Lens of Divine Oneness

The monotheistic perspective of Israel's later religious elites induced a certain cultural amnesia in some other representations of divinity found in the Bible. As we tracked the changes in the levels of Israelite divinity in chapter 3, we saw alterations made both to the levels and to the concepts of family and council. In view of that discussion, we can identify four major changes in divinity involving not just cultural memory but also cultural amnesia.

Yahweh and El

Perhaps the most important example of Israelite amnesia about divinity is the identification of Yahweh with El. Although some biblical texts preserved vestiges of the two gods' distinction, biblical traditions tended to read the distinction as continuity. It would appear that one factor in this identification involved the name El, which as the simple form of the word for "god" could be reread as a generic word for "the god." In the case of Israel, Yahweh was "the god." Exodus 6:2-3 shows explicitly that the god who had been understood as El (Shadday) was now to be identified with Yahweh: "I am Yahweh. I appeared to Abraham, to Isaac, and to Jacob as El Shadday, but my name Yahweh I did not make known to them." As this passage may also imply, perhaps it was El who was the god of the exodus, not Yahweh. It is possible that only through their later identification did Yahweh come to be viewed as the god responsible for the exodus.

There was further fallout from this identification of the two gods. Asherah was likely understood as Yahweh's wife, not El's. Moreover, the memory of El's family, conceptualized as the heavenly or astral hosts, was associated with Yahweh. So, the tradition preserved the memory of all these divinities, but their older separation from Yahweh was forgotten. Here cultural amnesia seems to result from long tradition, which included a process of interpreting older traditions no longer fully understood. In this instance, cultural amnesia seems to be unconscious and not deliberate.

Yahweh and His Home in Edom

In chapter 3 we discussed how Yahweh seems to be at least initially an outsider from Edom/Midian/Paran/Seir/Sinai (Sinai//Seir//Paran, Deuteronomy 33:2; Seir//Edom, Judges 5:4; Teman//Paran, Habakkuk 3:3; Sinai, Psalm 68:8, 17). This view is hardly the sort of claim created during the later monarchy when relations worsened between Israel and Edom. Instead, as we saw in chapter 1, the premonarchic period seems to be the time when Yahweh as an Edomite god (as noted by van der Toorn 1996, Lang 2002, and others) came to be rooted in the highland society of Israel. In chapter 1 we also noticed this close relationship with Edom within Israel's prosaic presentations of its ethnic relations in the book of Genesis. In time, Yahweh came to be recalled as "the god of Israel," with the memory of his origins in Edom remapped as the Mount Sinai experience of the earliest Israelites on their way from Egypt to the land promised to Abraham. Edom as Israel's "kin" and Yahweh as an Edomite god generally fell out of the Israelite script. The biblical tradition preserved the vestiges of the older religious situation, but forgot crucial aspects of it. Once again cultural amnesia as well as memory appear to be at work in an unconscious way.

Yahweh and the Divine Family

In ancient Israel, the concepts of the divine family and the divine council went through significant changes, as we saw in chapter 3. The divine family as a concept of polytheistic oneness is only vestigial in the Bible. The claim to be a god without family, generally anomalous in the ancient Near East, reflects a new situation in Israel whereby the family suffered terrible deterioration, first due to economic stratification in the eighth century, followed by the conquest of the north by the Assyrians around 732–722 and their conquest of the south in 701, with its massive deportation. These developments conclude with the conquest of the south in 597–586. As we also saw in chapter 3, the family no longer functioned as the sole or primary mode of social identification. Now the individual is no longer held responsible for the sins of her or his parents (Jeremiah 31:29-30; Ezekiel 18 and 33:12-20; Deuteronomy 24:16), and correspondingly the Israelite god could be seen as the individual deity responsible for the operation of the universe. The presentation of this god was also increasingly enlarged by notions of empire thanks to the incursions of the Assyrians: like Ashur and later Marduk, Yahweh becomes something of an empire-god over the whole cosmos. The result is the decrease in the intelligibility of the divine family as a governing conceptualization for divinity and an increase in the sense that monotheism would make. Thus the family falls into disuse as a means of conceptualizing divinity.

The emergent biblical monotheism seems to have grown in part out of a conscious rejection of foreign gods and a concomitant interpretation of Israel's own deities, apart from Yahweh, as foreign. As with the preceding examples of cultural memory and amnesia, reinterpretation of the past seems to be a basic ingredient in generating the developing understanding of the one God. This process of reinterpretation involved a rather deliberate agenda, especially on the part of the authors of Deuteronomy, for example, but this does not mean that Israel's old deities were all known to be ancient Israelite deities and then they were deliberately and consciously made into foreign deities. Instead, it may be that many of *alterity*

these divinities were vestigial and those that were not may have been interpreted within Israel's culture as foreign. For example, in chapter 3 we discussed the possibility that the old Israelite goddess (perhaps Astarte or Asherah) may have been identified as the Queen of Heaven of Mesopotamia in the sixth century. As a result, the deities that may have looked foreign in this period were understood by the author of a book like Deuteronomy as foreign, and other vestiges of older Israelite deities were understood in the same way. So a certain amount of unconscious cultural memory and amnesia may have been involved with this change, as with the other developments we have discussed so far. These stand in contrast to the more deliberate changes in the representation of the past that we saw earlier in this chapter with the biblical representations of Mount Sinai.

Interestingly, the divine council did not fall into disuse, but was reconfigured to express the new monotheistic perspective, with only two levels of deities, one the supreme king of the divine empire and the other the lowest tier of angels. The idea of the divine council in ancient Israel enjoyed a long literary history. It lasted through the period of the monarchy. For example, the picture of the heavenly seraphim in service to Yahweh enthroned appears in the eighth-century text of Isaiah 6, the biblical inspiration for both the Hosanna in Christian tradition ("holy, holy, holy is the Lord of Hosts . . ." recited in the Mass) and the Qedushah in Jewish services. (The relative antiquity of this section in Isaiah has been defended in Hartenstein 1997.) This picture of the heavenly council continued down through the second century (Daniel 7) and later. For these biblical works, however, these angels did not enjoy the same ontological status as the divine king. Instead, their functioning depended on the divine king whom they served. We may say that Power and powers represents the ancient world's way of expressing ontological status compared to the medieval philosophical concept of Being and beings (I expand on this point in the Postscript following this chapter). Viewed in these terms, the angels only have reality insofar as their power derives from and participates in the power of the One Supreme Power. The terms of power formerly attributed to the second level would be applied to the angels of the fourth level (both were called "divine sons" and "divinities"), and in turn these would be understood as "powers" derivative ultimately of the One Divine Power.

The fallout from this change can be seen in the handling of older Israelite material about gods. In chapter 3 we saw an example of the identification of the second level of divine children as angelic members of the fourth tier. I mentioned that the astral association lying behind the polemic against the king of Babylon in Isaiah 14:12-13 preserves an old story of divine conflict in heaven involving the celestial god Shahar (Dawn). From the allusion in this passage he seems to have *Lucifer* attempted to ascend into heaven and exalt his throne "above the stars of El." According to this story, Shahar was apparently viewed as trying to displace other astral deities and perhaps even El himself. In Israel this form of the story survived only as a little vestige in Isaiah 14:12-13, really only as an allusion. Its polytheistic background would be forgotten, but it would later become the basis for the story of the battle in heaven between God's angelic forces and the rebellious fallen angels cast into the underworld.

This story would enjoy a particular longevity, including New Testament references to the fall of Lucifer in Luke 10:18 and 2 Peter 2:4, and the heavenly battle in Revelation 12:7-9, as well as John Milton's profound *Paradise Lost;* the same story of angelic rebellion in heaven underlies the Hollywood movies *Devil's Advocate* and *Dogma.* In short, the old polytheistic narrative known in earlier Israel, which featured a level-two god, survived later in Israel as the story of a fourth-level angel. That this narrative ever applied to a level-two god was forgotten.

Angels and the God of the Fathers

The identification of second-level deities with fourth-level messenger deities (angels) issued in a further change: the occasional identification of the family god of the fathers with messenger divinities (angels). El was originally the patriarch of both the divine family and many human families in ancient Israel. In his help to humans, he was understood in part as a family or clan god, called in texts "the god of the fathers." With the loss of El and the melding of most of his functions with Yahweh's, the older role of the god of the fathers as one who accompanies the family (Genesis 35:3) shifted in some texts into the role of angelic accompaniment. This shift is apparent in a number of passages (1 Kings 19:5-9; Psalm 91: 11-12; compare Exodus 23:20-22), but especially in Genesis 48:15-16, where the accompanying "god of the father" and the protective angel stand in grammatical apposition:

> May the god before whom my fathers, Abraham and Jacob, went about,
> the god who has shepherded me from my time back till today,
> the messenger who has redeemed me from all evil,
> may he bless the boys.

In contrast to the biblical identification of these two divine functionaries stands the opposite situation attested in earlier texts, such as the Late Bronze Age texts from the city-state of Ugarit. These texts do not show messengers in the role of accompanying the family or people. Again this change in biblical tradition hardly seems like a deliberate, programmatic alteration. Instead, it shows both cultural memory and amnesia at work. The slippage of divine identity may have been facilitated because of the ambiguous character of the term *(ha)elohim.* As this word may refer to "god" or "gods" (whether minor or major) and serves as a generic term for Yahweh, it permits the effacing of older distinctions between minor and major divinities *(elohim)*, including messengers, the familial god, and Yahweh. This ambiguity facilitated the identification of the clan god and the divine messenger in some biblical texts, and the clan god with Yahweh in other passages. As a result, the memory of the clan god's functioning was effaced. From a sociological perspective, this shift in divine roles signals the reduction of family religion in shaping the dominant cultural memory under the force of the textually more dominant traditions represented by the priestly sections of the Torah (Pentateuch) and by Deuteronomy and the Deuteronomistic History. As a corollary of this shift, these traditions all criticize family religion and their religious practices, especially those pertaining to the dead in Leviticus 19:28, 31; 20:6, 27; Deuteronomy 14:1; 18:10-11; 26:14; 1 Samuel 28; and 2 Kings 21:6.

With these changes in Israel's cultural memory, we see how the divine figures in a sense become one, or continuous with the One. Amnesia about divinity appears to have been accomplished in part through the ambiguity of *elohim,* and in part due to changes in the understanding of divinity experienced during the monarchic period, and finally through the submersion caused by the growing importance of monistic developments in the Israelite cult, especially from the eighth century onward. The Bible's later commemorialists preserved some older vestiges about divinity in ancient Israelite religious life, vestiges that they themselves did not understand and that the tradition in the interim had largely forgotten. Such vestiges survived displacement, conflation, and diminishment as long as they could be read, interpreted, or rewritten according to later norms, especially a monotheistic view of God. As a result, the Bible preserves both the dominant views of later commemorialists and the vestiges of earlier memories. The varying presentation of divinity in the past suggests that not only the past in general but also divinity in particular involved reconfigurations. The images of divinity in the biblical writings underwent realignments by which "facts" about Israel's divinity came into larger narratives.

To remember the divinity was to re-form, to re-member, an unwieldy series of older divine portraits of various levels and types of divinity into some sort of single coherence by accumulation of images, but also by omission, mediated and filtered by a monistic vision of divinity. The presentation of a single deity, read back into the biblical corpus, was a cornerstone of cultural memory in priestly tradition and in Deuteronomy and the Deuteronomistic History probably from the eighth–seventh centuries onward. In time, the various pieces and persona of divinity could be accommodated to one another as parts of a single portrait, though hardly a fully consistent one. For Israel's later priestly and Deuteronomic commemorators, to attribute various past acts of divine help one way or another to a single deity aided their fashioning of narratives resonant with their perceptions of divinity in time past and present. Time was on their side.

Like the Bible's commemorators, its later readers read with the monotheistic God in mind across the wide narrative contexts of the Pentateuch and the Deuteronomistic History, the Major and Minor Prophets, wisdom works, Psalms, and other writings. As a consequence, believers participate in a process begun already in the biblical period: they read for the monotheistic God in the religious writings of Israel, including earlier texts that contain vestiges of Israel's polytheistic past. With such a process of reading, believers, like the ancient transmitters of the Bible, interpret it with a monotheistic lens and see the monotheistic God as the original historical experience of ancient Israel at Sinai and afterward. As a result, like ancient Jewish and Christian traditions themselves, later believers belonging to these religious traditions view the complex and numerous biblical texts and their shaping as a single text now called the Bible, with one deity who spans all of its individual texts and beyond.

For the religious traditions of Judaism and Christianity, this view of the monotheistic God of Israel's past became normative. This past was no longer simply Israel's representation. It also became recognized as God's own revelation about the past. In other words, the process that interpreted Israel's religious writings as sacred scriptures and eventually the canonical Bible transformed Israel's representation of the past. The Bible's representation of the past became God's words to Israel about God in Israel's past. As a result of this transformation, the revelation of the Bible embodied God's definitive word to Israel about their covenantal relationship, all the way from Abraham through Moses and David and well beyond. In other words, Israel's past as represented in the Bible became the memoirs of God.

From a theological perspective, the Bible is the revelation of what God selected to be remembered and forgotten of God's relationship to Israel and the world. This extended to God's own character and configuration. Viewing the Bible in this way raises a number of theological issues, which are addressed in the following Postscript.

Postscript

Biblical Memory between Religion, Theology, and History

In my beginning is my end.
—T. S. Eliot, *Four Quartets*

In this Postscript, I offer some reflections and questions raised by various parts of this book. The Postscript's title employs the preposition "between," because (despite the ungrammatical usage) this word suggests for me the intellectually difficult "spaces" lying between a number of different fields that coexist rather uneasily. As we have seen, memory—and in particular biblical memory—bears on the spaces lying between the fields of religion, theology, and history. In part, my comments are motivated by what I see as the problematic role of history in biblical and theological studies, not to mention its effect on the wider context of modern Western religions. The issues raised by the interrelationships between these areas of inquiry as seen in various chapters of this book are important ones that deserve further consideration by people interested in the Bible and by scholars engaged in religion and theology.

In these comments, I step back a bit from this book's agenda and offer a broader and less formal perspective. From my vantage point as a student of the Bible and the ancient Near Eastern world, I make this limited effort in order to engage some questions of theology and religion. I acknowledge that I am not a professional theologian, unless historical biblical studies were to be seen as a branch of historical theology. Nor am I a historian of religions in the strict sense, although my work draws heavily from the history of religions. However, my comments that follow enter into these areas. It would be fair also to say that my identity as a Roman Catholic has affected some of my remarks. Given my limitations, I do not

159

intend to address the relationships between the fields of theology, religion, and history in general, but only as they pertain to the study of the Bible.

The issues discussed here are interrelated. As a result, this Postscript is not as structured as the preceding chapters. At the outset, I would say that close-minded attitudes about the Bible coming from different sides badly distort its reading. From my perspective the extremes represented by a blind fundamentalism on the one hand and a corrosive secularism and atheism on the other have generated some of the greatest distortions of what the Bible has to offer to either religious or nonreligious readers. The first alternative regularly ignores the historical, diachronic dimensions of the Bible, while the second often shows little empathy for the religious experiences and faith expressed by biblical texts. These extremes are a problem not only in general American culture, but also inside the academic context for studying the Bible. However, the difficulties in appreciating the Bible are hardly confined to steering some ideal course between these extremes. The study of Israel's religion and theological reflections on the Bible do not often mix well. The study of religion is not delimited by theology's traditional understanding of the Bible as revelation, nor does the study of religion privilege the Bible as a historical source over other sources.

Despite gaps between the fields of religion and theology, the study of religion remains a useful tool for providing background information to the Bible. As a result, biblical traditions—and especially how they work to assert themselves—are illuminated by a history of religions approach that unveils biblical traditions and their perspectives, in contrast to a tendency in some biblical theologies largely to repeat and reinscribe the viewpoints found in biblical traditions. The study of religion is in some ways better able than theology to take seriously the competitors to biblical traditions, to hear them out on their own terms, and thereby to elucidate them.

The relative merits of biblical theology and the history of Israelite religion as fields have been intensely debated in German circles, especially since Rainer Albertz began championing the study of Israelite religion over biblical theology in the early 1990s. As he argues in the introduction to his two-volume history of Israelite religion (1994), Albertz regards the history of religions approach as "the more meaningful comprehensive Old Testament discipline." Albertz touched off an intense discussion in Germany, represented, for example, in essays by Janowski, Lohfink, and others published in volume 10 of the *Jahrbuch für biblische Theologie* (1995). The discussion was largely ignored in the United States, where the two fields intersect rather little.

One might think that the two fields roughly correspond to the diachronic and synchronic dimensions of the Hebrew Bible. History of religion tends to view biblical literature as a diversity of witnesses to religious (diachronic) developments

deconstructs binary

over time, while biblical theology approaches biblical literature (as much as possible) as a whole, a Bible, produced as a single (synchronic) revelation in time. However, the synchronic takes place in time, just as diachronic dimensions inform any synchronic project. Because the Bible came to fruition in synchronic moments informed by a variety of diachronic dimensions, the Bible's fuller understanding requires recognizing both its synchronic and diachronic dimensions, brought together into some sort of dialogue. What shape that dialogue should take will remain debated, but what should not be debated is the need for it. The biblical traditions concerning Israel's religious past, as clarified by the study of religion, raise important theological issues. More on this momentarily, but first a word about theology in some of the biblical texts that we observed earlier in this book.

Biblical Narrative and Systematic Theology

With the biblical representation of the past, Israel's collective memory generated a master narrative that relates in Genesis–Kings a linear presentation of God's relationship with Israel. This master narrative was modified as it went on, with older modifications overwritten by later ones. The modified biblical narrative often left vestiges of older versions of the past, issuing in a text with a dialectic between the master narrative and other earlier, or even contemporary, conflicting versions. Israel's representation of its past in the Bible also incorporates competition and compromise over the meaning of that past. What becomes recognized as revelation is more than a single revelation about the past.

The biblical representations of the past served as a forum for voicing different views about the circumstances of the Israelite community in the times of their authors. In chapter 3, when we examined Psalms 74 and 104 and Genesis 1, we saw three different versions of creation presented in different genres (lament, hymn, and narrative). The priestly formation of the Torah (Pentateuch) ultimately gave pride of place to Genesis 1, itself an important theological claim enshrined in Scripture that expresses a foundational biblical effort at theology. Genesis 1 is first. Moreover, its structure shows a brilliant effort at understanding reality as informed by divine agency; in other words, theology. Psalms 74 and 104 show how poetic narratives also functioned as an important means for doing theology. Although not a traditional form of Christian theology, biblical representations of the past, whether narrative, hymn, or lament, in their own way present or presuppose an arrangement of the universe and God's relationship with it. The arrangement of elements in these biblical passages is analogous to the arrangement of logical relations in systematic theology.

We may go further with the comparison between biblical texts and later forms of theology, especially when it comes to Genesis 1 and Psalms 74 and 104. For the ancient Israelites, their texts contain an ancient form of metaphysics. To be sure, these ancient texts do not use the ontological language of "being" found in the works of the great metaphysicians of later ages such as Thomas Aquinas. Instead, a fundamental ontology used in the ancient world is embodied in language about power. In the reduced pantheon of late-monarchic Judah, the world and its beings derive their reality (or being), in ancient terms their power, from the one power of God (Being itself, in medieval terms). We saw in chapter 3 how the messenger divinities, the angels, ultimately derive their power from the power of the One God. It is true also of human kings: their power was thought to derive from the power of the divine King. Transposed into traditional metaphysical language, the power of lesser beings in the world participates in Power itself, identified with God.

Psalm 104 offers another ancient metaphysical paradigm, in the form of the divine life force (Hebrew *ruach*). In the Bible, the word does not always refer to "life force," but in Psalm 104 it is the divine life force that sustains all creatures; if God takes back this *ruach,* they die (vv. 29-30, NRSV "breath" and "spirit"). In presenting an alternative ontology of the universe, the paradigm of Psalm 104 is of tremendous importance for modern theology, for it shows that the picture of a violent deity—and an intensely male one at that—was hardly the only paradigm of divinity enshrined in the Bible. While we should try to understand that the paradigm of power is an ancient way to express the fundamental point that God can and does help human beings, it is not the only way to express this point. In Psalm 104 the ecological balance and harmonious order of the world, where the various parts of the universe serve one another, offers a nonhierarchical paradigm that does not exalt humanity over the rest of creation. In many ways Psalm 104 offers an intensely sacramental vision of the dynamic, divine presence in the world, a paradigm particularly powerful for our age, as people struggle against violence, gender hierarchy, discrimination of various sorts, and ecological disaster.

The forms of ancient metaphysics found in Psalms 74 and 104 as well as Genesis 1 are not original with ancient Israel. They can be found also in a number of ancient Near Eastern cultures. We already saw martial power as the basic terms of the Ugaritic story of Baal battling Sea (*CAT* 1.2 IV). In the form of solar power, divine life force informs the presentation of reality in ancient Egyptian texts, for example, in the hymns to the Aten in the time of the famous Pharaoh Akhenaten (see *ANET,* 370–71). These ontologies in Israel and the ancient Near East raise a particularly important question for theology, namely, the understanding of biblical revelation.

Revelation, Tradition, and the Idolatry of History

Historically speaking, revelation at Sinai, as it is presented in the Bible, did not "happen" at Israel's point of origin. Instead, as we saw in chapters 2 and 4, the biblical presentation of Sinai involved descriptions of origins constructed at various points in time, presented as a single narrative of origins. In the case of the Torah (Pentateuch), the idea of torah as Sinai revelation is attested first in the middle of Israel's history (for example, in Deuteronomy 33:2-5). Its inclusion in the Sinai corpus, especially its lengthy priestly material, was constructed as an original, pristine moment in time in ancient Israel interpreted as eternal in value and purpose. Similarly, the book of Psalms is presented largely as the original words of David, although this is a relatively late idea retrojected onto the figure of David.

The model operative in both the Torah and the book of Psalms is a prophetic one: both Moses and David are modifications of the prophetic model. In Moses' case, he is a super-prophet. The book of Deuteronomy ends by telling us that there was never a prophet like Moses (34:10). Over the course of Israel's tradition, David also became a prophetic figure. To his royal persona was added the mantle of prophecy, as we saw toward the end of chapter 2. According to a Psalms scroll from the Dead Sea Scrolls (11QPs^a), David spoke the psalms under the influence of prophetic inspiration, and another scroll (4Q171, a Psalms *pesher* or interpretation) presents psalms as to be interpreted like the prophetic books that predict the future. Texts from different levels of Israelite tradition became attached to these figures, thereby becoming parts of the original revelation attributed to them. In other words, revelation is the complex of traditions retrojected literarily to a single original moment or period by applying the idea of prophecy to foundational figures (compare 2 Peter 1:20-21).

The idea that the original biblical revelation could be a product of biblical tradition, secondarily retrojected and created as an original moment of contact with the Divine, can be unsettling for people who regard the Bible as divine revelation. Many people want to believe that the presentation of revelation in the Bible was the way it actually happened. The logical implication of this idea is a kind of fundamentalism about the Bible. Indeed, part of the appeal of fundamentalism is its inherent simplicity. It does not ask people to understand anything of the Bible's complexities (although many biblical scholars who are fundamentalistic in their approach to the Bible are fully aware of such complexities). For people of this persuasion, it is unsettling to analyze the biblical traditions and to see the portrayals of biblical figures such as Moses or David as products of Israel's religious history, even its religious imagination. The unsettling nature of an academic approach to the Bible, however, is not simply a problem with critical biblical studies. Contrary to a view popular among some fundamentalists, biblical scholars are not evil people or misguided people trying to sabotage religious faith. On the contrary, many biblical scholars are intensely devoted to their religious traditions and to their God.

The bigger problem that I see is what I would call the "idolatry of history." Many people devoted to the Bible as divine revelation share a major assumption with people who are critical of religious faith and devotion to the Bible. Strangely, curiously, many in both camps operate with the assumption that the truth of the Bible stands or falls on whether the Bible is always historically true. However, this working assumption about history as the main criterion of biblical truth is at best implicit in the Bible itself. It is true that the Bible presents revelation as having come in the course of Israel's past. Furthermore, it is true that some basic "biblical events" stand on biblical claims about their actually having occurred. For Christians, one obvious example is the resurrection of Jesus (as expressed in 1 Corinthians 15:12-19). However, this is not the same as saying that the Bible stands or falls as revelation depending on whether or not every single fact recorded in the Bible was historically true. Indeed, the Bible itself provides multiple witnesses to the same event. Several episodes from the Gospels occur in multiple versions (such as the birth of Jesus or the Last Supper), which could not have all happened exactly as portrayed if all the biblical texts are historical transcripts of the events that they present. Another strong argument against an emphasis on the Bible as history involves whole biblical books that are parallel but differ in their presentation of the past. The events at Sinai are related in Exodus–Numbers and in Deuteronomy in different ways. Similarly, the Gospels relate the life of Jesus with quite a number of wide variations. The traditions that brought the Hebrew Bible (Old Testament) and New Testament into recognizable collections preserved the multiplicity of witnesses as to what "happened." So the formation of biblical tradition itself constitutes a powerful biblical argument against viewing the Bible as exact transcripts of biblical events.

Whether one accepts or criticizes the Bible as historical truth, historical veracity is hardly the single biblical standard for truth. Instead, the Bible fundamentally proclaims the reality of God in human lives and the implications that flow from that reality. It is not the Bible but our culture as it developed over the last half-millennium that has elevated the category of historical truth above other sorts or categories of truth. It is this exaltation of history as the absolute or primary measure of truth in the Bible that I view as the "idolatry of history."

By this I am not suggesting that revelation or other religious phenomena in the Bible have no grounding in time, that they stand outside time or are unaffected by temporal conditions. On the contrary, this entire book has shown the valuable service that historical research performs in bringing readers of the Bible, including religious believers, closer to the Bible's traditions. Historical research helps to illuminate the nature of revelation and its context. Religious believers should be satisfied with whatever historical research can provide, since to do otherwise would ill serve both historical research and faith. For the goal of historical research is not to "prove faith" or to "prove the Bible," nor does faith rely on the witness simply of historical research but on what Scripture teaches. What the Scripture proclaims can be better understood thanks to historical research, but the two are not the same. So to the degree that historical research serves the understanding of what the Bible teaches (and how ancient Israel and the Christian church understood that witness), it is an aid to religious traditions.

By the same token, religious traditions do not need to regard the biblical presentation as transcripts of events, and indeed should not view them in this way, in view of the positive results of historical research. Historical research helps to show how biblical revelation was understood, received, and transmitted. It can even identify the sorts of religious experience that inform biblical revelation. However, historical research cannot verify the truth claims of revelation that pertain to events in time—nor should it try to do so. For faith entails hope in things unseen. Faith does not stand or fall on historical proofs; it does not regard history as the primary basis for proving the truth of its claims. Thus I am stressing that the Bible does not proclaim history as the only or even the main factor of revelation. Revelation is highly conditioned by historical context, but it is not reducible to a simple paraphrase of human conditions.

The problem of history is not only a religious problem; it remains a central problem dividing the field of biblical studies. The contemporary crisis over what history is, and how to pursue it as an intellectual matter, have created intellectual fissures in the biblical field. In North America, biblical scholars may be divided, roughly speaking, between those who relate the Bible to its historical context in terms of both language and culture and those who, in applying to the Bible modern methods, lack an interest in Israel's past. In the hands of the former group, the Bible seems to be confined to Israel's past and seems to have little to say to the modern world. In the hands of the latter, the past represented by the Bible need not be related to the ancient world; it is a construct, an act of imagination. This world of imagination represented by the Bible is treated apart from the ancient world of its authors. The result is study of the Bible that in effect denies or ignores the Israel of the past. While such treatments can speak powerfully to the modern world, what they relate is freed from the ancient cultural context of Israel, and becomes more often than not modern acts of imagination rather than representations of Israel's own acts of imagination. To be sure, many scholars try to bridge the gap between the two sides of the divide, but this is becoming increasingly difficult.

It is not clear to me that the situation with respect to the Bible and history is much better elsewhere, for example, in Germany. Many German biblical scholars work almost exclusively in literary analysis of the texts, in their compositional levels and redaction as well as their tradition history. This study sometimes takes place with little sense of the culture in which this ancient activity took place and to which this tradition history belonged. As in North America, a number of German scholars are trying to bridge the gap. Israeli scholarship too is going through a deep questioning about the Bible's historicity, and we likewise see there some divide between history-oriented scholarship and literary approaches to the Bible with little interest in historical context. To my mind, this divide is intellectually problematic for the study of ancient Israel. As we saw in chapter 3, the imaginative world of Genesis 1 makes sense only if one knows the tradition of creation stories that the author of Genesis 1 is playing off of. If someone is unaware of the cosmic battle traditionally expected at the beginning of such a narrative, the shift in Genesis 1 to divine word ("he said") in verse 3 loses its power.

Thus some appreciation of the text itself and its context within ancient Israel is indispensable. Despite this conclusion, we are left with the problem of history in the field, and it represents a crisis not only within biblical studies but also within the humanities more broadly. We find that we are not free of historical context; our understandings of reality remain inextricably rooted in historical experience, and there is no way to escape this condition of life. Thus, just as we understand ourselves in time, so we should appreciate the Israelites in their biblical writings in their own time. By the same token, we do not and cannot restrict the meaning of ancient texts to what or how they spoke to their ancient audiences. Ancient writings are not simply of antiquarian interest, but speak to the larger human condition across time. And for religious people for whom these writings are Holy Scripture, the Bible is more than a group of interesting texts from the past. It is a text—the text—that has inspired generations that include many, if not most, of its most brilliant interpreters. Still, this recognition does not free the church from appreciating the audiences who first received the texts; they too belong to the whole history of audiences that have received and cherished the biblical texts. Accordingly, the larger enterprise of interpretation necessitates a historical interest in the earliest biblical witnesses, their inner-biblical audiences, and their interpretations of biblical texts, as well as their postbiblical interpreters. All of these are to be read in dialectic with one another. So, without worshiping history as the most important criterion for truth, as a theological matter we should value Israel's past despite the current lack of appreciation for the ancient past.

The Paradox of Revelation: Eternal yet Temporal

Many people of religious faith do not "worship history" in the sense that I have mentioned. They can live with the idea of the Bible both as revelation and as historically problematic. As we observed in chapter 4, this very complexity is part of the biblical record itself. For an important illustration, let me return to the Sinai revelation recorded in Exodus 19–Numbers 10. This complex of material in the Bible is a stunning example of the biblical witness to the complex relationship between revelation and history. For in adding collections to the Sinai event, Israel's later priestly and Deuteronomic commemorialists would attribute to ancient revelation what had been developed later during the monarchic, exilic, and postexilic periods. In other words, the Sinai complex enshrines as the eternal teaching of God what had developed in later history. This central paradox of collective memory also constitutes a religious or theological paradox: revelation is at once eternal and temporal, a single divine reality consisting of multiple parts from different periods; in short, a divine and eternal unity, yet also a human, time-bound amalgamation. In the Sinai material, we see that biblical traditions undergirded what became Scripture, and an increasing sense of Scripture in turn informed the formation of biblical traditions. Thus, already within the biblical period, Scripture and tradition stand in a complex dialectical relationship.

Those who study the Bible as only a single eternal or synchronic witness fail to understand the Bible's own witnesses to the historical complexity of biblical revelation. Here I am not simply speaking of fundamentalists who may be expected to ignore the deep historical complexities of biblical revelation. I am referring to biblical theologians, learned Scripture scholars, whose accounts exclude the religious complexity of the biblical witness that they otherwise claim to champion as their own and to acknowledge as revelation. When biblical theologians or Scripture scholars dismiss or minimize the potential contribution to be made by the field of the history of religion of Israel to understanding biblical revelation, this is, from a theological point of view (not to mention from an intellectual perspective), insufficient to the diachronic dimension of the biblical witness, to God's revelation about Israel's past. As a source for Israel's memory and amnesia about itself and its divinity, the Bible retained significant information about the history of Israel's religion. As a result, the historical approach has a significant role to play in informing and expanding biblical theology.

At the same time, an engagement with history of religion does not resolve many questions about biblical revelation. The biblical senses of what revelation means remain in great need of further understanding and probing, beyond what history of religions approaches have provided. Revelation does not constitute only what is recounted in the historically conditioned record of the Bible. It also involves a dialectic between the Bible and its immediate context in Israel and the rest of the ancient Near East. Subsequent to the emergence of Jewish and Christian Scriptures (and later Bibles), revelation has further engendered a dialectic between the Bible and the world, with tradition serving as a guide to help bridge the two. I formulate the matter in this way probably because I am a Roman Catholic, yet I see tradition serving an interpretive guide and bridge not only in Catholic tradition but also in other Christian communities, as well as in Judaism. I also tend to recognize tradition as a formative, historically conditioned dimension of religious faith and practice not only in contemporary religious traditions but also in ancient Israel. Tradition and Scripture deeply affected one another. This approach hardly settles many of these difficult issues about the Bible as revelation and history, but to my mind it provides some help for reflecting on these questions.

Those who think that they rely on Scripture alone for guidance on these matters often overlook or minimize that they are indebted to earlier religious traditions that choose to exalt Scripture alone over tradition. To be sure, the proclamation of Scripture alone has been a much-needed antidote to the exaltation of tradition, and in its history Roman Catholicism has sometimes forgotten the power of the biblical word. At the same time, it remains true that some form of tradition informs any religious life that claims the Bible as its central source of guidance. In the language of Christian theology, Scripture is much like Jesus Christ, fully divine and fully human, fully embedded in and shaped by history and acting in it. The human part of Scripture includes historically problematic, even incorrect, details. Where people are involved in the equation, human foibles are there as well. Contrary to fundamentalists, I think that the Bible's human side is better understood thanks to the God-given reason that scholars apply to it, and contrary to fundamentalists' severest secular critics, I believe the Bible's divine side remains a matter of respectable faith that inspires great good and hope in the world. Both sides of the Bible remain important to believers who stand between the two extremes. The twin sides of the Bible further affect the understanding of the Bible as revelation and canon.

Revelation and the Limits of the Biblical Canon

When looking at specific metaphors for the divine, revelation does not lie simply in the metaphors themselves, but in how the metaphors changed and recombined over the course of Israelite religion and then became enshrined in the Bible. In chapter 3 we noted that to understand the story of God in the Bible, it helped to back up to Israel's early expressions about divinity. In this intellectual enterprise, the Ugaritic texts may function for heuristic purposes as "the Old Testament of the Old Testament," to borrow an expression coined by Moberly (1992). Moberly used this phrase to characterize his understanding of the theological relationship of Genesis to the rest of the Pentateuch. With certain restrictions in mind, we may extend this expression to the Ugaritic texts vis-à-vis the Hebrew Bible. Of course, the beginning of the time frame for investigating biblical God-talk has, by tradition, been marked by the biblical canon. This is a theological judgment, by virtue of Christian and Jewish traditions, which have chosen to understand the

Trad

God of the Bible by restricting revealed discourse about God to what the Bible presents. For theological reasons, this cannot and will not change, nor do I think it should change. It is not the delimitation of the canon that should change; it is our ways of thinking about the works in the canon that should change. The Bible's understanding has developed throughout Christian tradition, and a comparable process is evident in Jewish tradition. Indeed, from Israel's own experience the limits of the canon do not delimit revelation.

This question involves in part the relationship of Israel's Scriptures to their ancient Near Eastern context. Ancient Near Eastern texts lie outside the Bible and therefore have no theological claim to inclusion in theological discussion. If ancient Near Eastern texts have no claim to inclusion, it is equally true that no theology has really advanced a constructive, reasoned theological basis for using ancient Near Eastern texts as a foil or contrast to the Bible. Nonetheless, from early church fathers to modern academics, many have cast ancient Near Eastern texts as a foil to the Bible; but this interpretive move has been made without a careful theological argument over inclusion or exclusion.

One possible basis worth considering for bringing the two into a theological dialogue involves the dialectical dynamic between the Bible and the larger ancient context that the Bible itself acknowledges. Given that both the Bible and many extrabiblical texts draw from the same fund of ancient tradition, understanding of the revelation of the Bible cannot be neatly restricted to the Bible. In other words, it is not enough to say that fuller understanding of revelation issues from only studying Israel's own realization of these metaphors; what came to be enshrined as biblical revelation issued from the interaction and the engagement with the older polytheistic contexts within Israel from which its monotheistic understanding developed. This polytheistic context was Israel's own, not simply one it was combating because of other peoples and their deities. Israel's own production of what came to be viewed as revelation involved a process of dialogue and debate with many currents within its own culture and beyond. Accordingly, for heuristic purposes we need models of revelation that are not simply assertions about biblical material rejecting and surpassing all ancient Near Eastern views. Instead, new models will need to take into account cultural interaction. Such interaction involves adoption from others and conflict with others, as well as various sorts of engagement in between.

We know that extrabiblical texts were occasionally borrowed by biblical tradition, for example, the proverbs of Amenemope (translated in *ANET,* 421–44), cited in Proverbs 22:19—24:22. In turn, we have become aware recently that some Israelite texts made their way into non-Israelite contexts, for example, Psalm 20 as found in Papyrus Amherst 63 (see Zevit 2001). Following these antecedents, we could benefit from a dialectical approach that addresses interaction on two levels:

between the Bible and the larger Israelite and ancient Near Eastern culture, and between our traditions and our culture as well as the larger universe around us. Revelation emerged from a comparable dialectic in the Bible, and while Christian tradition sees the basis, the genesis, of revelation ultimately with the Scriptures themselves, the biblical tradition also reveals a model for engaging the world beyond the Bible. In a world (even a universe) that is becoming smaller and more threatened by humanity, tendencies to restrict discourse about the Divine in the world to the Bible runs a risk of denying the full meaning of biblical revelation. Based on the diversity of biblical images, not to mention the different ways these are presented, one may argue that they constitute a kaleidoscope of divinity that the biblical Deity chose to leave as the record of divine identity. Ultimately, there can be no biblical center or core to biblical theology that emphasizes some notion of God at the expense of others, if only because the Deity, even within the confines of Scripture, cannot be confined to a center; this is the lesson we saw in chapter 3 with the book of Job. Instead, the question is how we can take in the vast breadth and depth about God that the Bible offers.

Biblical Supersessionism

Supersessionism is perhaps best known today as an old Christian view of Christianity over and against Judaism. In Christian supersessionism, Christianity is understood to have superseded and replaced Judaism as the divinely chosen religion. Although nowadays Christianity has largely given up this view of Judaism, its influences and its background have a long history. This supersessionist approach to older religious traditions has its roots in the Hebrew Bible itself (as insightfully discussed by Levenson [1993]). In chapter 3 we surveyed the levels of divinity in Ugaritic and biblical texts. It is apparent that the schema of divine levels in each phase of Israelite religion makes alterations to the preceding ones. In a number of instances, one stage constitutes a reformatting of a preceding one, with a religious judgment of this stage as normative and the preceding as heterodox to some degree. In other words, we see a process of supersessionism at work. Monotheism thus represents a form of supersessionism within Israelite religion, whereby a relatively late stage is believed to represent Israel's oldest religious configuration.

Supersessionism was not restricted to late-monarchic or postexilic Israelite religion. We also saw a case of supersessionism involving the relationship between Israel and its neighbors of Edom. One of the important observations made in chapter 4 involves Yahweh's origins in Edom. This view is based on references to Yahweh coming from Edom. These appear in some of Israel's earliest literature, and it is hardly the sort of claim created during the monarchy, when relations worsened between Israel and Edom. Instead, the premonarchic period seems to

be the time when Yahweh the Edomite god came to be rooted in the highland society of Israel, perhaps due to the trade relations between the two in this period.
This understanding was lost in time, itself part of the process of supersessionism.
In view of this apparent development, we may ask if it is possible to maintain the
integrity of a religious tradition without denigrating its antecedents. Theologically,
how will religious readers of the Bible appreciate its organic relations with extrabiblical texts and cultures, and maintain their sense of the Bible as revelation?
This question leads us to a final issue about the Bible and the modern world.

World Theology

As we saw in chapter 3, Israel went from a world theology relating its god to the
gods of other nations headed by El Elyon to a cosmic theology of a single deity. In
many circles of twentieth-century Christianity, traditional trinitarian monotheism moved into a world theology that tries to address the Christian Deity vis-
à-vis other religious views of reality and divinity. A common idea today about the
world's religions is that they pursue different paths toward reality and truth. Sometimes the metaphor used is that the different world religions take alternative
routes up the sides of the mountain that will eventually meet at the top.

We can see that both Israel's monotheism and modern Western Christianity
have been affected by a new world awareness in their own times. To some extent,
world empires were the impetus for these changes. As we saw in chapter 3, Assyria
and then Babylon moved westward, and as a result, Israel's vision of divinity was
affected by the challenges presented by the Assyrian and Babylonian empires and
their gods. Similarly, as Western nation-states moved out into the world, they
came into contact with other religious traditions, whose peoples they colonized.
The modern "Western" situation is the historical inversion of the situation of Israel,
as it became a colonized reality. As Israel was losing its land and political independence, it fostered new visions of one deity over all. As the modern "West" (itself a
form of colonization), colonized what has become known as the "third world" (a
term resulting from "Western" colonization), its own monotheistic worldviews
gradually required engagements with non-Western religions and their conceptu-
alizations of the Divine. Empire was key both for the distant past of Israel and for
our more recent experience in the West. In view of this observation, it seems
worth considering how to identify and to critique political imperialism in religious thinking.

To return to the terms of "center" and "periphery" used in chapter 3, what do
we favor in our ideas of God and the world? In other words, what notions of God
in the Bible do we implicitly or explicitly consider as the "center" (truth) and
what ideas do we banish to the "periphery" (untruth) in our thinking, especially

as these influence the way we think about other people in the world? As Job 38:1 reminds us, God is the mystery that challenges our efforts to classify the Divine. Ultimately, the same point applies to how we understand other people. For all these questions, we will need the humility to acknowledge our responsibility and to critique ourselves in how we understand the world as a result of reading the Bible. How will the Bible's record of Israel's struggles with the challenges it faced help us modern readers of the Bible to understand and engage the challenges of our own times? How will readers of the Bible be changed for the better by the visions of the Divine offered by biblical revelation? For those of us who are religious readers of the Bible or those of us nonreligious readers engaged by what the Bible has to say, how will our probing of Israel's past inform and transform us and our world? The Bible is not a simple book providing easy answers to life's problems. It is the record of God's questions to Israel in its time and to us in ours.

Sources and Bibliography

Sources

For many texts outside the Bible, I decided to cite Pritchard (1969b), abbreviated above as *ANET*, because of its wide accessibility for the general reader. However, I would highly recommend that interested readers become familiar with the three-volume work edited by Hallo and Younger (1997, 2000, 2002), which offers many more texts than *ANET*. These volumes include a number of ancient Hebrew inscriptions from Israel as well as some writings by or about Judeans living outside of Israel. Readers interested in looking further into Hebrew inscriptions will enjoy McCarter (1996).

For pictorial depictions, I have cited Pritchard (1969a), abbreviated as *ANEP*, because of its general accessibility. However, I would also recommend Keel and Uehlinger (1998).

Readers interested in the Ugaritic texts quoted in this book may find them in Parker (1997). The text numbers used for the Ugaritic texts come from the standard edition of Manfried Dietrich et al. (1997), abbreviated as *CAT*.

Some postbiblical Jewish religious works outside the Bible have been cited in this book. These include works from the Dead Sea Scrolls, which, except for the biblical scrolls, are conveniently collected in García Martínez and Tigchelaar (1997). Other Jewish works, such as the book of *Jubilees*, may be found in Charlesworth (1983–85). The passage from Josephus's *Jewish Antiquities* discussed in chapter 1 is conveniently translated with notes and discussion by Schiffman (1998, 92–93).

Bibliography

Most of the following bibliography is devoted to works in biblical studies and related areas. A short bibliography for the modern studies of collective memory used in this study is cited following the bibliography on the Bible and ancient Israel.

Bibliography on the Bible and Ancient Israel

Ackerman, Susan. 1992. *Under Every Green Tree: Popular Religion in Sixth-Century Judah.* HSM 46. Atlanta: Scholars.

Ahlström, Gösta W. 1993. *The History of Ancient Palestine from the Palaeolithic Period to Alexander's Conquest.* JSOTSup 146. Sheffield: JSOT Press.

Albertz, Rainer. 1994. *A History of Israelite Religion in the Old Testament Period*. Vol. 1: *From the Beginnings to the End of the Monarchy*. Translated by John Bowden. OTL. Louisville: Westminster John Knox.

―――. 2003. *Israel in Exile: The History and Literature of the Sixth Century B.C.E.* Translated by David Green. Studies in Biblical Literature. Atlanta: Society of Biblical Literature.

Assmann, Jan. 1990. "Guilt and Remembrance: On the Theologization of History in the Ancient Near East." *History and Memory* 2:5–33.

―――. 1997. *Moses the Egyptian: The Memory of Egypt in Western Monotheism*. Cambridge: Harvard Univ. Press.

Barrick, W. Boyd. 2002. *The King and the Cemeteries: Toward a New Understanding of Josiah's Reform*. VTSup 88. Leiden: Brill.

Becker, Adam H., and Annette Yoshiko Reed, editors. 2003. *The Ways That Never Parted*. Texts and Studies in Ancient Judaism 95. Tübingen: Mohr/Siebeck.

Becking, Bob, Meindert Dijkstra, Marjo C. A. Korpel, and Karel J. H. Vriezen. 2001. *Monotheism in Ancient Israel and the Veneration of the Goddess Asherah*. Biblical Seminar 77. Sheffield: Sheffield Academic.

Berlin, Adele. 2001. *Esther*. Jewish Publication Society Bible Commentary. Philadelphia: Jewish Publication Society.

Biran, Avraham. 1994. *Biblical Dan*. Jerusalem: Israel Exploration Society/Hebrew Union College—Jewish Institute of Religion.

―――. 1999. "Two Bronze Plaques and the *Ḥuṣṣot* of Dan." *IEJ* 49/1–2:43–54.

―――. 2001. "The High Places of Biblical Dan." In *Studies in the Archaeology of Iron Age in Israel and Jordan*, edited by Amihai Mazar with the assistance of G. Mathias, 148–55. JSOTSup 331. Sheffield: Sheffield Academic.

Bloch-Smith, Elizabeth. 1992. *Judahite Burial Practices and Beliefs about the Dead*. JSOTSup 129. American Schools of Oriental Research Monographs 7. Sheffield: Sheffield Academic.

―――. 1994. "'Who Is the King of Glory?' Solomon's Temple and Its Symbolism." In *Scripture and Other Artifacts: Essays on the Bible and Archaeology in Honor of Philip J. King*, edited by Michael David Coogan, J. Cheryl Exum, and Lawrence E. Stager, 18–31. Louisville: Westminster John Knox.

―――. 2003. "Israelite Ethnicity in Iron I: Archaeology Preserves What Is Remembered and What Is Forgotten in Israel's History." *JBL* 122:401–25.

Blomquist, Tina H. 1999. *Gates and Gods: Cults in the City Gates of Iron Age Palestine. An Investigation of the Archaeological and Biblical Sources*. ConBOT 46. Stockholm: Gleerup.

Brandfon, Frederic. 1987. "Limits of Evidence: Archaeology and Objectivity." *Maarav* 4/1: 5–43.

Bregstein, Linda B. 1993. "Seal Use in the Fifth Century B.C. Nippur, Iraq: A Study of Seal Selection and Sealing Practices in the Muraśû Archive." Ph.D. dissertation, University of Pennsylvania.

Brettler, Marc Z. 1989. "The Book of Judges: Literature as Politics." *JBL* 108:395–418.

―――. 1995. *The Creation of History in Ancient Israel*. London: Routledge.

―――. 2001. "Memory in Ancient Israel." In *Memory and History in Christianity and Judaism*, edited by Michael Signer, 1–17. Notre Dame, Ind.: Univ. of Notre Dame Press.

Bright, John. 1959. *A History of Israel*. Philadelphia: Westminster. (This work has been published in four editions, the latest in 2000.)

Burnett, Joel. 2001. *A Reassessment of Biblical Elohim*. SBLDS 183. Atlanta: Society of Biblical Literature.

Carr, David M. 1996. *Reading the Factures of Genesis: History and Literary Approaches.* Louisville: Westminster John Knox.

Charlesworth, James. 1983–85. *The Old Testament Pseudepigrapha.* 2 vols. Garden City, N.Y.: Doubleday.

Childs, Brevard S. 1962. *Memory and Tradition in Israel.* Studies in Biblical Theology 1/37. London: SCM.

Cogan, Mordechai. 2001. *1 Kings.* AB 10. New York: Doubleday.

Cohen, Shaye J. D. 1999. *The Beginnings of Jewishness: Boundaries, Varieties, Uncertainties.* Hellenistic Culture and Society 31. Berkeley: Univ. of California Press.

Coogan, Michael D., editor. 2001. *The Oxford History of the Biblical World.* New York: Oxford Univ. Press.

Cooper, Alan, and Bernard Goldstein. 1992. "Exodus and *Maṣṣôt* in History and Tradition." In *Let Your Colleagues Praise You: Studies in Memory of Stanley Gevirtz* (= *Maarav* 7-8), edited by Robert Ratner et al., 2:15–37. Rolling Hills Estates, Calif.: Western Academic Press.

Cross, Frank Moore. 1973. *Canaanite Myth and Hebrew Epic: Essays in the History of the Religion of Israel.* Cambridge: Harvard Univ. Press.

Crüsemann, Frank. 1996. *The Torah: Theology and Social History of Old Testament Law.* Translated by Allan W. Mahnke. Minneapolis: Fortress Press.

Damrosch, David. 1987. *The Narrative Covenant: Transformations of Genre in the Growth of Biblical Literature.* Ithaca, N.Y.: Cornell Univ. Press.

Day, Peggy L. 1988. *An Adversary in Heaven: Satan in the Hebrew Bible.* HSM 43. Atlanta: Scholars.

———. 1989. "From the Child Is Born the Woman: The Story of Jephthah's Daughter." In *Gender and Difference in Ancient Israel,* edited by Peggy L. Day, 58-74. Minneapolis: Fortress Press.

Dever, William. 2001. *What Did the Biblical Writers Know and When Did They Know It? What Archaeology Can Tell Us about the Reality of Ancient Israel.* Grand Rapids: Eerdmans.

Dietrich, Manfried, Oswald Loretz, and Joaquín Sanmartín, editors. 1997. *The Cuneiform Alphabetic Texts from Ugarit, Ras Ibn Hani and Other Places.* 2d ed. Münster: Ugarit-Verlag.

Dietrich, Walter, and Martin A. Klopfenstein, editors. 1994. *Ein Gott allein? JHWH-Verehrung und biblischer Monotheismus im Kontext der israelitischen und altorientalischen Religionsgeschichte.* OBO 139. Göttingen: Vandenhoeck & Ruprecht.

Faust, Avraham. 1999. "Differences in Family Structure between Cities and Villages in Iron II." *TA* 26:233–52.

———. 2003a. "The Farmstead in the Highlands of Iron Age II Israel." In *The Rural Landscape of Ancient Israel,* edited by Aren M. Maeir, Shimon Dar, and Ze'ev Safrai, 91–104. BAR International Series 1121. Oxford: Archaeopress.

———. 2003b. "Judah in the Sixth Century B.C.E.: A Rural Perspective." *Palestine Exploration Quarterly* 135:37–53.

———. 2003c. "Residential Patterns in the Ancient Israelite City." *Levant* 35:23–28.

Finkelstein, Israel. 2003. "City States to States: Polity Dynamics in the 10th–9th Centuries B.C.E." In *Symbiosis, Symbolism, and the Power of the Past: Canaan, Ancient Israel, and Their Neighbors from the Late Bronze Age through Roman Palaestina. Proceedings of the Centennial Symposium W. F. Albright Institute of Archaeological Research and American Schools of Oriental Research Jerusalem, May 29–31, 2000,* edited by William G. Dever and Seymour Gitin, 75–83. Winona Lake, Ind.: Eisenbrauns.

Fishbane, Michael. 1985. *Biblical Interpretation in Ancient Israel.* Oxford: Clarendon.

———. 2003. *Biblical Myth and Rabbinic Mythmaking.* Oxford: Oxford Univ. Press.

Fitzgerald, Aloysius. 2002. *The Lord of the East Wind.* CBQMS 34. Washington, D.C.: Catholic Biblical Association of America.

Fleming, Daniel. 1998. "Mari and the Possibilities of Biblical Memory." *Revue d'assyriologie* 92:41–78.

Fox, Nili Sacher. 2000. *In the Service of the King: Officialdom in Ancient Israel and Judah.* Monographs of the Hebrew Union College 23. Cincinnati: Hebrew Union College Press.

Friedman, Richard Elliott. 1989. *Who Wrote the Bible?* 2d ed. San Francisco: HarperCollins.

———. 2003. *The Bible with Sources Revealed: A New View into the Five Books of Moses.* San Francisco: HarperSanFrancisco.

García Martínez, Florentino, and Eibert J. C. Tigchelaar, editors. 1997. *The Dead Sea Scrolls Study Edition.* Leiden: Brill.

Gerhardsson, Birger. 1961. *Memory and Manuscript: Oral Tradition and Written Transmission in Rabbinic Judaism and Early Christianity.* Acta seminarii neotestamentici upsaliensis 22. Lund: Gleerup.

Ginsberg, H. Louis. 1969. "A Strand in the Cord of Hebrew Psalmody." *Eretz-Israel* 9:45–50.

———. 1982. *The Israelian Heritage of Judaism.* Texts and Studies of the Jewish Theological Seminary of America 14. New York: Jewish Theological Seminary of America.

Gnuse, Robert K. 2000. "Redefining the Elohist?" *JBL* 119:201–20.

Grabbe, Lester L., editor. 2003. *"Like a Bird in a Cage": The Invasion of Sennacherib.* JSOTSup 263; European Seminar in Historical Methodology 4. London: Sheffield Academic.

Hadley, Judith M. 2000. *The Cult of Asherah in Ancient Israel and Judah: Evidence for a Hebrew Goddess.* University of Cambridge Oriental Publications 57. Cambridge, England: Cambridge Univ Press.

Hahn, Scott W., and John S. Bersma. 2004. "What Laws Were 'Not Good'? A Canonical Approach to the Theological Problem of Ezekiel 20:25-26." *JBL* 123:201–18.

Hallo, William H., and K. Lawson Younger Jr., editors. 1997, 2000, 2002. *The Context of Scripture.* 3 vols. Leiden: Brill.

Halpern, Baruch. 1982. *The Emergence of Israel in Canaan.* SBLMS 29. Chico, Calif.: Scholars.

———. 1987. "'Brisker Pipes Than Poetry': The Development of Israelite Monotheism." In *Judaic Perspectives on Ancient Israel,* edited by Jacob Neusner, Baruch A. Levine, and Ernest S. Frerichs, 77–115. Philadelphia: Fortress Press.

———. 1988. *The First Historians: The Hebrew Bible and History.* San Francisco: Harper & Row.

———. 1991. "Jerusalem and the Lineages in the 7th-Century B.C.E.: Kinship and the Rise of Individual Moral Liability." In *Law and Ideology in Monarchic Israel,* edited by Baruch Halpern and Deborah W. Hobson, 11–107. JSOTSup 124. London: Sheffield Academic.

———. 1993. "The Baal (and the Asherah) in Seventh-Century Judah: Yhwh's Retainers Retired." In *Konsequente Traditionsgeschichte: Festschrift für Klaus Baltzer zum 65. Geburtstag,* edited by Rüdiger Barthelmus, Thomas Krüger, and Helmut Utzschneider, 115–54. OBO 126. Göttingen: Vandenhoeck & Ruprecht.

———. 1996. "Sybil, or the Two Nations? Archaism, Kinship, Alienation, and the Elite Redefinition of Traditional Culture in Judah in the 8th–7th Centuries B.C.E." In *The Study of the Ancient Near East in the 21st Century: The William Foxwell Albright Centennial Conference,* edited by Jerrold S. Cooper and Glenn M. Schwartz, 291–338. Winona Lake, Ind.: Eisenbrauns.

————. 2001. *David's Secret Demons: Messiah, Murderer, Traitor, King.* Grand Rapids: Eerdmans.

Handy, Lowell. 1994. *Among the Host of Heaven: The Syro-Palestinian Pantheon as Bureaucracy.* Winovia Lake, Ind.: Eisenbrauns.

————. 2001. "Wolkendunkel und Himmelsfeste: Zur Genese und Kosmologie der Vorstellung des himmlischen Heiligtums JHWHs." In *Das biblische Weltbild und seine altorientalischen Kontext,* edited by Bernd Janowski and Beata Ego, 125–79. FAT 32. Tübingen: Mohr/Siebeck.

————. 2003a. "Religionsgeschichte Israels—ein Überblick über die Forschung seit 1990." *Verkündigung und Forschung* 48:2–28.

————. 2003b. "Die unvergleichliche 'Gestalt' JHWHs: Israels Geschichte mit den Bildern im Licht von Deuteronomium 4,1-40." In *Die Sichtbarkeit des Unsichtbaren: Zur Korrelation von Text und Bild im Wirkungskreis der Bibel,* edited by Bernd Janowski and Nino Zchomelidse, 49–77. Arbeiten zur Geschichte und Wirkung der Bibel 3. Stuttgart: Deutsche Bibelgesellschaft.

Hartenstein, Friedhelm. 1997. *Die Unzugänglichkeit Gottes im Heiligtum: Jesaja 6 und der Wohnort JHWHs in der Jerusalemer Kulttradition.* WMANT 75. Neukirchener-Vluyn: Neukirchener Verlag.

Hendel, Ronald S. 1988. "The Social Origins of the Aniconic Tradition in Ancient Israel." *CBQ* 50:365–82.

————. 1988–89. "Images of God in Ancient Israel." *Bulletin of the Anglo-Israel Archaeological Society* 8:81–82.

————. 2001a. "The Exodus in Biblical Memory." *JBL* 120:601–22.

————. 2001b. "Of Doubt, Gadflies and Minimalists." *BR* 17/3:8.

————. 2002a. "Exodus: A Book of Memories." *BR* 18/4:38–45, 52–53.

————. 2002b. "Israel among the Nations: Biblical Culture in the Ancient Near East." In *Cultures of the Jews: A New History,* edited by David Biale, 42–75. New York: Schocken.

Hess, Richard S. 2003. "Israelite Identity and Personal Names from the Book of Judges." *Hebrew Studies* 44:25–39.

Himbaza, Innocent. 2002. "Dt 32, 8, une correction tardive des scribes: Essai d'interprétation et de datation." *Bib* 83:527–48.

Holloway, Steven W. 2002. *Aššur Is King! Aššur Is King! Religion in the Exercise of Power in the Neo-Assyrian Empire.* Culture and History of the Ancient Near East 10. Leiden: Brill.

Hurtado, Larry W. 2003. *Lord Jesus Christ: Devotion to Jesus in Earliest Christianity.* Grand Rapids: Eerdmans.

Janowski, Bernd, Norbert Lohfink, et al. 1995. *Religionsgeschichte Israels oder Theologie des Alten Testaments.* Neukirchen-Vluyn: Neukirchener Verlag (= *Jahrbuch für biblische Theologie* 10).

Jonker, Gerdien. 1995. *The Topography of Remembrance: The Dead, Tradition and Collective Memory in Mesopotamia.* Studies in the History of Religions 68. Leiden: Brill.

Keel, Othmar, and Christoph Uehlinger. 1998. *Gods, Goddesses, and Images of God in Ancient Israel.* Translated by Thomas H. Trapp. Minneapolis: Fortress Press.

King, Philip J., and Lawrence E. Stager. 2001. *Life in Biblical Israel.* Library of Ancient Israel. Louisville: Westminster John Knox.

Knohl, Israel. 1995. *The Sanctuary of Silence: The Priestly Torah and the Holiness School.* Minneapolis: Fortress Press.

————. 2003. *The Divine Symphony: The Bible's Many Voices.* Philadelphia: Jewish Publication Society.

Knoppers, Gary N. 2001. "Rethinking the Relationship between Deuteronomy and the Deuteronomistic History: The Case of Kings." *CBQ* 63:393–415.

Koch, Klaus. 1994. "Monotheismus und Angelologie." In *Ein Gott allein? JHWH-Verehrung und biblischer Monotheismus im Kontext der israelitischen und altorientalischen Religionsgeschichte*, edited by W. Dietrich and M. A. Klopfenstein, 565–81. OBO 139. Freiburg: Universitätsverlag.

Lang, Bernard. 2002. *The Hebrew God: Portrait of an Ancient Deity*. New Haven: Yale Univ. Press.

Lemaire, André. 1994. "Déesses et dieux de Syrie-Palestine d'après les inscriptions (c. 1000–500 av. N. è.)." In *Ein Gott allein? JHWH-Verehrung und biblischer Monotheismus im Kontext der israelitischen und altorientalischen Religionsgeshichte*, edited by W. Dietrich and M. A. Klopfenstein, 127–58. OBO 139. Freiburg: Universitätsverlag.

Levenson, Jon D. 1993. *The Death and Resurrection of the Beloved Son: The Transformation of Child Sacrifice in Judaism and Christianity*. New Haven: Yale Univ. Press.

Levine, Baruch A. 1993. *Numbers 1–20*. AB 4. New York: Doubleday.

———. 2000. *Numbers 21–36*. AB 4A. New York: Doubleday.

Levinson, Bernard M. 1997. *Deuteronomy and the Hermeneutics of Legal Innovation*. Oxford: Oxford Univ. Press.

———. 2002. "Goethe's Analysis of Exodus 34 and Its Influence on Wellhausen: The *Pfropfung* of the Documentary Hypothesis." *Zeitschrift für die alttestamentliche Wissenschaft* 114:212–23.

———. In preparation. *Rethinking Revelation and Redaction: Biblical Studies at the Boundaries*. Oxford: Oxford Univ. Press.

Lewis, Theodore J. 1998. "Divine Images and Aniconism in Ancient Israel." *Journal of the American Oriental Society* 118:36–53.

Lindsay, John. 1999. "Edomite Westward Expansion: The Biblical Evidence." *Ancient Near Eastern Studies* 36:48–89.

Lipschits, Oded, and Joseph Blenkinsopp, editors. 2003. *Judah and the Judeans in the Neo-Babylonian Period*. Winona Lake, Ind.: Eisenbrauns.

MacDonald, Nathan. 2003. *Deuteronomy and the Meaning of "Monotheism."* FAT 2/1. Tübingen: Mohr/Siebeck.

Machinist, Peter. 1994. "Outsiders or Insiders: The Biblical View of Emergent Israel and Its Contexts." In *The Other in Jewish Thought and History: Constructions of Jewish Culture and Identity*, edited by L. J. Silberstein and R. L. Cohn, 35–60. New York: New York Univ. Press.

———. 2003. "The Voice of the Historian in the Ancient Near Eastern and Mediterranean World." *Interpretation* 57:117–37.

Maier, Aren M., Shimon Dar, and Ze'ev Safrai, editors. 2003. *The Rural Landscape of Ancient Israel*. BAR International Series 1121. Oxford: Archaeopress.

Mankowski, P. V. 2000. *Akkadian Loanwords in Biblical Hebrew*. HSS 47. Winona Lake, Ind.: Eisenbrauns.

Mazar, Amihai. 1990. *Archaeology of the Land of the Bible 10,000–586 B.C.E.* Anchor Bible Reference Library. New York: Doubleday.

———. 2003. "Remarks on Biblical Traditions and Archaeological Evidence concerning Early Israel." In *Symbiosis, Symbolism, and the Power of the Past: Canaan, Ancient Israel, and Their Neighbors from the Late Bronze Age through Roman Palaestina. Proceedings of the Centennial Symposium W. F. Albright Institute of Archaeological Research and American Schools of Oriental Research Jerusalem, May 29–31, 2000*, edited by William G. Dever and Seymour Gitin, 85–98. Winona Lake, Ind.: Eisenbrauns.

McCarter, P. Kyle, Jr. 1996. *Ancient Inscriptions: Voices from the Biblical World*. Washington, D.C.: Biblical Archaeology Society.

McKenzie, Steven L. 2000. *King David: A Biography*. New York: Oxford Univ. Press.

Mettinger, T. N. D. 1995. *No Graven Image? Israelite Aniconism in Its Ancient Near Eastern Context*. ConBOT 42. Stockholm: Almqvist & Wiksell.

Moberly, R. W. L. 1992. *The Old Testament of the Old Testament: Patriarchal Narratives and Mosaic Yahwism*. Overtures to Biblical Theology. Minneapolis: Fortress Press.

Mullen, E. Theodore. 1980. *The Divine Council in Canaanite and Early Hebrew Literature*. HSM 24. Chico, Calif.: Scholars.

Na'aman, Nadav. 1993. "Population Changes in Palestine following Assyrian Deportations." *TA* 20:104–24.

———. 1995. "Historiography, the Fashioning of Collective Memory, and the Establishment of Historical Consciousness in Israel in the Late Monarchical Period." (Hebrew.) *Zion* 60:449–72.

———. 2002. "In Search of Reality behind the Account of David's War with Israel's Neighbors." *IEJ* 52:200–24.

Na'aman, Nadav, and Ran Zadok. 2000. "Assyrian Deportations to the Province of Samerina in the Light of Two Cuneiform Tablets from Tel Hadid." *TA* 27:159–88.

Nocquet, Dany. 2004. *Le "livret noir de Baal": La polémique contre le dieu Baal dans la Bible hébraïque et l'ancien Israël*. Actes et recherches. Geneva: Labor et Fides.

Olson, Dennis T. 1985. *The Death of the Old and the Birth of the New: The Framework of the Book of Numbers and the Pentateuch*. Brown Judaic Studies 71. Chico, Calif.: Scholars.

Olyan, Saul M. 1988. *Asherah and the Cult of Yahweh in Israel*. SBLDS 34. Atlanta: Scholars.

———. 2003. " 'We Are Utterly Cut Off': Some Possible Nuances of נגזרנו לנו in Ezek 37:11." *CBQ* 65:43–51.

Parker, Simon B. 1995. "The Beginning of the Reign of God." *Revue biblique* 102:532–59.

———, editor. 1997. *Ugaritic Narrative Poetry*. SBL Writings from the Ancient World 9. Atlanta: Scholars.

Patrick, Dale. 1985. *Old Testament Law*. Atlanta: John Knox.

Pritchard, James B., editor. 1969a. *The Ancient Near East in Pictures Relating to the Old Testament*. 2d ed. Princeton: Princeton Univ. Press.

———. 1969b. *The Ancient Near Eastern Texts relating to the Old Testament*. 3d ed. Princeton: Princeton Univ. Press.

Riesner, Rainer. 1988. *Jesus als Lehrer: Eine Untersuchung zum Ursprung der Evangelien-Überlieferung*. Wissenschaftliche Untersuchungen zum Neuen Testament 2/7. Tübingen: Mohr/Siebeck.

Rofé, Alexander. 2000. "Clan Sagas as a Source in Settlement Traditions." In *"A Wise and Discerning Mind": Essays in Honor of Burke O. Long*, edited by Saul M. Olyan and Robert C. Culley, 191–203. Brown Judaic Studies 325. Providence: Brown Judaic Studies.

Römer, Thomas, and Albert de Pury. 2000. "Deuteronomistic Historiography (DH): History of Research and Debated Issues." In *Israel Constructs Its History: Deuteronomistic Historiography in Recent Research*, edited by Albert de Pury, Thomas Römer, and Jean-Daniel Macchi, 24–141. JSOTSup 306. Sheffield: Sheffield Academic.

Rosenberg, Stephen. 1998. "The Siloam Tunnel Revisited." *TA* 25/1:116–30.

Sack, Ronald H. 2004. *Images of Nebuchadnezzar: The Emergence of a Legend*. 2d ed. Selinsgrove, Pa.: Susquehanna Univ. Press.

Sanders, Paul. 1996. *The Provenance of Deuteronomy 32*. Oudtestamentische Studiën 37. Leiden: Brill.

Schiffman, Lawrence H. 1998. *Texts and Traditions: A Source Reader for the Study of Second Temple and Rabbinic Judaism.* Hoboken, N.J.: Ktav.

Schloen, J. David. 1993. "Caravans, Kenites and Casus Belli: Emnity and Alliance in the Song of Deborah." *CBQ* 55:18–38.

———. 2001. *The House of the Father as Fact and Symbol: Patrimonialism in Ugarit and the Ancient Near East.* Studies in the Archaeology and History of the Levant 2. Winona Lake, Ind.: Eisenbrauns.

Schniedewind, William M. 1996. "The Problem with Kings: Recent Study of the Deuteronomistic History." *Religious Studies Review* 22/1:22–27.

———. 2004. *How the Bible Became a Book: The Textualization of Ancient Israel.* New York: Cambridge Univ. Press.

Schottroff, Willy. 1967. *"Gedenken" im Alten Orient und im Alten Testament.* 2d ed. WMANT 15. Neukirchen-Vluyn: Neukirchener Verlag.

Schroeder, Christoph O. 2001. *History, Justice and the Agency of God: A Hermeneutical and Exegetical Investigation of Isaiah and the Psalms.* Biblical Interpretation Series 52. Leiden: Brill.

Segal, Alan F. 1997. *Two Powers in Heaven: Early Rabbinic Reports about Christianity and Gnosticism.* Studies in Judaism in Late Antiquity 25. Leiden: Brill.

Seitz, Christopher R. 1985. "The Crisis of Interpretation over the Meaning and Purpose of the Exile." *Vetus Testamentum* 35:78–97.

Seow, C. Leong. 1989. *Myth, Drama, and the Politics of David's Dance.* HSM 46. Atlanta: Scholars.

———. 1997. *Ecclesiastes.* AB 18C. New York: Doubleday.

Sharpe, Carolyn J. 2003. *Prophecy and Ideology in Jeremiah: Struggles for Authority and the Deutero-Jeremianic Corpus.* London: T. & T. Clark.

Smith, Mark S. 1990. *The Early History of God: Yahweh and the Other Deities in Ancient Israel.* San Francisco: Harper & Row.

———. 1997. *The Pilgrimage Pattern in Exodus.* With contributions by Elizabeth M. Bloch-Smith. JSOTSup 239. Sheffield: Sheffield Academic.

———. 2001. *The Origins of Biblical Monotheism: Israel's Polytheistic Background and the Ugaritic Texts.* Oxford: Oxford Univ. Press. (Paperback edition, 2003.)

———. 2002a. *The Early History of God: Yahweh and the Other Deities in Ancient Israel.* 2d ed. Biblical Resource Series. Grand Rapids: Eerdmans.

———. 2002b. "Remembering God: Collective Memory in Israelite Religion." *CBQ* 64: 631–51.

Stager, Lawrence E. 1988. "Archaeology, Ecology, and Social History: Background Themes to the Song of Deborah." In *Congress Volume: Jerusalem 1986,* edited by John A. Emerton, 221–34. VTSup 40. Leiden: Brill.

———. 2003. "The Patrimonial Kingdom of Solomon." In *Symbiosis, Symbolism, and the Power of the Past: Canaan, Ancient Israel, and Their Neighbors from the Late Bronze Age through Roman Palaestina. Proceedings of the Centennial Symposium W. F. Albright Institute of Archaeological Research and American Schools of Oriental Research Jerusalem, May 29–31, 2000,* edited by William G. Dever and Seymour Gitin, 63–74. Winona Lake, Ind.: Eisenbrauns.

Steiner, Richard C. 2003. *Stockmen from Tekoa, Sycomores from Sheba.* CBQMS 36. Washington, D.C.: Catholic Biblical Association.

Stordalen, Terje. 2000. *Echoes of Eden: Genesis 2–3 and Symbolism of the Eden Garden in Biblical Hebrew Literature.* Contributions to Biblical Exegesis and Theology 25. Louvain: Peeters.

Tappy, Ron E. 1992–2001. *The Archaeology of Israelite Samaria.* 2 vols. HSS 44 and 50. Winona Lake, Ind.: Eisenbrauns.

Tigay, Jeffrey, editor. 1985. *Empirical Models for Biblical Criticism.* Philadelphia: Univ. of Pennsylvania Press.

Toews, Wesley I. 1993. *Monarchy and Religious Institution in Israel under Jeroboam I.* SBLMS 47. Atlanta: Scholars.

Toorn, Karel van der. 1992. "Anat-Yahu, Some Other Deities and the Jews of Elephantine." *Numen* 39:80–101.

———. 1996. *Family Religion in Babylonia, Syria and Israel: Continuity and Change in the Forms of Religious Life.* Studies in the History and Culture of the Ancient Near East 7. Leiden: Brill.

———, editor. 1997. *The Image and the Book: Iconic Cults, Aniconism, and the Rise of Book Religion in Israel and the Ancient Near East.* Contributions to Biblical Exegesis and Theology 21. Louvain: Peeters.

Toorn, Karel van der, Bob Becking, and Pieter W. van der Horst, editors. 1999. *Dictionary of Deities and Demons in the Bible.* 2d ed. Leiden: Brill.

Tov, Emanuel. 2001. *Textual Criticism of the Hebrew Bible.* 2d ed. Minneapolis: Fortress Press.

Van De Mieroop, Marc. 1999. *Cuneiform Texts and the Writing of History.* London: Routledge.

Vaughn, Andrew G. 1999. *Theology, History, and Archaeology in the Chronicler's Account of Hezekiah.* Archaeology and Biblical Studies 4. Atlanta: Scholars.

Weippert, Manfred. 1997. *Jahwe und die anderen Götter: Studien zur Religionsgeschichte des antiken Israel in ihrem syrisch-palästinischen Kontext.* FAT 18. Tübingen: Mohr/ Siebeck.

Wiggermann, Franz. 1992. *Mesopotamian Protective Spirits: The Ritual Texts.* Cuneiform Monographs 1. Groningen: Styx.

———. 1996a. "Scenes from the Shadow Side." In *Mesopotamian Poetic Language: Sumerian and Akkadian,* edited by M. E. Vogelzang and H. L. J. Vantiphout, 207–20. Cuneiform Monographs 6. Groningen: Styx.

———. 1996b. "Transtigridian Snake Gods." In *Sumerian Gods and Their Representations,* edited by I. L. Finkel and M. J. Geller, 33–55. Cuneiform Monographs 7. Groningen: Styx.

Wright, J. Edward. 2000. *The Early History of Heaven.* Oxford: Oxford Univ. Press.

Yadin, Azzan. 2003. "קול as Hypostasis in the Hebrew Bible." *JBL* 122:601–26.

Zadok, Ran. 1998. "On the Reliability of the Genealogical and Prosopographical Lists of Israelites in the Old Testament." *TA* 25:228–54.

———. 2002. *The Earliest Diaspora: Israelites and Judeans in Pre-Hellenistic Mesopotamia.* Publications of the Diaspora Research Institute 151. Tel Aviv: Diaspora Research Institute, Tel Aviv University.

Zevit, Ziony. 2001. *The Religions of Ancient Israel: A Synthesis of Parallactic Approaches.* New York: Continuum.

Modern Studies of Collective Memory and Amnesia

Ariès, Philippe. 1962. *Centuries of Childhood: A Social History of Family Life.* Translated by R. Baldick. New York: Vintage.

Carruthers, Mary J. 1990. *The Book of Memory: A Study of Memory in Medieval Culture.* Cambridge Studies in Medieval Culture. Cambridge: Cambridge Univ. Press.

Funkenstein, Amos. 1993. *Perceptions of Jewish History.* Berkeley: Univ. of California Press.

Gedi, Noa, and Yigal Elam. 1996. "Collective Memory—What Is It?" *History and Memory* 8:30–50.

Halbwachs, Maurice. 1975. *Les cadres sociaux de la mémoire.* New York: Arno. (Originally published in 1925.)

———. 1971. *La topographie légendaire des évangiles en terre sainte.* Edited by Fernand Dumont. Paris: Presses Universitaires de France. (Originally published in 1941.)

———. 1980. *The Collective Memory.* Translated by Francis J. Ditter and Vida Yazdi Ditter. New York: Harper & Row. This book has an introduction written by Mary Douglas, "Introduction: Maurice Halbwachs (1877–1945)," 1–21. (Originally published as *La mémoire collective,* 1950.)

Hervieu-Léger, Danièle. 2000. *Religion as a Chain of Memory.* Translated by S. Lee. New Brunswick, N.J.: Rutgers. (Originally published as *La religion pour mémoire,* 1993.)

Hutton, Patrick. 1993. *History as an Art of Memory.* Hanover, N.H.: Univ. Press of New England.

Le Goff, Jacques. 1992. *History and Memory.* Translated by S. Rendell and E. Claman. New York: Columbia Univ. Press. (Originally published as *Histore et mémoire.* Paris: Gallimard, 1977.)

Le Goff, Jacques, Jacques Revel, and Rogier Chartier, editors. 1978. *Dictionnaire de la Nouvelle Histoire.* Paris: Retz.

Le Goff, Jacques, and Pierre Nora, editors. 1974. *Faire de l'histoire.* 3 vols. Paris: Gallimard. (Selected essays from the three volumes were translated and published as *Constructing the Past: Essays in Historical Methodology* [Cambridge: Cambridge Univ. Press, 1985].)

Nora, Pierre, editor. 1996–98. *Realms of Memory: The Construction of the French Past.* Translated by A. Goldhammer. Edited by L. D. Kritzman. 3 vols. New York: Columbia Univ. Press. (Originally published as *Les lieux de mémoire.* 3 vols. Paris: Gallimard, 1984–92.)

Schachter, Daniel L. 2001. *The Seven Sins of Memory: How the Mind Forgets and Remembers.* Boston: Houghton Mifflin.

Woods, Nancy. 1994. "Memory's Remains: Les lieux de mémoire." *History and Memory* 6:123–49.

Yerushalmi, Yosef Hayim. 1989. *Zakhor: Jewish History and Jewish Memory.* Rev. ed. Seattle: Univ. of Washington Press. (Original edition 1982.)

Yerushalmi, Y. H., N. Loraux, H. Mommsen, J.-C. Milner, and G. Vattimo. 1988. *Usages de l'oubli: Au Colloque de Royaumont.* Paris: Seuil.

Index

Who owns history?
How are the "horizons of interpretation" different for historiography, foundational narrative, and sacred text?

Who is "Moses" in today's public discourse?

Where are the women?

How is oral culture different from literate culture?

We can't step out of time and minister to different age groups as if we were exempt from classification

effect of repetition

significance of "hardening pharaoh's heart"